Rechtssprache des Auslands

Anglo-Amerikanisches Vertrags- und Deliktsrecht

D1721209

The Law & Language of Contracts and Torts

Anglo-Amerikanisches Vertrags- und Deliktsrecht

von

B. Sharon Byrd

C.H. Beck'sche Verlagsbuchhandlung, München
Manz'sche Verlags- und Universitätsbuchhandlung, Wien
Verlag Stämpfli AG, Bern
1998

Über die Autorin

Die Autorin, derzeit Leiterin des "Law & Language" Programms an der Universität Jena und Honorarprofessorin für anglo-amerikanisches Recht an der Universität Erlangen, verfügt aufgrund ihrer akademischen Ausbildung (J.D. University of California, Los Angeles; LL.M., J.S.D. Columbia University, New York) über langjährige Erfahrungen mit dem amerikanischen Recht. Als Stipendiatin der Alexander von Humboldt Stiftung studierte sie darüberhinaus zwei Jahre deutsches Recht. Die Autorin hat mehrere Jahre als Dozentin für anglo-amerikanisches Recht in Augsburg Erfahrungen gesammelt, bevor sie nach Jena ging, um dort das "Law & Language" Programm aufzubauen.

Die Deutsche Bibliothek – CIP-Einheitsaufnahme

Byrd, Sharon:
The Law & Language of Contracts and Torts = Anglo-Amerikanisches Vertrags- und Deliktsrecht / von B. Sharon Byrd. –
München : Beck; Wien : Manz; Bern : Stämpfli, 1998
(Rechtssprache des Auslands)
ISBN 3-406-43984-5 (Beck)
ISBN 3-214-02941-X (Manz)
ISBN 3-7272-9044-7 (Stämpfli)

C.H. Beck ISBN 3-406-43984-5
Manz ISBN 3-214-02941-X
Stämpfli ISBN 3-7272-9044-7

© C.H. Beck'sche Verlagsbuchhandlung, München
Satz: Herbert Kloos, München
Umschlag: Christiane Rauert, München
Druck und Bindung: C.H. Beck'sche Buchdruckerei, Nördlingen
Gedruckt auf säurefreiem, alterungsbeständigem Papier
(hergestellt aus chlorfrei gebleichtem Zellstoff)

Meinem Mann

Vorwort

Dieses Buch ist in gewisser Weise eine Fortsetzung meiner vor einem Jahr erschienenen *Introduction to Anglo-American Law & Language*. Ebenfalls erwachsen aus vielen Jahren Lehrerfahrungen an deutschen Universitäten, verfolgt es dieselben didaktischen Ziele wie die Einführung. Wieder bin ich meinen Freunden und meinen Studenten dankbar für die Hilfestellung, die sie mir gegeben haben.

Jena, Februar 1998   *B. Sharon Byrd*

Einführung und methodische Hinweise

I. Lernziele

The Law & Language of Contracts and Torts baut auf der in dieser Reihe bereits erschienenen Einführung *Introduction to Anglo-American Law & Language* auf. Im vorliegenden Buch werden zwei der wichtigen Rechtsgebiete – Vertragsrecht und Deliktshaftungsrecht – eingehend behandelt. Genauso wie von dem Einführungsbuch sollten Sie auch von diesem Buch erwarten,

- daß Sie mit seiner Hilfe ca. 300 neue juristische Fachbegriffe im Kontext lernen können, was es Ihnen ermöglicht, sich mit Juristen und Juristinnen in einem englischsprachigen Land über Rechtsprobleme zu unterhalten; Sie schaffen sich damit eine Grundlage, auf der aufbauend Sie Ihren Fachwortschatz später selbständig erweitern können;
- daß Sie sich mit seiner Hilfe eine Arbeitsmethode aneignen können, die Sie befähigt, eigenständig englischsprachige juristische Texte aufzufinden, zu lesen und genau zu verstehen;
- daß Sie mit seiner Hilfe ein Verständnis für die fundamentalen Unterschiede zwischen anglo-amerikanischem und deutschem Vertrags- und Deliktshaftungsrecht gewinnen können;
- daß Sie mit seiner Hilfe einen Einblick in die Grundlagen dieser ausgewählten Rechtsgebiete bekommen können, was Sie befähigt, sich in diesen Rechtsgebieten selbständig weiter auszubilden, die Lösungen juristischer Probleme selbständig zu erforschen und die dafür notwendige Rechtsterminologie zu verstehen.

II. Adressaten und Benutzer

The Law & Language of Contracts and Torts ist gedacht als

- eine Unterstützung für den Fachsprachen-Unterricht im Rahmen eines Studiengangs an einer Universität oder einer anderen Institution für den Unterricht von Rechtssprachen (Dolmetscher- und Übersetzerinstitute);
- eine Einführung für Anwälte, die sich wegen ihrer beruflichen Tätigkeit selbständig einen Einblick in das anglo-amerikanische Vertrags- und Deliktshaftungsrecht und seine Rechtssprache verschaffen möchten;

- eine Vorbereitung für Studenten, die vorhaben, ein Aufbaustudium (LL.M.) oder ein Praktikum in einem Land mit einem common law-System zu absolvieren, d.i. in Australien, England, Irland, Kanada, Neuseeland oder in den Vereinigten Staaten, auch in Indien oder in Schottland, die beide vom common law-System beeinflußt sind;
- eine Grundlage für Rechtsreferendare, die eine Auslandswahlstation in einem Land mit einem common law-System verbringen möchten.

Englischkenntnisse, wie sie in 7 bis 9 Jahren an einem Gymnasium, und juristiche Grundkenntnisse, wie sie in 2 Semestern an einer Universität erworben werden können, werden für die Lernenden vorausgesetzt. Für das Unterrichten mit Hilfe dieses Buches sind Rechtskenntnisse zwar nützlich, aber nicht unbedingt erforderlich. *The Law & Language of Contracts and Torts* versucht, die Rechtsprobleme, die in den verschiedenen Orginaltexten ans Licht kommen, auch im Detail sprachlich und fachlich zu untersuchen, damit sie für jeden Leser klar sind. Das Buch liefert ein Lehr- und Lernprogramm, das die Studierenden auch auffordert, zwischen ihrem eigenen Rechtssystem und dem common law-System Vergleiche zu ziehen. Diese Orientierung erleichtert dem Nicht-Juristen das Unterrichten insofern, als er sich in aktiven Diskussionen während des Unterrichts die Lösungen der Rechtsprobleme, die in dem Buch angesprochen werden, von den Studierenden nach dem einheimischen Recht erläutern lassen kann. Darüber hinaus werden die Studierenden dadurch veranlasst, über ihr eigenes Rechtssystem in der englischen Fachsprache zu reden.

III. Struktur und Aufbau des Lehr- und Lernprogramms

The Law & Language of Contracts and Torts besteht aus zwei Einheiten, die jeweils in mehrere Kapitel unterteilt sind. Wenn das Buch als Unterstützung für den Unterricht im Rahmen eines Recht- und Sprachenprogramms oder einer fachspezifischen Fremdsprachenausbildung an einer Hochschule benutzt wird, kann es bei einer Unterrichtsdauer von 2 SWS innerhalb von 2 bis 3 Semestern durchgearbeitet werden, und zwar nach dem folgenden Zeitplan:

    Unit I. Contracts (1 bis 2 Semester)
    Unit II. Torts (1 Semester)

Unit I: Contracts bietet Ihnen
- in *Chapter 1* einen allgemeinen Überblick über die Voraussetzungen und die Wirkungen eines Vertrages, über die Rechtsfolgen eines Vertragsbruchs und über die verschiedenen Vertragstypen,
- in *Chapter 2* Ausführungen über die Schließung von Verträgen durch Angebot und Annahme, über Widerrufsmöglichkeiten, über die bindende Wirkung der Annahme und über Optionsrechte,

- in *Chapter 3* eine ausführliche Erklärung der "Consideration"-Doktrin, die Leistung und Gegenleistung als Kern der bindenden Wirkung einer Vereinbarung ansieht,
- in *Chapter 4* eine Darstellung der wichtigsten Gründe, warum eine Vertragspartei von der Verpflichtung zur Leistung befreit wird, und
- in *Chapter 5* eine Einführung in den *Uniform Commercial Code*, die die unterschiedlichen rechtlichen Voraussetzungen für einen Kaufvertrag zwischen Privaten und einen Kaufvertrag zwischen Kaufleuten erläutert.

Unit II: Torts bietet Ihnen
- in *Chapter 1* Ausführungen über vorsätzliche unerlaubte Handlungen wie beispielsweise vorsätzliche Körperverletzungen,
- in *Chapter 2* Ausführungen zu den fahrlässigen unerlaubten Handlungen und einer Reihe damit verwandter Problembereiche und
- in *Chapter 3* eine Einführung in das Produkthaftungsrecht, das besonders in den USA im Privatrecht eine zentrale Rolle spielt.

Es ist nicht so, daß die Grundzüge des Vertrags- und Deliktsrechts lediglich abstrakt angesprochen würden. Statt dessen führt *Contracts and Torts* in das Lesen von englischen und U.S.-amerikanischen Gerichtsentscheidungen – die wichtigste Quellen der common law-Rechtsprinzipien – ein und versucht, den Studierenden nahezubringen, wie sie diese Rechtsprinzipien in den Entscheidungen erkennen können. Die Studierenden sollten dabei auch lernen, Fälle miteinander zu vergleichen und voneinander zu unterscheiden, damit sie Analogien zu weiteren Fällen bilden können und dadurch lernen, in der Weise englischsprachiger Juristen zu argumentieren. Darüberhinaus enthält das Buch Gesetzestexte und Sekundärliteratur zu diesen Themen.

The Law & Language of Contracts and Torts will die Fähigkeiten, die die Studierenden bereits durch ihre Arbeit mit *Introduction to Anglo-American Law & Language* entwickeln konnten, noch weiter fördern. Insofern setzt das Buch Grundkenntnisse des common law-Systems voraus. Damit Sie aber mit diesem Buch auch selbständig arbeiten können, habe ich die Terminologie, die für das Verständnis der Texte notwendig, aber schon in meiner *Introduction* erklärt worden ist, in einer "*Terminology Review*," die jedem einzelnen Kapitel folgt, besonders aufgeführt.

Natürlich ist es nicht möglich, in *The Law & Language of Contracts and Torts* eine umfassende Darstellung des Vertrags- und Deliktsrechts zu geben. Doch habe ich versucht, dadurch eine solide Grundlage zu schaffen, daß die Darstellung etwas mehr in die Tiefe der juristischen Problematik eindringt. Die ausführliche Darstellung der relevanten Terminologie, die Fragen zum Text, die Erklärungen der prozeßrechtlichen Aspekte der Fallentscheidungen und die fachsprachlichen Übungen sollen Sie aber in der Lage versetzen, vertrags- und deliktsrechtliche Texte jeder möglichen Art ohne Probleme selbständig zu lesen und zu verstehen.

IV. Arbeiten mit *The Law & Language of Contracts and Torts*

Aus welchem Grunde auch immer Sie Interesse an diesem Buch gefunden haben, sollten Sie – um den höchsten Erfolg zu erzielen – folgendes beachten:

- Dieses Buch baut Ihre Sprachkompetenz und Ihr Verständnis für die common law-Lösung von Rechtsfragen kontinuierlich auf und sollte deswegen langsam von vorne nach hinten durchgearbeitet werden; dabei sollte die Rechtsterminologie im ersten Kapitel verstanden und gelernt sein, bevor Sie mit dem zweiten Kapitel anfangen, usw.

- Bevor Sie mit den verschiedenen Rechtstexten konfrontiert werden, führt das Buch Sie erst einmal in jedes der einzelnen Rechtsgebiete ein. Dabei wird die für das Verstehen der Texte notwendige Terminologie durch **Fettdruck** hervorgehoben und erläutert. Die Terminologie wird auch in Listen aufgeführt, die Sie in den einzelnen Kapiteln finden. Dort finden Sie auch Definitionen und, soweit das sinnvoll ist, Übersetzungen oder Übertragungen ins Deutsche. Darüber hinaus versucht das Buch, Ihren allgemeinen Wortschatz dadurch zu erweitern, daß es auch solche englische Wörter in Wortschatzlisten aufführt und definiert, die nach meiner Erfahrung Studenten oft nicht geläufig sind.

- Wenn Sie die Einführung verstanden und die Terminologie gelernt haben, sollten Sie die orginalen Rechtstexte durchlesen und dabei versuchen, ihren Sinn auch ohne die mitgelieferten Analysen der Rechtsprobleme so gut wie möglich zu verstehen. Überlegen Sie sich, was Ihnen noch nicht klar ist und wie Sie vorgehen würden, um die Unklarheiten selbständig zu beseitigen.

- Nach jedem Text finden Sie eine ausführliche Analyse der Rechtsprobleme und der benutzten Rechtsterminologie. Achten Sie darauf, wie sich Probleme lösen lassen, die beim Verständnis eines Textes immer noch bestehen bleiben. Sie werden sehen, daß das Buch oft ein Rechtswörterbuch "Englisch-Englisch" sowie Kommentare und andere Sekundärliteratur als Hilfsmittel heranzieht. Diese Methode sollte Ihnen klar werden, damit Sie lernen, solche Verständnisprobleme selbständig zu lösen. Ich habe bewußt die Hilfsmittel, die ich bei der Analyse benutze, danach ausgesucht, daß Sie sie auch in einer relativ schlecht ausgestatteten juristischen Bibliothek noch finden können.

- Wenn Sie einen Text als ganzen verstanden und sich mit der Terminologie vertraut gemacht haben, sollten Sie ihn nochmals durchlesen und sich dieses Mal darauf konzentrieren, die genaue Bedeutung jedes einzelnen Satzes zu verstehen.

- Im Anschluß an die Texte finden Sie Übungen ("Questions on the Text"), die Sie anregen sollen, das Gelernte noch einmal zu überdenken und sich dabei selbst zu prüfen, ob Sie die im Text angespochenen Probleme wirklich verstanden haben. Diese Übungen sind auch für die aktive Diskussion im Rahmen eines Lehrprogramms besonders geeignet.

- Bei der Bearbeitung der Texte sollten Sie sich den sprachlichen Rahmen merken, in dem die Terminologie benutzt wird. Um Sie dabei zu unterstützen, liefert das Buch zusätzliche Terminologie-Übungen ("Language Exercises"), die Sie am Ende jedes Kapitels finden.

- Jeweils am Ende der Lehr-Einheiten ("Units") mache ich Vorschläge, was Sie lesen können, um sich weiter in das jeweilige Rechtsgebiet zu vertiefen. Die Gerichtsentscheidungen, die ich anführe, sind dafür geeignet, daß Sie sie gewissermaßen als Hausaufgabe lesen und bearbeiten und dann Ihren Freunden vortragen. Auf diese Weise wird Ihre Fähigkeit gefördert, juristische Texte selbständig zu verstehen, zu erläutern und darüber zu diskutieren. Darüber hinaus ist die Methode fraglos dafür geeignet, in das Rechtsgebiet, um das es jeweils geht, immer weiter einzudringen.

- Am Endes des Buches finden Sie ein vollständiges Glossar, das die juristische Terminologie mit Definitionen und deutschen Übersetzungen und Übertragungen enthält. Das Glossar gibt auch Hinweise darauf, wo die Ausdrücke in dem Buch zu finden sind, und kann deshalb auch als Sachregister benutzt werden.

Eine Bemerkung zum Thema "Politically Correct Speech": In diesem Buch verwende ich in den Beispielen, bei denen es um Kläger, Rechtsanwälte, Richter usw. geht, die Ausdrücke "he" und "she" gleichermaßen. Das ist in Großbritannien und in den U.S.A. heute üblich. Sie sollten deswegen nicht denken – was viele Leser schon gedacht haben -, daß es sich um einen Druckfehler handelt, wenn "The judge.... she" vorkommt.

Eine Bemerkung zum Unterschied zwischen britischem und amerikanischem Englisch: Sie werden in diesem Buch authentische Texte sowohl aus England als auch aus den USA finden. Dabei werden Sie sicher merken, daß in der Rechtssprache die Unterschiede nicht so groß sind, wie sie auf der Konversationsebene Ihnen vielleicht erscheinen mögen. Sogar die Rechtsterminologie im engeren Sinne ist meistens dieselbe oder doch so ähnlich, daß die Unterschiede als nicht sehr problematisch bewältigt werden können. Nichtsdestoweniger habe ich mich in den Fällen einer Differenz in der Terminologie darum bemüht, sowohl die englischen als auch die U.S.-amerikanischen Ausdrücke und Begriffe zu liefern. Auch versuche ich, auf die manchmal unterschiedliche Schreibweise in England und in den Vereinigten Staaten hinzuweisen.

Table of Contents

Vorwort   VII

Einführung und methodische Hinweise   IX

Unit I: *Contracts*   1

Chapter 1: Contract Formation and Breach   3

   A. Specialty and Simple Contracts   3

   B. Unilateral and Bilateral Contracts   4

   C. Consideration for Simple Contracts   5

   D. Breach of Contract   7

      Carlill v. Carbolic Smoke Ball Co   10

      Analysis 10, 12, 13, 16, 17

      Questions on the Text 11, 13, 19

      Lefkowitz v. Great Minneapolis Surplus Store   19

      Terminology   21

      Terminology Review   24

Language Exercises Chapter 1   28

Chapter 2: Offer and Acceptance   31

   A. Validity of Acceptance   31

      Analysis   32

   B. Right to Revoke the Offer and the Acceptance   33

      Questions on the Text   34

   C. Consideration and Option Contracts   35

      Petterson v. Pattberg   36

      Analysis   37

      Questions on the Text 38, 39

      Terminology   44

      Terminology Review   46

Language Exercises Chapter 2   47

Chapter 3: Consideration.   50

    A. Exclusive Dealership Contracts   50

       Wood v. Lucy, Lady Duff-Gordon   50

       Questions on the Text 51, 53

    B. Apparent Give-Aways   54

       Maughs v. Porter   54

       Questions on the Text 55, 57, 58

    C. Detrimental Reliance   59

       Allegheny College v. National Chautauqua County Bank   59

       Questions on the Text 60, 65, 66

       Analysis   63

       Terminology   67

       Terminology Review   69

Language Exercises Chapter 3   72

Chapter 4: Defenses to Claims of Breach and Rights of Avoidance   74

    A. Impossibility   74

       Taylor and Another v. Caldwell and Another   74

       Questions on the Text 75, 80

       Analysis   77

    B. Frustration of Purpose   81

       Krell v. Henry   81

       Questions on the Text   83

    C. Mistake, Misrepresentation and Fraud   83

       Wood v. Boynton   83

       Analysis 84, 86, 89

       Questions on the Text 85, 88, 91

       Terminology   91

       Terminology Review   95

Language Exercises Chapter 4   97

Chapter 5: Uniform Commercial Code   100

    A. Application of the *U.C.C.*   102

       1. Choice of Law   103

       2. Conflict of Laws   103

    B. Scope of the *U.C.C*   104

    C. Modifications of the Requirements for Effective Acceptance of an Offer   105

1. Demise of the Mirror-Image Rule 106
      Analysis 107
      Questions on the Text 108
2. Method and Medium of Acceptance 109
      Analysis 110
      Questions on the Text 111
3. Open Terms and Gap Fillers 112
      Questions on the Text 115
D. Modification of the Consideration Requirement 115
  1. Options 116
  2. Pre-Existing Legal Duty Rule 116
      Questions on the Text 118
      Terminology 118
      Terminology Review 121
      Suggested Reading & Web Sites 121

Language Exercises Chapter 5 123

Unit II: *Torts* 125

Chapter 1: Intentional Torts 127
A. Battery 127
  Analysis 128
  Mink v. University of Chicago 129
  Analysis 130, 134, 135, 137
  Questions on the Text 138
B. Assault 139
  Prosser & Keeton on The Law of Torts: Assault 139
  Questions on the Text 140
  Terminology 141
  Terminology Review 143

Language Exercises Chapter 1 145

Chapter 2: Negligent Torts 148
A. Duty of Care 148
B. Breach of Duty 150
  United States et al. v. Carroll Towing Co., Inc., et al. 151
  1. The Master - Servant Relationship 155

Questions on the Text.. 157

   2. *Contributory and Comparative Negligence* 160

   3. *The Standard of Care* 162

C. Cause in Fact.. 162

Untaken Precautions (Mark F. Grady) 163

Questions on the Text.. 164

D. Proximate Cause 164

Palsgraf v. Long Island Railroad................................... 166

Questions on the Text.. 166, 167

   1. *Transferred Intent*... 169

   Prosser & Keeton on The Law of Torts 169

   2. *The Domains of Judge and Jury in Negligence Cases* 170

      Questions on the Text................................. 171, 173, 177

      Terminology 178

      Terminology Review 181

Language Exercises Chapter 2 184

Chapter 3: Products Liability...................................... 186

A. Construction Defects... 187

Escola v. Coca Cola Bottling Co 187

Analysis... 188

Res Ipsa Loquitur 189

Questions on the Text 191, 193

B. Design Defects.. 193

Greenman v. Yuba Power Products, Inc 193

Analysis.. 194, 195, 197

Questions on the Text 196

C. Failure to Warn 200

Sindell v. Abbott Laboratories.................................... 201

Questions on the Text 203, 205, 208

Terminology 208

Terminology Review 211

Suggested Reading & Web Sites 213

Language Exercises Chapter 3 214

Answers to Language Exercises 217
Answers to Questions on the Text 231
Bibliography 259
Glossary of Terminology 265

Unit I
Contracts

This Unit on contract law contains five chapters. The first Chapter will give you a general overview of the types of contracts recognized by the **common law,** the general requirements for their validity and the **remedies** available for their breach. This Chapter also includes one detailed case analysis. The case selected for this chapter is *Carlill v. Carbolic Smoke Ball Co.*, an English case decided around the turn of the century. This case is quite popularly used for introducing the topic, because it covers every step of the contracting process. In Chapter 2, we will delve deeper into the contract formation process by considering the offer and its acceptance. Chapter 3 is devoted to the concept of consideration, which is a basic requirement for a simple contract to be binding under the common law, but which is not necessary under the law of most continental European systems. Chapter 4 will consider defenses an individual who has been sued for breach of contract can raise on his behalf and rights the parties may have to declare certain contracts void. Finally, in Chapter 5 we will consider the *Uniform Commercial Code.* In particular we will deal with Article 2 of this code in an effort to indicate what changes it makes in the common law regarding contracts for the sale of goods.

Chapter 1
Contract Formation and Breach

A. Specialty and Simple Contracts

A contract represents the agreement of two parties, who are called **parties to the contract**. The agreement process is initiated by the **offeror**, who makes an **offer** to the **offeree.** If the offeree **accepts** the offeror's offer, the contract is **closed.** The contract will be legally **binding** only if one of two requirements is fulfilled. Either the contract must be **formalized** or it must be **supported by consideration.**

Formalization consists of having the contract **signed, sealed and delivered.** Some laws require that the signature be **witnessed** by at least one other person. A **seal** may be wax, or a paper wafer, or even some sign or mark on the document if the document itself makes clear that this sign or mark is intended to be a seal. In England, a formalized contract is referred to as a **deed** or a **contract by deed.** In the United States, a formalized contract is called a **sealed contract.**

Consideration is a complex concept and at the heart of the difference between the common law concept of contract and continental European legal concepts. It is often defined as a **mutually bargained-for exchange** between the parties. A mutually bargained-for exchange is something akin to the idea *do ut des* meaning "give in order to receive." Suffice it to say for the present that for a non-formalized contract to be binding, the parties each have to receive something they negotiated for in exchange for whatever it is they gave the other party to the contract. The doctrine of consideration will be dealt with on a step-by-step basis as we proceed and will be given particular attention in Chapter 3.

Accordingly, the common law divides contracts into two major categories:
1) **specialty contracts**: contracts that are binding only if **formalized.** A typical example of a specialty contract is a **donative (gratuitous)** contract, which involves a promise to make a gift.
2) **simple contracts** (also referred to as **informal** contracts): contracts that are binding only if **supported by consideration.** The typical **sales contract** is usually a simple contract.

Hence the elements of a binding contract under the common law are: 1) **offer**, 2) **acceptance**, and 3) **formalization**, for **specialty contracts**, or **consideration**, for **simple contracts**. Since the vast majority of contracts actually closed are simple contracts, the remainder of this Unit will be devoted to them.

B. Unilateral and Bilateral Contracts

Simple contracts are either **unilateral** or **bilateral** contracts. A **unilateral contract** is a promise in exchange for an act. A **bilateral contract** is a promise in exchange for a promise.

A typical example of an **offer for a unilateral contract** is the posting of a reward. "I will give anyone who brings back my lost dog $50.00." Here the **offeror** is bargaining for the act of bringing back the dog, and not for a promise to bring back the dog. Accordingly, the contract is **unilateral** and not bilateral. The **offeree** accepts the offer by doing what the offeror requests. Doing what the offeror requests is also the **consideration** the offeree gives to the offeror for the offeror's promise to pay the reward. Hence for unilateral contracts performance of the act requested by the offeror is simultaneously both **acceptance of the offer** and **consideration for the contract**. The consideration the offeror provides in return for the act requested is the promise to pay the $50 reward. *Nota bene*: It is important not to confuse the German legal notion of *einseitiges Rechtsgeschäft* with the common law unilateral contract even though the meaning of the word **unilateral** may appear to correspond to the idea of *einseitig*. German law does not characterize promises in exchange for acts as constituting a separate category of contracts, so any attempt to simply translate these terms is doomed to failure from the start. Furthermore, an *einseitiges Rechtsgeschäft* involves only one person's **declaration of will**, whereas a unilateral contract involves two declarations of will. The offeror makes this declaration by posting the reward. The offeree makes it by performing the act.

A typical example of an **offer for a bilateral contract** is the offer to sell goods. "I will sell you my automobile for $5,000." Here the offeror expects the offeree to respond by promising to pay $5,000 for the automobile. The offeror in this type of case is not requesting the offeree to immediately hand over the money (perform an act), but rather to accept the offer through giving a return promise. The return promise is the **acceptance** of the offer. Here the **consideration** the offeror provides the offeree is the promise to sell the automobile for $5,000. The consideration the offeree provides the offeror is the promise to pay $5,000 for the automobile.

Contracts under the common law can be illustrated through the following chart:

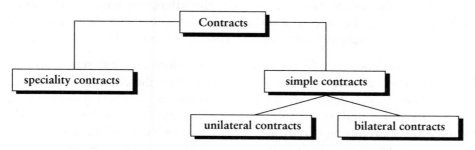

C. Consideration for Simple Contracts

Let us briefly introduce the idea of **consideration** by looking at the following sections of the *Restatement (Second) Contracts*. The *Restatement (Second)* was adopted in 1979 by the American Law Institute. It represents the efforts of scholars and practitioners to **codify** the common law of contracts, at least as it has developed over the years in the United States. Although the *Restatement* is **codified law,** it has not been uniformly adopted by the individual states in the United States. Still, because it codifies the **common law of contracts,** courts consider it to be good authority for deciding cases, even in the absence of legislative enactment:

§ 17 Requirement of a Bargain

(1) Except as stated in Subsection (2), the formation of a contract requires a bargain in which there is a manifestation of mutual assent to the exchange and a consideration.

(2) Whether or not there is a bargain a contract may be formed under special rules applicable to formal contracts ...

§ 71 Requirement of Exchange; Types of Exchange

(1) To constitute consideration, a performance or a return promise must be bargained for.

(2) A performance or return promise is bargained for if it is sought by the promisor in exchange for his promise and is given by the promisee in exchange for that promise.

(3) The performance may consist of

    (a) an act other than a promise, or

    (b) a forbearance, ...

Section 17 states what you already know, namely that 1) a contract is formed through a **manifestation of mutual assent. Mutual assent,** or the agreement of both of the contracting parties, is **manifested**, or shown, through the making of an offer and the acceptance of that offer; the **offeror** manifests her assent in making her offer; the **offeree** manifests it by accepting that offer; and 2) the contract has to be supported by consideration or formalized to be binding.

Section 71(1) refers to consideration as either a performance or a return promise. If consideration consists of some performance, then the contract is **unilateral**. Furthermore, § 71(3) defines what types of performance can be given in exchange for an offer for a unilateral contract. The performance might be an act (other than the act of promising in return, in which case we have a bilateral rather than a unilateral contract) or a **forbearance**. In the example we have already discussed, the consideration for the promise to pay $ 50 was the act, not of promising ("other than a promise"), but of actually bringing back the dog. But we can imagine a case in which the offeror does not want the offeree to do something, but rather to refrain (**to forbear**) from doing something that she perhaps otherwise would do. Consider the case of A, who is concerned about his daughter's (D's) health. A promises to give D a mink coat if D forbears from drinking alcohol and smoking for one year. Here A is not bargaining for D's promise not to drink alcohol or smoke. Accordingly, A is not bound to give D the mink coat until the year is actually over and D has in fact refrained as specified in A's promise. It is important to note that one cannot forbear from doing something that one is physically unable to do. I cannot **forbear** from jumping to the moon, for example, because it is not within my physical capacity to undertake that act anyway. Consequently, a forbearance is always something that a person otherwise could do, but in fact does not do.

If consideration is a return promise we have a **bilateral contract**. Here the offeree is required to give a promise in return for the offeror's promise. Since the offeror initiated the contracting process, he has already made a promise that becomes binding as soon as it is accepted by the offeree's making a return promise. As a result, each party to a **bilateral contract** has given the other party a promise in return for the promise made by that other party. At the point at which the promises have been exchanged, which occurs with the offeree's acceptance, both parties are contractually bound. Note the difference to the unilateral contract, where the offeror is not bound until the offeree has actually performed the act requested.

Finally, § 71(1) and (2) refer to the requirement that the consideration be **bargained for**. This apparently simple requirement can cause considerable confusion. Consider the example of a wealthy philanthropist (P) who sees a poor tramp (T) sitting on the street. P says to T that she will buy him a good solid meal. All T need do is go around the corner to the restaurant where P is a regular customer and order whatever food he would like on P's account. Although it is true that T will have to perform the act of going to the restaurant in order to take advantage of P's promise, P is not bargaining for T to perform that act. Instead she is making a promise to give T a donation. T merely has to accept the gift by going to the restaurant. A gift, or a promise to make a gift, can, by its very nature, never become a binding simple contract because it is not supported by consideration. In our example discussed above of A promising D to give her a mink coat if she refrains from using alcohol and tobacco for one year, A is bargaining for the forbearance, and not merely making a gift of the mink coat to D. One way of answering the question of whether a contract is supported by consideration or not, is to consider what motivated the parties to make their promises, or to perform, or forbear from performing, a certain act. Our philanthropist is motivated by the desire to help T and not by any personal interest in having T walk around the corner and order food at a restaurant. A, however, is motivated by the prospect of stopping D's excessive lifestyle for a year, and not by any desire to make a donation of a mink coat.

Note that Section 71(2) refers to the parties as the **promisor** and the **promisee**. The terms **promisor** and **promisee** are used more broadly than the terms **offeror** and **offeree**. Since many contracts consist of the exchange of promises, each of the parties is both a promisor and a promisee. The promisor is the person making a promise and the promisee is the person to whom a promise is made. The **offeror**, however, is always the person who initiates the contracting process by making an offer. The **offeree** is always the person to whom the offer is made and who therefore has the power to accept and close the contract. Accordingly, by using the terms **promisor** and **promisee**, § 71(2) refers to *both* the bargain the offeror makes with the offeree and the bargain the offeree makes with the offeror. Each party must use his promise, act or forbearance in order to attain something he wishes to have in return. Otherwise the consideration is not bargained for.

D. Breach of Contract

When a party fails to fulfill her obligation under a contract that party is **in breach of contract**. Here again, the common law way of thinking about this issue is very different from the way German law approaches the problem. Perhaps under the influence of an **adversary system of trial**, where the parties confront one another in open court with their individual claims, the common law lawyer tends to think about the law in terms of the parties' opposition to each other. When performance is due and the party does not perform, we would say the party is **in breach of contract**. There may be **defenses** for breach of contract that the breaching party can argue on his behalf, such as **impossibility of performance** or **immateriality of** the breach, but these arguments are exactly what they are called, *defenses* **to a claim of breach.** Contrarily, the German lawyer would not jump to the conclusion that a party is in breach of contract merely because he has not performed when performance is due. Instead, the German approach tends to analyze what we would consider defenses to the claim of breach of contract, such as **impossibility of performance** or **immateriality of the breach,** on a level prior to any final determination that the contract has been breached. The term **breach,** to the extent used at all, would be reserved for the final conclusion that the non-performing party, although capable of performing, simply refuses to do so. This difference in approaching **breach of contract** within the two systems does not have as many consequences for the final conclusions drawn in individual cases, but it does strongly influence the way lawyers talk about the issues.

If a contract has been breached, the **non-breaching party** can file a law suit against the **breaching party.** In this context, one would call the **non-breaching party** the **promisee,** because she is claiming that the **breaching party,** called the **promisor,** promised her something but did not fulfill the promise. In this sense the terms are used very similarly to *Gläubiger* and *Schuldner* in the German *Civil Code* (*BGB*) sections relating to contractual obligations, the Gläubiger, or promisee, being the person to whom something is owed, and the Schuldner, or promisor, being the person who owes it.

The typical **remedy** under the common law for breach of contract is **money damages.** The word **remedy** designates what it is that a court can award an injured party to make up for that party's injury. **Money damages,** which are also called **compensatory damages,** are designed to put the **non-breaching party** in the position he would have been in had the contract not been breached. Consider the typical sales contract where A promises to sell B an automobile for $ 5,000. The money damages that would make up for B's injuries or losses if A breaches the contract would be the difference between what B promised to pay A for the automobile ($ 5,000) and the amount B would have to pay to buy a comparable automobile elsewhere.

Although **money damages** is the typical **remedy for breach of contract,** in some cases the court may award the **equitable remedy** of **specific performance.** Here the breaching party is required to do whatever he promised to do under the contract (**to perform specifically**). This remedy will be awarded only in cases in which the court determines that justice cannot be done by merely awarding money damages. One classic example of a case where courts will award **specific performance** is when the **subject matter of the contract** is **unique.** In cases of unique goods, such as an original Picasso, money damages usually cannot place the non-breaching party in the position she would have been in had the contract been performed, because no amount of money can buy a "comparable" Picasso.

On the question of **remedies for breach of contract,** consider the following sections from the *Restatement (Second) Contracts*:

§ 347. Measure of Damages in General

Subject to the limitations stated in §§ 350–53, the injured party has a right to damages based on his expectation interest as measured by

(a) the loss in the value to him of the other party's performance caused by its failure or deficiency, plus

(b) any other loss, including incidental or consequential loss, caused by the breach, less

(c) any cost or other loss that he has avoided by not having to perform.

§ 357. Availability of Specific Performance ...

(1) Subject to the rules stated in §§ 359–69, specific performance of a contract duty will be granted in the discretion of the court against a party who has committed or is threatening to commit a breach of the duty ...

§ 359. Effect of Adequacy of Damages

(1) Specific performance ... will not be ordered if damages would be adequate to protect the expectation interest of the injured party.

§ 360. Factors Affecting Adequacy of Damages

In determining whether the remedy in damages would be adequate, the following circumstances are significant:

(a) the difficulty of proving damages with reasonable certainty,

(b) the difficulty of procuring a suitable substitute performance by means of money awarded as damages, and

(c) the likelihood that an award of damages could not be collected.

As you can see from §§ 347 and 359 of the *Restatement*, the **remedy for breach of contract** is **money damages,** rather than **specific performance,** assuming that the remedy in damages would be adequate. Money damages are not adequate, for example, when the non-breaching party cannot obtain a suitable substitute for the promised performance with the money he receives as damages (§ 360 (b)). One typical example of inability to obtain a substitute performance is when the promised performance concerns transferring ownership in unique goods. In such cases the court, in its discretion, can recognize a **cause of action for the remedy of specific performance** (§ 357).

Now that you have gained a very general understanding of the common law of contracts and the terminology used to discuss it, read the following case, which will be interrupted to provide you with a step-by-step analysis to facilitate understanding:

Carlill v. Carbolic Smoke Ball Co.

1 Q.B. 256 [1893]

Appeal from a decision of Hawkins J. [1892].

5   The defendants, who were the proprietors and vendors of a medical preparation
called "The Carbolic Smoke Ball," inserted in the *Pall Mall Gazette* of November 13,
1891, and in other newspapers, the following advertisement:

> £100 reward will be paid by the Carbolic Smoke Ball Company to any person
> who contracts the increasing epidemic influenza, colds, or any disease caused
10   > by taking cold, after having used the ball three times daily for two weeks
> according to the printed directions supplied with each ball. £1,000 is de-
> posited with the Alliance Bank, Regent Street, showing our sincerity in the
> matter ...

The plaintiff, a lady, on the faith of this advertisement, bought one of the balls at a
15   chemist's, and used it as directed, three times a day from November 20, 1891, to
January 17, 1892, when she was attacked by influenza. Hawkins J. held that she was
entitled to recover the £100. The defendants appealed.

Analysis

Notice the forms: **vendor**: seller and **vend<u>ee</u>**: buyer, purchaser. The endings **-or**
and **-ee** are commonly used by English speaking lawyers, the former indicating
a person who undertakes to do something and the latter a person for or to whom
the thing is done. Other examples include: **lessor**, or the person leasing out
property, and the **lessee**, or the person to whom the property is leased; **donor**, or
the person making a gift, and **donee**, or the person to whom the gift is made; and,
as we have already seen, the offer**or** and the offer**ee**, the promis**or** and the promis**ee**.

The trial court in this case held in favor of Ms. Carlill saying that she was **entitled
to recover** £ 100, which is another way of saying that she was awarded the
remedy of **money damages**. Admittedly, money damages and specific performance in this case would be the same, because in either event the defendant has to
hand over £100 to Ms. Carlill. Still, in a common law system we speak of money
damages rather than specific performance as being the remedy for the defendant's breach in this case. Ms. Carlill would have a right to specific performance
only if the reward were something unique that she could not purchase with the
money damages she might receive, or, for any of the other reasons listed in § 360
of the *Restatement*, money damages would be inadequate to compensate for the
defendant's breach.

Questions on the Text

☐1 Give a short statement of the **facts of this case**. Use the appropriate terminology: "The plaintiff in this case ... "

☐2 What is the **legal history of the case**? What was the decision of the lower court? "The lower court held ... " As you know from *Einführung in die anglo-amerikanische Rechtssprache / Introduction to Anglo-American Law & Language*, Unit I, Chapter 1, p. 15 et seq., when you read a case, you should always be able to discuss the **facts of the case**, the **legal history of the case**, the **issue raised on appeal**, the **holding**, and the **ratio decidendi** of the case. The **facts of the case** refer to the facts that are relevant for the legal issue raised in the case. The **legal history of the case** is the treatment of the case by any of the lower courts which considered it before it reached the court whose decision you are currently reading. The **issue raised on appeal** is the legal problem confronting the court whose decision you are reading. The **holding** is the resolution of that legal problem. The **ratio decidendi** is the legal principle, theory, or reasoning that permits the court to reach the holding it reached. You should have these questions in mind anytime you read a case.

☐3 Discuss the solution to this case within your own legal system. Who would win the case? What arguments can you make for each of the two parties? Regardless of your own legal system's solution to this case, who do you think should win the case out of considerations of justice and fairness?

☐4 Who is the **offeror** and the **offeree** in this case under the common law?

☐5 Is this a **specialty** contract or a **simple** contact?

☐6 Is the offer an offer for a **bilateral** or **unilateral** contract?

☐7 Was the offer accepted and if so how?

☐8 What were the parties bargaining for? What could be the **consideration** for the agreement passing from Ms. Carlill to the company and passing from the company to Ms. Carlill?

Continue reading the case:

Bowen L.J.: We were asked to say that this document was a contract too vague to be enforced.

20   The first observation which arises is that the document itself is not a contract at all, it is only an offer made to the public. The defendants contend next that it is an offer the terms of which are too vague to be treated as a definite offer, inasmuch as there is no limit of time fixed for the catching of the influenza, and it cannot be supposed that the advertisers seriously meant to promise to pay money to every person who catches

25   the influenza at any time after the inhaling of the smoke ball. It was urged also that if you look at this document you will find much vagueness as to the persons with

whom the contract was intended to be made – that, in the first place, its terms are wide enough to include persons who may have used the smoke ball before the advertisement was issued; at all events, that it is an offer to the world in general, and,
30   also, that it is unreasonable to suppose it to be a definite offer, because nobody in their senses would contract themselves out of the opportunity of checking the experiment which was going to be made at their own expense. It is also contended that the advertisement is rather in the nature of a puff or a proclamation than a promise or offer intended to mature into a contract when accepted. But the main point seems to
35   be that the vagueness of the document shows that no contract whatever was intended.

It seems to me that in order to arrive at a right conclusion we must read this advertisement in its plain meaning, as the public would understand it. It was intended to be issued to the public and to be read by the public. How would an
40   ordinary person reading this document construe it? It was intended unquestionably to have some effect, and I think the effect which it was intended to have, was to make people use the smoke ball, because the suggestions and allegations which it contains are directed immediately to the use of the smoke ball as distinct from the purchase of it. It did not follow that the smoke ball was to be purchased from the defendants
45   directly, or even from agents of theirs directly. The intention was that the circulation of the smoke ball should be promoted, and that the use of it should be increased.

Analysis

In this section of the case, the court concentrates on the company's intent in placing the advertisement. In fact the court is careful to point out that the defendant company did not require the smoke ball to be purchased from the company itself or from its agents (**agents** are those who act for another, those who conduct business for another party, who is called the **principal**). Instead, the purpose or motivation for the company to place the advertisement was to promote the use of the smoke ball. What is the reason for this distinction? In answering this question, try to analyze the issue of **consideration** in this case. What is the consideration for the *sales contract*, or the contract between Ms. Carlill and the druggist where she purchased the smoke ball? What is the consideration for the contract with the Carbolic Smoke Ball Co.? Is it important when trying to determine what the parties were bargaining for that one consider their individual motivations in acting the way they did?

The Carbolic Smoke Ball Co. claimed that the advertisement was intended to be a puff and not an **offer to contract**. Certainly, the company would have preferred to promote their sales without ever having to pay anyone the £100. If they only intended to attract customers but not to pay anyone the £100, why does the court consider the meaning of the advertisement as the public would understand it? Why does it not simply accept the company's own statement of its intent in placing the advertisement? Does it make any difference what an offeror subjectively intended? What is the difference between the company's motivation for placing the advertisement when trying to determine whether there was consideration for the agreement, and the company's claim regarding what it subjectively intended?

Questions on the Text

1. What issue is the judge discussing in this passage? It is one of several **issues raised on appeal** to this court.
2. What arguments did the defendant advance on its behalf? Could the defendant have made the same arguments under the law of your legal system?
3. What counter-arguments can you advance for Ms. Carlill?
4. From reading this passage, what can you say about the nature of an offer to contract? What requirements must the offeror's manifestation of intent meet in order to be viewed by a court as an offer to contract?

Continue reading the case:

> It was also said that the contract is made with all the world – that is, with everybody; and that you cannot contract with everybody. It is not a contract made with all the world. There is the fallacy of the argument. It is an offer made to all the world; and
> 50 why should not an offer be made to all the world which is to ripen into a contract with anybody who comes forward and performs the condition? It is an offer to become liable to anyone who, before it is retracted, performs the condition, and although the offer is made to the world, the contract is made with that limited portion of the public who come forward and perform the condition on the faith of
> 55 the advertisement. It is not like cases in which you offer to negotiate, or you issue advertisements that you have got a stock of books to sell, or houses to let, in which case there is no offer to be bound by any contract. Such advertisements are offers to negotiate – offers to receive offers – offers to chaffer, ... If this is an offer to be bound, then it is a contract the moment the person fulfils the condition.

Analysis

Offers to negotiate: In this last section of the case, the court distinguishes between an offer to negotiate and an offer to contract. What is the difference?

Consider the following sections and illustrations from the *Restatement (Second) Contracts*:

§ 26. Preliminary Negotiations

A manifestation of willingness to enter into a bargain is not an offer if the person to whom it is addressed knows or has reason to know that the person making it does not intend to conclude a bargain until he has made a further manifestation of assent.

Illustrations:

1. A, a clothing merchant, advertises overcoats of a certain kind for sale at $50. This is not an offer, but an invitation to the public to come and purchase. The addition of the words "Out they go Saturday; First Come First Served" might make the advertisement and offer.

2. A advertises that he will pay $5 for every copy of a certain book that may be sent to him. This is an offer, and A is bound to pay $5 for every copy sent while the offer is unrevoked.

§ 32. Invitation of Promise or Performance

In case of doubt an offer is interpreted as inviting the offeree to accept either by promising to perform what the offer requests or by rendering the performance, as the offeree chooses.

Who is the offeree? The court also considers the problem of identifying the offeree. The Carbolic Smoke Ball Co. argued that the newspaper advertisement was addressed to everyone, the whole world, and therefore was not individualized sufficiently to create a power of acceptance in any particular person. Consider the following section of the *Restatement (Second) Contracts*:

§ 29. To Whom an Offer is Addressed

(1) The manifested intention of the offeror determines the person or persons in whom is created a power of acceptance.

(2) An offer may create a power of acceptance in a specified person or in one or more of a specified group or class of persons, acting separately or together, or in anyone or everyone who makes a specified promise or renders a specified performance.

§ 52. Who May Accept an Offer

An offer can be accepted only by a person whom it invites to furnish the consideration.

To retract, or revoke, an offer: The court also states: "It is an offer to become liable to anyone who, before it is retracted, performs the condition ... " Consider the following sections of the *Restatement (Second) Contracts* on the retraction of offers:

§ 35. The Offeree's Power of Acceptance

(1) An offer gives to the offeree a continuing power to complete the manifestation of mutual assent by acceptance of the offer.

(2) A contract cannot be created by acceptance of an offer after the power of acceptance has been terminated in one of the ways listed in § 36.

§ 36. Methods of Termination of the Power of Acceptance

(1) An offeree's power of acceptance may be terminated by

(a) rejection or counter-offer by the offeree, or

(b) lapse of time, or

(c) revocation by the offeror, or

(d) death or incapacity of the offeror or offeree.

(2) In addition, an offeree's power of acceptance is terminated by the non-occurrence of any condition of acceptance under the terms of the offer.

Continue reading the case:

60 Then it was said that there was no notification of the acceptance of the contract. One cannot doubt that, as an ordinary rule of law, an acceptance of an offer made ought to be notified to the person who makes the offer, in order that the two minds may come together. Unless this is done the two minds may be apart, and there is not that consensus which is necessary according to the English law – I say nothing about the
65 laws of other countries – to make a contract. But there is this clear gloss to be made upon that doctrine, that as notification of acceptance is required for the benefit of the person who makes the offer, the person who makes the offer may dispense with notice to himself if he thinks it desirable to do so, and I suppose there can be no doubt that where a person in an offer made by him to another person, expressly or im-
70 pliedly intimates a particular mode of acceptance as sufficient to make the bargain binding, it is only necessary for the other person to whom such offer is made to follow the indicated method of acceptance; and if the person making the offer, expressly or impliedly intimates in his offer that it will be sufficient to act on the proposal without communicating acceptance of it to himself, performance of the
75 condition is a sufficient acceptance without notification.

Now, if that is the law, how are we to find out whether the person who makes the offer does intimate that notification of acceptance will not be necessary in order to constitute a binding bargain? In many cases you look to the offer itself. In many cases you extract from the character of the transaction that notification is not required,
80 and in the advertisement cases it seems to me to follow as an inference to be drawn from the transaction itself that a person is not to notify his acceptance of the offer before he performs the condition, but that if he performs the condition notification is dispensed with. It seems to me that from the point of view of common sense no other idea could be entertained. If I advertise to the world that my dog is lost, and
85 that anybody who brings the dog to a particular place will be paid some money, are all the police or other persons whose business it is to find lost dogs to be expected to sit down and write me a note saying that they have accepted my proposal? Why, of course, they at once look for the dog, and as soon as they find the dog they have performed the condition. The essence of the transaction is that the dog should be
90 found, and it is not necessary under such circumstances, as it seems to me, that in order to make the contract binding there should be any notification of acceptance. It

follows from the nature of the thing that the performance of the condition is sufficient acceptance without the notification of it, and a person who makes an offer in
an advertisement of that kind makes an offer which must be read by the light of that
95   common-sense reflection. He does, therefore, in his offer impliedly indicate that he
does not require notification of the acceptance of the offer.

Analysis

In this passage the court focuses on acceptance of the defendant's offer. Consider
the following sections of the *Restatement (Second) Contracts* on the acceptance
of offers:

§ 50. Acceptance of Offer Defined ...

(1) Acceptance of an offer is a manifestation of assent to the terms thereof made by
the offeree in a manner invited or required by the offer ... .

In *Carlill*, the defendant company impliedly indicated that it did not require
notification. Therefore, Ms. Carlill made her acceptance in a manner "invited ...
by the offer," in the words of the *Restatement (Second) Contracts*, and was thus
permitted to dispense with notification.

§ 23. Necessity That Manifestations Have Reference to Each Other

It is essential to a bargain that each party manifest assent with reference to the
manifestation of the other.

Suppose A announces a reward for the return of her lost cat. B, who is A's
neighbor, returns the cat in ignorance of the announcement. Is B entitled to the
reward under the common law? Under German law the result would be different.
Explain the treatment German law would give to this type of case. Consider the
fact that German law treats cases of the so-called *Auslobung* as *einseitige Rechts-
geschäfte* where only one person, the person posting the reward is giving a declaration of his will. Under the common law of contracts, acceptance of the unilateral contract is the act of doing whatever it is that the offeror requested in the
offer. Since the act is acceptance of the offer, it can also be seen as an implied
declaration of will. Would that explain why the offeree would have to know of
the reward announcement in order to effectively accept the offer it contains?

§ 54. Acceptance by Performance; Necessity of Notification to Offeror

(1) Where an offer invites an offeree to accept by rendering a performance, no
notification is necessary to make such an acceptance effective unless the offer requests such a notification ...

Does this section of the *Restatement (Second) Contracts* correspond to the determination of the court in the *Carlill* case? Does it matter whether general prin-

ciples of law are announced by the courts or adopted by the legislature in the form of statutes? If being announced by a court is enough for a principle to become binding law, as it is in a common law system, is it important that the courts be bound by their past decisions in deciding future cases?

Continue reading the case:

A further argument for the defendants was that this was a *nudum pactum* – that there was no consideration for the promise – that taking the influenza was only a condition, and that using the smoke ball was only a condition, and that there was no
100 consideration at all; in fact, that there was no request, express or implied, to use the smoke ball. Now, I will not enter into an elaborate discussion upon the law as to requests in this kind of contracts ... The short answer, to abstain from academical discussion, is, it seems to me, that there is here a request to use involved in the offer. Then as to the alleged want of consideration. The definition of "consideration" ... is
105 this: "Any act of the plaintiff from which the defendant derives a benefit or advantage, or any labour, detriment, or inconvenience sustained by the plaintiff, provided such act is performed or such inconvenience suffered by the plaintiff, with the consent, either express or implied, of the defendant." Can it be said here that if the person who reads this advertisement applies thrice daily, for such time as may seem
110 to him tolerable, the carbolic smoke ball to his nostrils for a whole fortnight, he is doing nothing at all – that it is a mere act which is not to count towards consideration to support a promise (for the law does not require us to measure the adequacy of the consideration). Inconvenience sustained by one party at the request of the other is enough to create a consideration. I think, therefore, that it is consideration enough
115 that the plaintiff took the trouble of using the smoke ball. But I think also that the defendants received a benefit from this use, for the use of the smoke ball was contemplated by the defendants as being indirectly a benefit to them, because the use of the smoke balls would promote their sale ... if you once make up your mind that there was a promise made to this lady who is the plaintiff, as one of the public – a
120 promise made to her that if she used the smoke ball three times daily for a fortnight and got the influenza, she should have £100, it seems to me that her using the smoke ball was sufficient consideration. I cannot picture to myself the view of the law on which the contrary could be held when you have once found who are the contracting parties. If I say to a person, "If you use such and such a medicine for a week I will give
125 you £5, and he uses it, there is ample consideration for the promise.

Analysis

In this passage the court discusses the **sufficiency and adequacy** of consideration for a contract. **Sufficient consideration** refers to the fact that the consideration has to be real and not just claimed to exist. It must be something that is in fact bargained for. Accordingly, the question of whether consideration for an agreement is **sufficient** is really the question of whether there was any consideration at all. This problem can arise, for example, when an individual who really intends to make a gift, but wants to avoid gift tax, claims to have sold the property to the donee for a small sum of money. Here there would be no real consideration and we would say that the consideration is **insufficient. Adequate consideration** refers to the amount of consideration given. The law will not interfere with the bargains people actually make. If a person wants to sell something below the market price for that object, the courts will not inquire into whether the price is fair. Indeed, the so-called **peppercorn doctrine** states that even a peppercorn, if actually bargained for, is sufficient to constitute consideration. It may seem difficult to distinguish between inadequate consideration and no real consideration at all (insufficient consideration), and in fact this determination must be made by a court in the light of all of the facts relevant to the case. Note in the *Carlill* case, the judge determined that using the smoke ball was sufficient consideration for the company's promise to pay the £100. Considering the value of £100 in 1893, do you think using the smokeball was adequate consideration?

This section of the court's decision includes a definition of consideration (lines 105–108) that is different from the definition you read in *Restatement (Second) Contracts § 71*. What are the differences? Consider the following text:

> [B]y the end of the nineteenth century, at least in the United States, the traditional requirement that the consideration be either a benefit to the promisor or a detriment to the promisee had begun to give way to a requirement that the consideration be "bargained for." At first it was said that the benefit or detriment had to be bargained for. But when the Restatement of Contracts was promulgated in 1933, it defined *consideration* exclusively in terms of something that was "bargained for," with no mention of benefit or detriment ... Something is said to be bargained for "if it is sought by the promisor in exchange for his promise and is given by the promisee in exchange for that promise."

> E. Allan Farnsworth, *Contracts*, Little Brown & Co.: Boston/Toronto, 1982, pp. 41–42.

The court discusses **conditions** and the defendant's argument: "that taking the influenza was only a condition, and that using the smoke ball was only a condition, ... " The court concludes that using the smoke ball was not just a condition, but rather consideration for the defendant's promise to pay £100. But the court never discusses what taking the influenza has to do with the contract. Consider the following section of the *Restatement (Second) Contracts*:

§ 224. Condition Defined

A condition is an event, not certain to occur, which must occur, ... , before performance under a contract becomes due.

§ 230. Event that Terminates a Duty

(1) ... [I]f under the terms of the contract the occurrence of an event is to terminate an obligor's duty of immediate performance ... , that duty is discharged if the event occurs.

The **condition** discussed in § 224 is usually referred to as a **condition precedent**, whereas the condition referred to in § 230 is referred to as a **condition subsequent**. The former is a condition which requires that something happen before the other party is bound to perform at all under the contract. The latter is a condition which specifies that if something occurs after the contract has been closed and perhaps even after some performance has been due under that contract the contractual relation is terminated. How would you now characterize "taking the influenza" within the contract between Ms. Carlill and the company?

Questions on the Text

❏ *Read the facts of the following case:*

Lefkowitz v. Great Minneapolis Surplus Store
251 Minn. 188, 86 N.W.2d 689 (1957)

5 Murphy, J. This is an appeal from an order of the Municipal Court of Minneapolis denying the motion of the defendant for ... a new trial. The order for judgment awarded the plaintiff the sum of $138.50 as damages for breach of contract.

This case grows out of the alleged refusal of the defendant to sell the plaintiff a certain fur piece which it had offered for sale in a newspaper advertisement. It appears from the record that ... on April 13, the defendant ... published an advertise-
10 ment in the ... newspaper as follows:

> "Saturday 9 A.M ... .
> 1 Black Lapin Stole
> Beautiful,
15 worth $139.50 ... .$1.00
> First Come
> First Served"

The record supports the findings of the court that on ... the Saturday..following the
20 publication of the above described ad ... the plaintiff was the first to present himself at the appropriate counter in the defendant's store and ... demanded the ... stole so

advertised and indicated his readiness to pay the sale price of $1 ... The defendant refused to sell the merchandise to the plaintiff, stating ... that by a "house rule" the offer was intended for women only and sales would not be made to men ...

1 Give a statement of the **facts of the case** and the **legal history of the case.**

2 Argue the case for the plaintiff and for the defendant. Use the sections of the *Restatement (Second) Contracts* and the *Carlill* case as authority in making your arguments. Try to use the new terminology you have learnt in this chapter.

3 Write the opinion of the appellate court judge as you think the case was decided. Include a discussion of each of the arguments the plaintiff and defendant might have made in this case and respond to them as the judge in the *Carlill* case did.

When you have finished, read the rest of the case excerpt. Note the vocabulary and terminology used in the opinion. It is surprisingly similar to the language used in the *Carlill* case, even though the *Carlill* opinion was written by an English judge before the turn of the century and the *Lefkowitz* opinion was written by a U.S. American judge in the middle of the twentieth century. In fact, you should already be familiar with all of the terminology used in this case:

25   The defendant contends that a newspaper advertisement offering items of merchandise for sale at a named price is a "unilateral offer" which may be withdrawn without notice. He relies upon authorities which hold that, where an advertiser publishes in a newspaper that he has a certain quantity or quality of goods which he wants to dispose of at certain prices and on certain terms, such advertisements are not offers

30   which become contracts as soon as any person to whose notice they may come signifies his acceptance by notifying the other that he will take a certain quantity of them. Such advertisements have been construed as an invitation for an offer of sale on the terms stated, which offer, when received, may be accepted or rejected and which therefore does not become a contract of sale until accepted by the seller; and

35   until a contract has been so made, the seller may modify or revoke such prices or terms ... On the facts before us we are concerned with whether the advertisement constituted an offer, and, if so, whether the plaintiff's conduct constituted an acceptance ...

The test of whether a binding obligation may originate in advertisements addressed

40   to the general public is 'whether the facts show that some performance was promised in positive terms in return for something requested.' 1 Williston, Contracts (Rev. ed.) § 27.

The authorities above cited emphasize that, where the offer is clear, definite, and explicit, and leaves nothing open for negotiation, it constitutes an offer, acceptance

45   of which will complete the contract ... Whether in any individual instance a newspaper advertisement is an offer rather than an invitation to make an offer depends on the legal intention of the parties and the surrounding circumstances ... We are of the

view on the facts before us that the offer by the defendant of the sale of the Lapin fur was clear, definite, and explicit, and left nothing open for negotiation. The plaintiff
50 having successfully managed to be the first one to appear at the seller's place of business to be served, as requested by the advertisement, and having offered the stated purchase price of the article, he was entitled to performance on the part of the defendant. We think the trial court was correct in holding that there was in the conduct of the parties a sufficient mutuality of obligation to constitute a contract of
55 sale.

The defendant contends that the offer was modified by a 'house rule' to the effect that only women were qualified to receive the bargains advertised. The advertisement contained no such restriction. This objection may be disposed of briefly by stating that, while an advertiser has the right at any time before acceptance to modify
60 his offer, he does not have the right, after acceptance, to impose new or arbitrary conditions not contained in the published offer ...

4 What were the **issues raised on appeal**?

5 What was the **holding** of the court?

6 What is the **ratio decidendi** of the opinion?

Terminology

party to a contract	an individual who has entered into a contractual relationship with one or more persons (**Vertragspartei**)
offeror	the person who initiates the contracting process by making an offer (**Antragender**)
offeree	the person to whom an offer to enter into a contract is made (**Angebotsempfänger**)
promisor	the person who makes a promise, hence either party to a bilateral contract and the offeror for a unilateral contract; the term is usually used for the defendant to a breach of contract suit, because the plaintiff claims that the defendant has promised something and not performed (**Schuldner einer Verbindlichkeit aus Vertrag**)
promisee	the person to whom s.th. has been promised, hence either party to a bilateral contract and the person performing the act requested by an offer for a unilateral contract; the term is usually used to designate the plaintiff to a breach of contract suit, because he claims that the defendant has promised something and not performed (**Gläubiger eines Anspruchs aus Vertrag**)

specialty contract	contract that has to be formalized to be binding (**formgebundener Vertrag, formbedürftiger Vertrag**)
formalization	method of recognition of the binding nature of a contract, usually by a notary who either stamps or seals the contract, often in the presence of witnesses to the contracting parties' signatures (**öffentliche Beglaubigung**)
deed	(UK) formalized contract (**formgerechter Vertrag**); (US) document used to transfer ownership in land
donative contract **gratuitous contract**	contract to make a gift (**Schenkungsvertrag**)
simple contract **informal contract**	contracts that have to be supported by consideration to be binding (**formfreier Vertrag**)
offer	proposal for a specific contract; initiation of the contracting process by the making of a promise which, if accepted and supported by consideration, legally binds the person making it (**Angebot**)
acceptance	agreement to the terms of an offer; closes the contract (**Annahme**)
manifestation of intention	communication, explicitly or implicitly, of will (**Willenserklärung**)
manifestation of assent	communication, express or implied, of agreement (**Erklärung der Zustimmung**)
consideration	mutually bargained-for exchange; requirement for a simple contract to be binding on the parties; whether a contract is supported by consideration is a legal evaluation (**Gegenleistung**)
sufficient consideration	consideration that is viewed by a court to be real in the sense that it was actually bargained for and not just nominal or a sham (**hinreichende Gegenleistung**)
adequate consideration	enough to be a fair return for s.th. in the light of general market prices; not a requirement for a contract to be binding, since the parties are free to decide what they want to exchange (**angemessene Gegenleistung**)
peppercorn doctrine	principle that even something as valueless as a peppercorn can be sufficient consideration to support a contract if a contracting party actually bargained to get it
unilateral contract	promise in exchange for an act; the act is both acceptance of the offer and consideration for the promise made by the offeror (*nicht:* einseitiges Rechtsgeschäft!; ein Beispiel dieses Vertragstyps ist die Auslobung) (ca. **einseitig verpflichtender Vertrag**)
bilateral contract	promise in exchange for a promise (ca. **zweiseitig verpflichtender Vertrag**)

breach of contract	failure to fulfill a contractual obligation when due (**Nichterfüllung einer vertraglichen Verbindlichkeit zum Fälligkeitszeitpunkt**)
defense to a claim of breach	anything a defendant to a law suit for breach of contract can claim on his behalf (**Einwendung gegen eine Klage wegen Nichterfüllung**)
impossibility of performance	one defense to a law suit for breach of contract, whereby the defendant claims that through no fault of his own he has become unable to perform his promise (**nicht zu vertretende Unmöglichkeit**)
immateriality of breach	failure to perform as required by a contract but in a relatively insignificant manner, such as by being in delay for an amount of time that is irrelevant in light of the entire contract; if a breach is **material** it permits the non-breaching party to terminate his own performance and sue the breaching party for damages; if the breach is **immaterial**, the breaching party may insist that the non-breaching party not terminate the contract, or may claim this immateriality in his own defense to an action for breach of contract (**Unerheblichkeit der Nichterfüllung**)
breaching party	person who fails to perform on a contract when performance is due (**Schuldner, der seine vertraglichen Pflichten nicht erfüllt**)
non-breaching party	person who has either performed or is prepared to perform on a contract that has been breached by the other party to the contract (**vertragstreuer Teil**)
money damages **compensatory damages**	primary common law remedy for breach of contract; puts the non-breaching party in the position he would have been in had the contract been performed (**Schadensersatz wegen Nichterfüllung**)
specific performance	equitable remedy for breach of contract which requires the breaching party to actually perform as he promised under the contract (**Anspruch auf Vertragserfüllung**)
to recover damages	to receive a court's award of money damages to be paid by the defendant to a law suit in order to compensate, e.g. for the defendant's breach of contract
equitable remedy	remedy, such as specific performance, which was awarded plaintiffs by courts of equity, rather than by courts of law (**Klagebegehren aus Prinzipien von Treu und Glauben, entwickelt für Fälle, die nach reinen Rechtsprinzipien nicht gerecht gelöst werden konnten**)
vendor	seller (**Verkäufer**)
vendee	buyer (**Käufer**)
proprietor	owner (**Eigentümer**)

lease	agreement whereby one party, the **lessor**, lets real or personal property to another party, the **lessee**, who pays a certain amount of money to the lessor for the use of that property (**Miete, Pacht, Leasing**)
lessor	person who owns or possesses property and leases it to another, the **lessee** (**Verpächter, Vermieter, Leasinggeber**)
lessee	person to whom property is let for that person's use under the condition that he or she pay a specified amount of money as rent (**Pächter, Mieter, Leasingnehmer**)
principal	person who conducts business through another person, who is the agent (**Geschäftsherr, Prinzipal**)
agent	person who conducts business for another person, who is the principal (**Geschäftsführer, Vertreter**)
to retract an offer	to withdraw an offer before it has been accepted (**ein Angebot widerrufen**)
termination of an offer	end to the validity of an offer; once an **offer is terminated**, it can no longer be accepted by the offeree (**Erlöschen eines Angebots**)
offer to negotiate **offer to receive offers** **offer to chaffer**	invitation to another person to make an offer (**invitatio ad offerendum**)
to negotiate	to deal, to discuss in order to reach an agreement or bargain (**verhandeln**)
condition precedent	some event that must occur before a duty to perform on a contract arises (**aufschiebende Bedingung**)
condition subsequent	some event that if it occurs terminates the duty to perform on a contract (**auflösende Bedingung**)

Terminology Review

Number after term indicates Book, Unit, and Chapter in which term originally appeared and was explained, e.g. I.I.2 = Book I (*Einführung in die anglo-amerikanisches Rechtssprache*), Unit I, Chapter 2. Book II = this book.

common law system (I.I.1)	a system of law such as found in England and in countries influenced by England with the main source of law in the opinions of judges
remedy (I.I.1)	what plaintiff to law suit is suing to obtain from defendant to compensate plaintiff for injury defendant is claimed to have caused him; what court can order defendant to do to compen-

	sate for causing injury to plaintiff (ca. **Klagebegehren**); for breach of contract the remedy is usually money damages or specific performance
adversary system (I.I.3)	system of trial in which the parties, as opponents, present evidence most favorable to their own view of the case in an attempt to convince either judge or jury of their right to prevail; (UK **adversarial system** (im Zivilrecht: **Parteienprozeß**)
evidence (I.I.1)	proof offered at trial (**Beweismaterial**)
equity (I.I.1)	body of principles that developed in England to compensate for the rigidity of the common law; permitted courts of equity to do justice in cases that could not be resolved justly under common law principles alone (**Billigkeit; Billigkeitsrecht; Recht nach Prinzipien von Treu und Glauben**)
cause of action (I.I.1)	set of facts that permit a person to file a law suit against s.o. else (**Klagegrund**); also **right of action**
plaintiff (I.I.1)	in a private law dispute, person who sues, who initiates the law suit (**Kläger**); also called the **complainant,** because it is the plaintiff who files a complaint to initiate a law suit
defendant (I.I.1)	in a private law dispute, the person against whom a law suit has been brought (**Beklagter**); in a criminal case, the person who has been formally charged with a crime (**Angeklagter**)
complaint (I.I.1)	formal document setting forth the plaintiff's claims against the defendant to a private law suit (**Klage, Klageschrift**); the law suit is initiated by the plaintiff's filing the complaint with the appropriate court
allegation (I.I.1)	claim; used primarily in a legal context (**Behauptung**); **to allege** (**behaupten**)
trial (I.I.1)	the first proceeding in which a legal dispute is resolved (**Hauptverhandlung**)
trial court (I.II.1)	first court to hear a case, considers both issues of fact and issues of law, convenes with one judge and possibly a jury (**Tatsacheninstanz**)
liability (I.I.1)	responsibility in the legal sense; meaning person responsible has to pay for damage he has caused (**Haftung**); conclusion of a private law dispute determining that defendant has to pay for plaintiff's injuries; also used in a criminal context but only if specifically referenced, as **criminal liability** (**strafrechtliche Verantwortung**); **liable** (adj.) as in: **to be held liable, to become liable; to be liable**
to hold s.o. liable (I.I.1)	to determine as a court that s.o. is responsible and must pay for damage caused (ca. **jemanden haftbar machen**)
to appeal (I.I.1)	(US) to turn to a higher court with the argument that a legal

	error occurred during the trial (**in die Revision gehen**); **on appeal**: during the appeal (**in der Revision**); (UK) appeals may be taken on points of law and fact, hence **to appeal** on points of law (**in die Revision gehen**); **to appeal** on points of fact (**in die Berufung gehen**)
appellant (I.I.1)	person bringing the appeal (**Revisionskläger** [Zivilrecht]; **Revisionsführer** [Strafrecht]);
appellee (I.I.1)	the person against whom the appeal has been brought (**Revisionsbeklagter** [Zivilrecht]; **Revisionsgegner** [Strafrecht]); (UK) respondent
appellate (I.I.1)	of or relating to an appeal, as the **appellate** court, meaning the **court of appeal(s)** (**Revisions-**)
appellate court (I.II.1)	intermediate court; considers only issues of law on appeal, namely errors that it is claimed the trial court made in the law; convenes with a panel of judges (usually three) and no jury; also called the **court of appeals** (US **Revisionsgericht** [and *not* **Berufungsgericht!**]; UK **Berufungs-** oder **Revisionsgericht**)
record (I.I.1)	all of the documents relevant to a law suit assembled by the court (ca. **Gerichtsakten, Protokoll**)
motion (I.I.2)	formal request addressed to judge in a law suit (**Antrag**); one **files** or **makes** a motion (**einen Antrag stellen**)
motion for a new trial (I.I.2)	motion claiming that some significant error affected the outcome of the trial such that a new trial should be held (**Antrag auf Wiederaufnahme eines Verfahrens, das aufgrund schwerer Rechtsfehler als ungültig behauptet wird**)

Vocabulary

to abstain from	to not do something
akin to	similar to, related to
ample	plenty, enough
consensus	agreement
to contract a disease	to catch a disease, to become ill from a disease
to delve	to dig into, to go deeper into s.th.
detriment	s.th. negative, such as loss, expense, disadvantage
to dispense with	to do without, to disregard
to dispose of	to get rid of, to do away with, to take care and get done with

elaborate	detailed, long
to extract from	to draw a conclusion from, to derive, to deduce
fallacy	something that is incorrect (false)
gloss	interpretation
immaterial	not essential, not of central importance
inference	conclusion drawn, deduction
nostrils	the holes in one's nose through which one breathes
nominal	in name only, a nominal amount is s.th. so minimal it is not worth discussing
to promulgate	to announce officially
puff	exaggerated advertising claim, not meant to be taken seriously
to sustain	to suffer, to undergo; as in **to sustain a loss, to sustain inconvenience**
to urge	to try to convince, to strongly suggest that s.o. do s.th.

Language Exercises
Chapter 1

I. Fill in the blanks. Some may require more than simply one word:

Contract Law Terminology

The person who initiates the agreement process is called the 1 , who makes an offer to the 2 . If the offer is 3 , a contract is 4 . The two major types of contracts under the common law are 5 , which have to be formalized to be binding, and 6 or 7 contracts, which have to be supported by 8 to be binding. In England a formalized contract is called a 9 , but in the United States it is called a 10 . A promise in exchange for an act is a 11 contract. The act is simultaneously 12 of the offer and 13 for the contract. A promise in exchange for a promise is a 14 . When a party fails to fulfill her obligation under a contract she is in 15 of contract. She then can be referred to as the 16 , or the 17 , and the other person as the 18 , or the 19 . She can be held 20 (legally responsible) by a court for this failure. The typical remedy under the common law for this failure to perform is 21 , but if the subject matter of the contract is unique the remedy will be 22 . If someone takes back their offer they 23 , or 24 , it. List three expressions for *invitatio ad offerendum*: 25 , 26 , 27 . If consideration for a promise is real, we say it is 28 , but even if it is real it still may be far below the normal market price for such a promise in which case it is 29 . If an event must occur before a party has a duty to perform under a contract, the occurrence of that event is a 30 . If the occurrence of an event terminates an individual's duty to perform under a contract, the occurrence of that event is a 31 .

The Legal System (review)

The person who files a law suit is the 1 . The person against whom the law suit is filed is the 2 . A law suit is initially filed with the 3 court, where both issues of 4 and issues of 5 are considered. The document that has to be filed with the court to initiate the law suit is called the 6 . The 6 must state facts that are legally recognized as making out a 7 , the legal basis for the suit. In addition the 6 requests that the court award a 8 , which is to compensate for the harm caused to the 1 . A party dissatisfied with the result reached by the first court may 9 to the 10 court. That person is then referred to as the 11 . The other party is referred to as the 12 . At this court only issues of 5 are considered.

General Legal Expressions

To have a right to something is to be 1 to it. A seller can also be called a 2 and the buyer the 3 . The person who makes a gift is the 4 and the person to whom the gift is made is the 5 . The person leasing out property is the 6 and the person to whom the property is leased is the 7 . Lawyers need a lot of different words for "argue" or "claim," such as 8 , 9 , 10 . A person who conducts business for another person is called an 11 and person for whom he conducts this business is the 12 . To not do something that you have the ability and right to do is to 13 , or 14 , from doing it. *Einwilligen* in English is 15 .

General Vocabulary

He caught the influenza = He 1 the disease of influenza. If an offer is not specific in its terms, it is 2 . How would you interpret the contract? = How would you 3 it? If an offer is terminated, it cannot be accepted at a later time = it cannot be 4 accepted. I will do without academic discussion = I will 5 with it. She stated the offer in words, so the offer was 6 . If she said nothing but we could conclude that she was making an offer from the way she acted, the offer would be 7 . An advantage is a 8 and a disadvantage is a 9 . There is plenty of evidence of his guilt = There is 10 evidence of his guilt.

II. Note the following English construction:

It is an offer **the terms of which** are too vague ... : it is an offer whose terms are too vague. (*Carlill*, line 21)

The **persons with whom** the contract was intended to be made: the contract was intended to be made with those persons. (*Carlill*, lines 25–26)

Complete the following using the above construction:

The company intended to contract with Ms. Carlill: Ms. Carlill was the person 1 the company intended to contract. The advertiser promised to pay money to every person who caught the influenza: Ms. Carlill is a person 2 the advertiser promised to pay money. It was issued to the public: It was the public 3 it was issued.

It is only necessary for the other person 4 the offer is made to follow the indicated method of acceptance. Any act of the plaintiff 5 the defendant derives a benefit could be consideration for a contract. I cannot picture to myself the view of the law 6 the contrary could be held when you have once found who are the contracting parties. It was the use of the smoke ball 7 the company had bargained. Such advertisements are not offers which become contracts as soon as any person

8 notice they may come signifies his acceptance. It constitutes an offer, acceptance 9 will complete the contract. It was the performance 10 he was entitled.

III. Decide whether the blanks should be filled in with "a," "an," "the" or left empty:

1 contract represents 2 agreement of 3 two parties, who are called 4 parties to 5 contract. 6 agreement process is initiated by 7 offeror, who makes 8 offer to 9 offeree. If 10 offeree accepts 11 offeror's offer, then 12 contract is closed. 13 offeror and 14 offeree are also referred to as 15 promisor and 16 promisee, although these latter terms are used more broadly. Since 17 many contracts consist of 18 exchange of 19 promises, each of 20 parties is both 21 promisor and 22 promisee. 23 contract will only be legally binding on 24 parties if 25 one of 26 two requirements is fulfilled. Either 27 contract must be formalized or supported by 28 consideration.

Chapter 2
Offer and Acceptance

When an offeror makes an offer, he gives the offeree the right to accept the offer until it is terminated (*Restatement (Second) Contracts § 35*). As we have already seen, an offer may be terminated in a number of ways, including termination by the **offeror's revocation of the offer** (*Restatement (Second) Contracts § 36(1)(c)*). In this section, we shall consider what constitutes valid **acceptance** and valid **revocation of an offer**. Once a valid acceptance has been made, the offeror and the offeree are bound. But until an offer has been accepted, the offeror usually has the right to **revoke the offer** at any time, even though he may have promised to keep the offer open. This common law rule represents a fundamental difference to the law of Germany, where an offer binds the offeror for either the time stated in the offer or for a normal period of time in the light of the circumstances.

A. Validity of Acceptance

Since an offer may be terminated at any time before it is accepted, the exact point in time at which the acceptance is valid is of central importance. We shall first deal with **offers for bilateral contracts**, where the parties exchange promises. The law on acceptance and revocation of offers for unilateral contracts is more complicated and will be dealt with afterwards. Consider the following section of the *Restatement (Second) Contracts*:

§ 63. **Time When Acceptance Takes Effect**

Unless the offer provides otherwise,

(a) an acceptance made in a manner and by a medium invited by an offer is operative and completes the manifestation of mutual assent as soon as put out of the offeree's possession, without regard to whether it ever reaches the offeror; ...

In the United States, this rule is referred to as the **mailbox rule** (UK **postal rule**) because it essentially provides that acceptance by post is valid as soon as the offeree places his letter of acceptance in the mailbox. The rule may seem harsh for the offeror, but consider the following text in its defense:

> In the context of a postal system that in the nineteenth century was remarkably swift and reliable, the mailbox rule had the virtue of creating maximum certainty at the earliest point. The promisee knew he had a deal as soon as he posted his acceptance, and he could proceed on that basis without awaiting a confirmation. True, the
> 5 promisor had to consider the risk that he might be bound to a contract without knowing it, but that is both a lesser and a controllable hardship: The promisor initiates the transaction by making the offer, so he can make enquiries if no answer is forthcoming. And if he does not wish to assume even this burden, he can reverse the law's presumption and require actual receipt of the acceptance as a term of his offer.
> 10 The contrary presumption – that the contract is complete only on receipt of the acceptance – would leave the promisee in exactly the same doubt about his situation as the mailbox rule leaves the promisor. And the effective date of the obligation would be delayed by that one step without any gain in certainty.

> Charles Fried, *Contract as Promise*, Harvard University Press: Cambridge, Massachusetts (1981) p. 51.

Analysis

A **presumption** is something that is assumed to be true whether it is actually true or not. The law makes certain presumptions when, for example, the individuals involved have not expressly provided for certain situations. Here the law presumes that the acceptance is valid when posted. Still the offeror has control over the situation because she is the one who is actually making the offer. Accordingly, she may state in the offer that acceptance is only valid once it is communicated to her and thus **reverse the law's presumption**. The law makes some presumptions that cannot be reversed or rebutted, which are called **irrebuttable presumptions**. A minor, for example, is considered by the law to **lack the capacity to contract**. We say someone has **legal capacity** if he is **above the age of legal majority**, which in England, Germany and the United States means above the age of eighteen. People below the **age of legal majority** are called **minors**. This presumption is irrebuttable and will always give the minor **a right of avoidance**. That is the right **to have the contract declared void** (empty of legal effect) if the minor, or his legal representative (usually his parents), later decides that he should not be bound by the contract. Other presumptions are **rebuttable** as we have seen here.

Another argument in favor of the **mailbox rule** is that it helps to balance the positions of the two parties. Under the common law, the offeror has more leeway than under the law of continental European legal systems, because he can revoke his offer at any time before it is accepted. The mailbox rule improves the position of the offeree, because it shortens the time during which the offeror can effectively revoke.

Consider the following example:

A posts an offer to B on January 1, which B receives on January 3. B then posts her acceptance of the offer on January 4, but the acceptance does not reach A until January 6. A is bound as of January 4. If the acceptance actually had to be communicated to the offeror, A could revoke until January 6.

Under German law, A is bound by an offer made through the post until the normal time has elapsed for receiving a reply, or in this example presumably January 6 or 7. Consequently, requiring that the offeror actually receive notice of the acceptance would not place the German offeree in any worse position, but it would, of course, the common law offeree.

B. Right to Revoke the Offer and the Acceptance

If the mailbox rule also applied to an offeror's revocation of her offer, a great deal of confusion could arise as to whether a binding contract has been closed or not and the benefit the offeree has under the mailbox rule would be lost.

Consider the following modification of our previous example:

A mails the offer on January 1; B receives it on January 3; A mails a revocation of the offer on January 4; B mails acceptance on January 4; B receives the revocation on January 5; A receives the acceptance on January 6.

In order to avoid this problem, the common law requires that a revocation actually be communicated to the offeree. In this example, the contract would be binding as of January 4 and A would not be permitted to revoke on that same day, unless of course B had not yet posted the acceptance. Any other rule would create problems of proof and would take away the benefit given the offeree under the mailbox rule. Consider the *Restatement (Second) Contracts* formulation of this rule:

§ 42. Revocation by Communication from Offeror Received by Offeree

An offeree's power of acceptance is terminated when the offeree receives from the offeror a manifestation of an intention not to enter into the proposed contract.

Of course, the mailbox rule also binds the offeree. Once the offeree has posted his acceptance, he may no longer reject the offer, for example by telephoning his rejection before the acceptance reaches the offeror. But what happens when the offeree first posts a rejection and then, regretting this decision, telephones his acceptance? If the telephone acceptance occurs before the offeror has received the rejection, the contract is binding. That seems proper because here the same rule on retraction applies to both parties, it is not valid until actually received. On the other hand, if the acceptance occurs after the rejection has been received by the offeror, the acceptance operates as a **counter-offer**. A counter-offer is an offer made by the offeree in response to the offeror's offer. It functions as a rejection of the original offer, unless otherwise expressly specified (*nota bene: here is another example of a rebuttable or reversible presumption*). It may be accepted by the original offeror any time before the original offeree communicates his retraction of the counter-offer, and is subject to the same rules that apply to offers in general. The principle on rejection of an offer and subsequent acceptance is stated in the *Restatement (Second) Contracts*:

> § 40. Time When Rejection ... Terminates the Power of Acceptance
>
> Rejection ... by mail or telegram does not terminate the power of acceptance until received by the offeror, but limits the power so that a letter or telegram of acceptance started after the sending of an otherwise effective rejection ... is only a counter-offer unless the acceptance is received by the offeror before he receives the rejection ...

Questions on the Text

1. Explain the mailbox rule in your own words. Discuss whether this rule has advantages or disadvantages. Think up hypothetical cases to test the fairness of the rule. One interesting example is provided by Charles Fried, the author of the text we read above: "A offers to sell corn to B at $5,000 a carload, the current market price. B dispatches his acceptance, the normal postal delay being three days. B knows that if within those three days the price of corn falls he can wire or telephone the withdrawal of his acceptance; if it rises or stays firm he will allow his acceptance to go through." (Charles Fried, op. cit. p. 13). Would B be able to take advantage of A in this way under the common law rules you have learnt? Is this a good argument for the rules?

2. One main argument in support of the mailbox rule is that it equalizes the situation for the offeree. Under the common law the offeror can revoke his offer at any time before it is accepted, which gives him a definite advantage over the offeree in controlling the agreement process. Why not simply

change the rule permitting the offeror to revoke his offer and adopt law such as that stated in §§ 145, 146 *BGB*? Re-consider the elements of a binding contract under the common law: 1) **offer**, 2) **acceptance**, and 3) **consideration**. Continental European legal systems emphasize the parties' declaration of their will to be legally bound as the central aspect of a private agreement making it a binding contract. But the common law requires that each party give consideration for the other party's promise in order for a contract to be legally binding. If A offers to sell B an automobile for $5,000 and promises to keep the offer open for B to ponder for a week, what consideration has B given A in return for A's promise to keep the offer open? If B has given A no consideration, can A's promise be binding under the common law?

C. Consideration and Option Contracts

In attempting to deal with the common law requirement of consideration, it may be helpful to consider a typical contract that is never supported by consideration, a **donative contract** (promise to make a gift). The very nature of a donative contract is that the **promisor** receives nothing in return for her promise to make the gift. Accordingly, such contracts are usually not enforceable, although there are a number of exceptions to this general rule. Now reconsider the case where A promises to keep an offer open for B to think about. Here B has given A nothing in return for A's promise to keep the offer open. For A's promise to be binding, B has to give A something in return that A bargained to get. Consider the following section of the *Restatement (Second) Contracts* on the creation of an **option contract**:

§ 25. Option Contracts

An option contract is a promise which meets the requirements for the formation of a contract and limits the promisor's power to revoke an offer.

Option contracts are quite common where people deal in shares of a company sold on the stock exchange. You may purchase the right either to buy (**call option**) or to sell (**put option**) a specified number of shares at a certain price for a certain period of time. If, for example, you purchase a thirty-day option to buy 100 shares in the ABC Company at $200 per share, the money you pay for the option gives you the right to accept the offer anytime within those 30 days. The promise to keep the offer open for 30 days is supported by consideration, namely the purchase price of the option. Similarly, if you want to bind an offeror to keep an offer open, you must give her consideration for that promise, even though you are not dealing in shares on the stock exchange. That is one of many consequences of the consideration requirement under the common law.

Read the following case:

Petterson v. Pattberg

248 N.Y. 86, 161 N.E. 428 (1928)

KELLOGG, J. The evidence given upon the trial sanctions the following statement of
5   facts: John Petterson, of whose last will and testament the plaintiff is the executrix, was the owner of a parcel of real estate in Brooklyn, known as 5301 Sixth Avenue. The defendant was the owner of a bond executed by Petterson, which was secured by a third mortgage upon the parcel. On April 4, 1924, there remained unpaid upon the principal the sum of $5,450. This amount was payable in installments of $250 on
10   April 25, 1924, and upon a like monthly date every three months thereafter. Thus the bond and mortgage had more than five years to run before the entire sum became due. Under date of the 4th of April, 1924, the defendant wrote Petterson as follows: "I hereby agree to accept cash for the mortgage which I hold against premises 5301 6th Ave., Brooklyn, N.Y. It is understood and agreed as a consideration I will allow
15   you $780 providing said mortgage is paid on or before May 31, 1924, and the regular quarterly payment due April 25, 1924, is paid when due." On April 25, 1924, Petterson paid the defendant the installment of principal due on that date. Subsequently, on a day in the latter part of May, 1924, Petterson presented himself at the defendant's home, and knocked at the door. The defendant demanded the name
20   of his caller. Petterson replied: "It is Mr. Petterson. I have come to pay off the mortgage." The defendant answered that he had sold the mortgage. Petterson stated that he would like to talk with the defendant, so the defendant partly opened the door. Thereupon Petterson exhibited the cash, and said he was ready to pay off the mortgage according to the agreement. The defendant refused to take the money.
25   Prior to this conversation, Petterson had made a contract to sell the land to a third person free and clear of the mortgage to the defendant. Meanwhile, also, the defendant had sold the bond and mortgage to a third party. It therefore became necessary for Petterson to pay to such person the full amount of the bond and mortgage. It is claimed that he thereby sustained a loss of $780, the sum which the defendant agreed
30   to allow upon the bond and mortgage, if payment in full of principal, less the sum, was made on or before May 31, 1924. The plaintiff has had a recovery for the sum thus claimed, with interest.

Analysis

Loans and Mortgages: A **bond** is defined by *Black's Law Dictionary* as:

> A written obligation, made by owner of real property, to repay a loan under specific terms, usually accompanied by a mortgage placed on land as security.

A **mortgage** is defined as:

> A mortgage is an interest in land created by a written instrument providing security for the performance of a duty or the payment of a debt.

Real property, also referred to as **real estate** or **realty** or **immovables,** is land and anything permanently attached to the land, such as buildings. It is contrasted to **personal property,** also referred to as **personalty** or **chattels** or **movables.** In *Petterson v. Pattberg*, Petterson, the owner of real property, borrowed money from Pattberg and gave Pattberg a **bond** specifying the terms of repayment of the debt and securing that debt with a **mortgage.** The fact that the **mortgage** is referred to as a **third mortgage** means that Petterson had already borrowed money from two other **creditors,** each of whom received a **mortgage to secure the debt.** The owner of the **first mortgage** has the first claim to proceeds from the sale of the property in case Petterson **defaults,** or fails to make payment on his loan. If, after the holder of the **first mortgage** has received full payment on the outstanding debt, money is left from the sale of the property, the holder of the **second mortgage** has the next claim, and so forth.

Principal is defined in *Black's Law Dictionary* as:

> The capital sum of a debt or obligation, as distinguished from interest or other additions to it. An amount on which interest is charged or earned. Amount of debt, not including interest. The face value of a note, mortgage, etc ... .

Here, Petterson still owed $5,450 on the **principal,** plus interest on that unpaid balance for somewhat longer than the next five years. Pattberg, not wanting to wait for the next five years to receive his money as originally agreed, promised to **allow** Petterson $780 against the total amount still owed, meaning that Petterson could deduct $780 from that amount, if he paid before he originally had promised to pay.

Last Will and Testament: This expression is actually redundant. At one time a **testament** disposed of **personal property** after the **testator**'s death, whereas a **will** disposed of **real property.** Today, a **will** can be used to dispose of both real and personal property after death. A man who leaves a will is called a **testator,** a woman a **testatrix.** A person who dies without leaving a will dies **intestate.** If a person leaves a will and designates in the will who is to manage the **decedent's,** namely the testator's or testatrix's, assets and liabilities after death and before they are distributed to the heirs, that person is referred to as an **executor** or an **executrix**, if male or female, respectively. If the decedent does not name an **executor** or **executrix** in the will, the **probate court**, which is a court dealing with family and inheritance law matters, will appoint someone to manage the estate. In that case the person is called an **administrator** or **administratrix**, again depending on the person's gender. In *Petterson v. Pattberg*, the plaintiff is the **executrix** of Petterson's estate and has a right to sue on behalf of the estate for the decedent, who had a potential breach of contract claim against Pattberg.

Questions on the Text

1. What are the facts of the case? Who won at the lower court?

2. Did the parties in this case close a binding contract?

3. What was the offer and the acceptance?

4. Was the offer an offer for a unilateral or a bilateral contract?

5. Does the answer to question no. 4 affect your decision on whether the parties closed a binding contract? Analyze the answer to question no. 2 assuming that a) the offer was an offer for a bilateral contract, and b) the offer was an offer for a unilateral contract.

6. What was the consideration for the agreement assuming that a) the offer was an offer for a bilateral contract, and b) the offer was an offer for a unilateral contract?

7. Who would prevail in this case under the law of your own legal system?

8. Did the offer bind Pattberg? Could he revoke the offer before he actually received the final payment from Petterson? Did he revoke the offer by telling Petterson that he had already sold the mortgage to a third party?

Continue reading the case:

> Clearly the defendant's letter proposed to Petterson the making of a unilateral contract, ... a promise in exchange for the performance of an act. The thing conditionally
> 35 promised by the defendant was the reduction of the mortgage debt. The act requested to be done, in consideration of the offered promise, was payment in full of the reduced principal of the debt prior to the due date thereof. "If an act is requested, that very act, and no other, must be given." Williston on Contracts, § 73 ... It is elementary that any offer to enter into a unilateral contract may be withdrawn
> 40 before the act requested to be done has been performed ... The offer of a reward in consideration of an act to be performed is revocable before the very act requested has been done ... So, also, an offer to pay a broker commissions, upon a sale of land for

the offeror, is revocable at any time before the land is sold, although prior to revocation the broker performs services in an effort to effectuate a sale ...

45 An interesting question arises when, as here, the offeree approaches the offeror with the intention of proffering performance and, before actual tender is made, the offer is withdrawn. Of such a case Williston says:

> The offeror may see the approach of the offeree and know that an acceptance
> 50 is contemplated. If the offeror can say "I revoke" before the offeree accepts, however brief the interval of time between the two acts, there is no escape from the conclusion that the offer is terminated. Williston on Contracts, § 60b.

In this instance Petterson, standing at the door of the defendant's house, stated to the
55 defendant that he had come to pay off the mortgage. Before a tender of the necessary moneys had been made, the defendant informed Petterson that the defendant could not perform his offered promise, and that a tender to the defendant, who was no longer the creditor, would be ineffective to satisfy the debt. "An offer to sell property may be withdrawn before acceptance without any formal notice to the person to
60 whom the offer is made. It is sufficient if that person has actual knowledge that the person who made the offer has done some act inconsistent with the continuance of the offer, such as selling the property to a third person." Dickinson v. Dodds, 2 Ch. Div. 463, headnote ... Thus it clearly appears that the defendant's offer was withdrawn before its acceptance had been tendered ... We think that in this particular
65 instance the offer of the defendant was withdrawn before it became a binding promise, and therefore that no contract was ever made for the breach of which the plaintiff may claim damages.

The judgment of the Appellate Division and that of the Trial Term should be reversed, and the complaint dismissed, with costs in all courts.

Questions on the Text

1. *Tenders*: The court uses the term **tender** in a number of places in the opinion (lines 46, 55, 57 and 64). **Tender** is defined in *Black's Law Dictionary* as:

> The actual proffer of money, as distinguished from mere proposal or proposition to proffer it. Hence mere written proposal to pay money, without offer of cash, is not 'tender'.

Did Petterson tender performance, namely actually hand the money over to Pattberg, before Pattberg revoked his offer, or did he just indicate his intent to **tender** payment to Pattberg?

2. *Revocation of Offers for Unilateral Contracts*: As you have read, an offer may be revoked at any time before it is accepted. For **bilateral contracts**, the acceptance takes effect as soon as the offeree sends it off to the offeror. When

does acceptance of an offer for a **unilateral contract** take effect? Reconsider the example of A, who is concerned about D's health and promises to buy her a mink coat if she abstains from using tobacco and alcohol for one year. Suppose D forbears from the use of these two drugs from January 1 to December 30. On December 31 before midnight, A revokes the offer. Is A bound under the rule announced in *Petterson v. Pattberg*? Is this result just? Is it at least logically consistent in light of the common law definition of a **unilateral contract** and the **consideration** requirement? If you were a legislator, what kind of law could you adopt that would cure the injustice of *Petterson v. Pattberg* for the offeree, but still be logically consistent with common law principles of contract? Reconsider the above section relating to revocation of offers for bilateral contracts. How is it that the **offeree** can bind the **offeror** to keep his offer open for a longer period of time? How could this idea be carried over to **unilateral contracts**? Read the following section of the *Restatement (Second) Contracts*:

§ 45. Option Contract Created by Part Performance or Tender

(1) Where an offer invites an offeree to accept by rendering a performance and does not invite a promissory acceptance, an option contract is created when the offeree tenders or begins the invited performance or tenders a beginning of it.

(2) The offeror's duty of performance under any option contract so created is conditional on completion or tender of the invited performance in accordance with the terms of the offer.

Comment:

b. Manifestation of contrary intention. The rule of this Section is designed to protect the offeree in justifiable reliance on the offeror's promise, and the rule yields to a manifestation of intention which makes reliance unjustified. A reservation of power to revoke after performance has begun means that as yet there is no promise and no offer ... In particular, if the performance is one which requires the cooperation of both parties, such as the payment of money or the manual delivery of goods, a person who reserves the right to refuse to receive the performance has not made an offer.

Illustrations:

1. B owes A $5000 payable in installments over a five-year period. A proposes that B discharge the debt by paying $4,500 cash within one month, but reserves the right to refuse any such payment. A has not made an offer. A tender by B in accordance with the proposal is an offer by B.

c. Tender of performance. A proposal to receive a payment of money or a delivery of goods is an offer only if acceptance can be completed without further cooperation by the offeror. If there is an offer, it follows that acceptance must be complete at the latest when performance is tendered. A tender of performance, so bargained for and given in exchange for the offer, ordinarily furnishes consideration and creates a contract ...

Illustration:

3. A promises B to sell him a specified chattel for $5, stating that B is not to be bound until he pays the money. B tenders $5 within a reasonable time, but A refuses to accept the tender. There is a breach of contract.

d. Beginning to perform. If the invited performance takes time, the invitation to perform necessarily includes an invitation to begin performance. In most cases the beginning of performance carries with it an express or implied promise to complete performance ... In the less common case where the offer does not contemplate or invite a promise by the offeree, the beginning of performance nevertheless completes the manifestation of mutual assent and furnishes consideration for an option contract ... If the beginning of performance requires the cooperation of the offeror, tender of part performance has the same effect. Part performance or tender may also create an option contract in a situation where the offeree is invited to take up the option by making a promise, if the offer invites a preliminary performance before the time for the offeree's final commitment.

[3] Assuming that § 45 *Restatement (Second) Contracts* had been adopted in New York at the time *Petterson v. Pattberg* was decided, would the court have reached the same result? Again, the question revolves around whether Petterson actually tendered performance or only gave an indication of his intention to perform. Remember that to bind Pattberg, Petterson's performance or tender of performance must have occurred before Pattberg revoked the offer.

[4] Does Petterson's payment of the "regular quarterly payment due April 25, 1924" constitute beginning the invited performance within the meaning of the *Restatement (Second) Contracts* § 45(1)? Consider the following section from the *Restatement (Second) Contracts*:

§ 73. Performance of Legal Duty

Performance of a legal duty owed to a promisor which is neither doubtful nor the subject of honest dispute is not consideration; but a similar performance is consideration if it differs from what was required by the duty in a way which reflects more than a pretense of bargain.

Illustrations:

1. A offers a reward to whoever produces evidence leading to the arrest and conviction of the murderer of B. C produces such evidence in the performance of his duty as a police officer. C's performance is not consideration for A's promise.

2. In Illustration 1, C's duties as a police officer are limited to crimes committed in a particular State, and while on vacation he gathers evidence as to a

crime committed elsewhere. C's performance is consideration for the promise.

5. Was Petterson only fulfilling a **pre-existing legal duty** when he paid the "regular quarterly payment due April 25, 1924"? If so, can this payment be the beginning of performance within the meaning of § 45 *Restatement (Second) Contracts*?

6. Consider the following cases (all taken from the *Restatement (Second) Contracts*) and determine whether the offeror is bound to his offer in light of § 45:

> a. A offers a reward for the return of lost property. In response to the offer, B searches for the property and finds it. A then notifies B that the offer is revoked. B makes a tender of the property to A conditional on payment of the reward, and A refuses. Has A breached the contract?

> b. A, a magazine, offers prizes in a subscription contest. At a time when B has submitted the largest number of subscriptions, A cancels the contest. Has A breached the contract?

> c. A writes to her daughter B, living in another state, an offer to leave A's farm to B if B gives up her home and cares for A during A's life, B remaining free to terminate the arrangement at any time. B gives up her home, moves to A's farm, and begins caring for A. Is A bound to her promise?

> d. A offers to sell a piece of land to B, and promises that if B incurs expense in employing experts to appraise the property the offer will be irrevocable for 30 days. B hires experts and pays for their transportation to the land. Is A bound by his promise?

7. Are the following statements true or false? (Examples taken in part from the *Restatement (Second) Contracts*):

a) Where an offer invites an offeree to accept by rendering a performance, notification is necessary to make such an acceptance effective.

b) It is essential to a bargain that each party manifest assent with reference to the manifestation of the other.

c) An acceptance made in a manner and by a medium invited by an offer is operative and completes the manifestation of mutual assent without regard to whether it ever reaches the offeror.

d) Dan offers to sell his car to Paula for $5,000. Paula is indecisive and Dan tells her she can have two weeks to think about it. Before the two weeks have expired, Dan tells Paula that he is revoking his offer. Dan then sells the car to Tertia. Paula is forced to pay $5,500 for a comparable car. She can sue Dan for $500.

e) A sends an offer to sell 500 pounds of corn to B on March 1. B receives the offer on March 4. B mails A his acceptance on March 5. On March 8, B telephones A and rejects A's offer. On March 9, A receives B's acceptance. A and B have closed a binding contract.

f) A reservation of the right to revoke an offer for a unilateral contract after performance has begun means that there is no offer.

g) Performance of a legal duty owed to a promisor which is neither doubtful nor the subject of honest dispute is consideration for the promisor's promise.

h) Rejection of an offer by mail destroys the power of acceptance as soon as it is posted.

i) A owes B $5,000, to be paid over the next two years. A offers to pay B $4,000 immediately in satisfaction of the debt. B accepts. The contract is not supported by consideration.

j) A claims he owes B $4,000. B claims A owes him $5,000. A offers to pay B $4,500 in satisfaction of the debt. The contract is not supported by consideration.

k) A offers to pay B $2 per bushel for 1000 bushels of corn if B ships the corn immediately. B ships the corn immediately on receipt of A's offer. Before the corn arrives, A telephones B and revokes his offer. The revocation is effective.

l) Same facts as in 7k, but B ships only 500 bushels immediately. Two weeks later, B ships another 500 bushels. A refuses to accept delivery of the second shipment. A has breached the contract.

m) A promises to leave B $500 in A's will if B attends A's funeral. B attends A's funeral, but A's executrix refuses to pay B the $500. B has a right to recover if he sues the estate.

n) A promises to forbear suit against B in exchange for B's promise to pay an undisputed debt to A. A's promise is not binding.

o) Same facts as in 7n. A's promise is consideration for B's promise.

p) A group of fishermen agreed to go to Alaska to perform duties for the defendant. The defendant agreed to pay each worker $50 for the season plus $.02 per each salmon caught. Upon arrival in Alaska the workers refused to perform unless they each received $100 for the season. The defendant agreed. The contact for $100 is enforceable.

q) The duty to keep a contract at common law means a prediction that you must pay damages if you do not keep it.

r) A agrees to pay $25 for one 1922 silver dollar. The contract is not binding for lack of consideration.

Terminology

revocation of an offer	cancellation of the effect of an offer; extinguishes the offeree's power of acceptance (**Widerruf eines Vertragsangebotes**)
rejection of an offer	offeree's communication of refusal to accept offeror's offer; terminates offeree's power of acceptance (**Ablehnung eines Vertragsangebotes**)
mailbox rule	principle that makes acceptance effective as soon as it is posted or otherwise sent off to the offeror, assuming that the manner of sending the acceptance was reasonable in light of the offer and the way it was communicated; (UK) **postal rule**
rebuttable presumption	legal assumption which is made when facts are insufficient to indicate real state of affairs but which can be refuted by contrary evidence (**widerlegliche Vermutung**)
irrebuttable presumption	legal assumption which is made regardless of what the factual situation might be and which cannot be refuted with any amount of evidence (**unwiderlegliche Vermutung**)
right of avoidance	right to have a contract declared void (**Anfechtungsrecht**)
minor	s.o. below the **age of legal majority**, or s.o. who cannot enter into binding legal relations because he or she is not yet old enough to understand the full nature of any obligation assumed (**Minderjährige**)
age of legal majority	age at which the law considers an individual sufficiently mature to enter into legal relations (ca. **Eintritt der Volljährigkeit**)
counter-offer	an offer the offeree makes in response to the offeror's original offer; does not function as an acceptance because the terms of the counter-offer are significantly different from the original offer (**Gegenangebot**)
option contract	agreement to keep an offer open for a specified period of time that binds the offeror (**Option**)
call option	option giving offeree the right to buy s.th. at a set price for a specified period of time (der Ausdruck **call option** wird auch in deutschen Texten verwendet)
put option	option giving offeree the right to sell s.th. at a set price for a specified period of time (der Ausdruck **put option** wird auch in deutschen Texten verwendet)
bond	instrument of security for a debt; document indicating existence of a debt and agreement to repay which is secured by a mortgage (**Schuldschein verbunden mit der Bewirkung einer Sicherheitsleistung**)
default on a mortgage	to fail to make timely repayment of a debt that is secured by a

	mortgage (**Verzug des Schuldners bei einer dinglich gesicherten Forderung**)
creditor	individual who has loaned money to another (**Gläubiger**), who is called the **debtor** (**Schuldner**); contrast to: **promisor** (**Schuldner**) and **promisee** (**Gläubiger**)
principal	the amount of the original debt excluding interest payments owed under loan agreement; the principal is reduced as repayments on the debt are made (**Kreditsumme**)
installment	regular partial repayment on a debt (**Rate**)
real property real estate realty immovables	all terms used for land and everything attached to the land (**Liegenschaften, unbewegliche Sachen**)
personal property personalty chattels movables	all terms used for property other than land (**Fahrnis, bewegliche Sachen**)
testament will	document containing instructions on how to dispose of a person's property after death; testament originally limited to the distribution of personal property and **will** to the distribution of real property, but today terms are synonymous (**Testament**)
testator testatrix	person who has left a last will or testament; **testator** is a male and **testatrix** a female (**Testator**)
to die intestate	to die without leaving a will or testament (**ohne letztwillige Verfügung sterben**)
executor executrix	individual designated in a will who is responsible for managing property left after death and eventually distributing it to the deceased's heirs; **executor** is a male and **executrix** a female (**Testamentsvollstrecker/Testamentsvollstreckerin**)
administrator administratrix	individual appointed by a court to perform the functions of an **executor** in all cases in which an executor has not been named by the decedent; **administrator** is male and **administratrix** is female (**gerichtlich ernannter Testamentsvollstrecker/ernannte Testamentsvollstreckerin**)
probate court	court that deals with inheritance law and family law matters (**Nachlaß- und Familiengericht**)
to tender performance to proffer performance	to actually hand s.th. over for acceptance as opposed to an offer or indication of intent to hand over for acceptance (**die Leistung, wie sie zu bewirken ist, tatsächlich anbieten**)
to render performance	to actually do what one is required to do under a contract (**den Vertrag erfüllen**)

promissory acceptance	to accept an offer by making a return promise (**Annahme des Vertragsangebots**)
justifiable reliance	to trust in what another person promises or says under circumstances in which rational people generally would put their trust (**berechtigtes Vertrauen**)
reservation of power to revoke	offeror's expressly retaining the right to cancel his offer at any time (**Vorbehalt des Widerrufs**)
pre-existing legal duty	a legal obligation one has toward another person which existed before one promises to do the same thing required by that legal obligation; cannot be consideration for a new contract since the person under the obligation no longer can bargain with a promise to fulfill the obligation he already has to fulfill anyway ((**Handlungs- oder Unterlassungs-)Pflicht, die schon vor einem Vertragsabschluß besteht**)

Terminology Review

recovery (I.I.1)	judge's award to successful plaintiff to be paid by defendant in order to make up for injury defendant caused plaintiff; also **redress, relief, remedy** (ca. **Klagebegehren**)

Vocabulary

to appraise	to estimate the value of s.th.
to dispatch	to send off
forthcoming	approaching, about to happen
to incur	to take on or suffer s.th. negative, such as debt, expenses, losses
leeway	room to manoeuver
to ponder	to think about in detail, to consider
premises	the locality, the place, where a dwelling or business is located
pretense	claim not supported by reality
to have the virtue of	to have the advantage of
to yield	to give in to, to give way to, to give s.th. else priority

Language Exercises
Chapter 2

I. Note the following construction:

If you purchase a **thirty-day** option, you have **thirty days** to decide whether to exercise that option.

Note that **thirty-day** is 1) hyphenated and 2) remains in the singular, even though we are talking about thirty days! That is because **thirty** and **day** function together to modify the noun "option." We would say: He has thirty days to exercise the option by purchasing the shares, but that he purchased a thirty-day option. Translate the following:

1. Ein dreijähriges Kind.
2. Das Kind ist drei Jahre alt.
3. Das ist ein 5,000–Dollar Auto.
4. Das Auto kostet 5,000 Dollar.
5. Er verkaufte die Aktien für 200 Dollar pro Stück.
6. Diese Option gibt dem Inhaber 30 Tage Zeit zu entscheiden, ob er die Aktien kaufen will oder nicht.

Read the following selecting the correct form and indicating where to place hyphens when necessary:

1. On April 4, 1924, there remained unpaid upon the principal the sum of $5,450.
2. There was a $5,450 balance remaining on April 4, 1924.
3. This amount was payable in installments of $250 on April 25, 1924, and upon a like monthly date every three month(s) thereafter.
4. Petterson paid $250 installment(s) payment(s) in a 3 month(s) cycle.
5. Thus the bond and mortgage had more than five year(s) to run before the entire sum became due.
6. The bond and mortgage had more than a five year(s) period to run before maturity.
7. Pattberg wrote that as consideration for Petterson's early payment, Pattberg would allow him $780 against the principal due.

8. Pattberg offered Petterson a $780 deduction from the principal in exchange for Petterson's early payment.

9. B owes A $5,000 payable in installments over a five year(s) period.

10. A proposes that B discharge the debt by paying $4,500 within one month. B then made a $4,500 payment.

11. A promises B to sell him a specified chattel for $5. A made B a $5 offer.

12. B tenders $5 within a reasonable time. B's $5 tender was made promptly.

13. A offers to sell corn to B at $5,000 per carload, the current market price.

II. Fill in the blanks, some of which may require more than one word:

In order to enter into contractual relations, you must be old enough to understand the nature of your conduct, or you must have 1 . If you are not old enough you are referred to as a 2 . If A pays B money so that B will keep his offer open for 2 weeks, A and B have closed an 3 contract. Another word for "to proffer" performance is 4 performance. A offers to sell his car for $5000 and B says he will buy it for $4500. B has made a 5 . *Liegenschaften* in English are called 6 , 7 , 8 , or 9 and *bewegliche Sachen* are 10 , 11 , 12 or 13 . The best definition of "consideration" is a 14 . A person who acts for someone else is an 15 . The person he acts for is the 16 . In English an *unwiderlegliche Vermutung* is an 17 .

III. Translate the following sections of the German Civil Code (BGB) into English:

§ 145 [Bindung an den Antrag] Wer einem anderen die Schließung eines Vertrags anträgt, ist an den Antrag gebunden, es sei denn, daß er die Gebundenheit ausgeschlossen hat.

§ 146 [Erlöschen des Antrags] Der Antrag erlischt, wenn er dem Antragenden gegenüber abgelehnt ... wird.

§ 147 [Annahmefrist] (2) Der einem Abwesenden gemachte Antrag kann nur bis zu dem Zeitpunkt angenommen werden, in welchem der Antragende den Eingang der Antwort unter regelmäßigen Umständen erwarten darf.

IV. Fill in the correct prepositions or prepositional phrases:

Clearly the defendant's letter proposed 1 Petterson the making 2 a unilateral contract, a promise 3 exchange 4 the performance 5 an act. The thing conditionally promised 6 the defendant was the reduction 7 the mortgage debt. The act requested to be done, 8 consideration 9 the offered promise, was payment 10 full 11 the reduced principal 12 the debt 13 the due date thereof. It is elementary that any offer to enter 14 a unilateral contract may be withdrawn 15 the act requested to be done has been performed. The offer 16 a reward 17 consideration 18 an act to be performed is revocable 19 the very act requested has been done. So, also, an offer to pay a broker commissions, 20 a sale 21 land 22 the offeror, is revocable 23 any time before the land is sold, although 24 revocation the broker performs services 25 an effort to effectuate a sale.

V. Fill in the correct verbs:

A formalized contract must be 1 , 2 , and 3 . To be valid a simple contract must be 4 by consideration. To be sufficient, consideration must actually be 5 for. If the offeree accepts the offeror's offer, a contract 6 . The offeror and the offeree 7 their mutual assent to the agreement through their offer and acceptance. The contract then 8 both parties 9 their obligations under the contract. If a party fails to perform, that party 10 the contract. He will then have to 11 the other party by paying money damages, or if the subject matter of the contract is unique by 12 specifically. An offeror may 13 his offer at any time before the offeree accepts it. Otherwise the offer is 14 , for example, by the death of the offeror. If under the terms of a contract the occurrence of an event is to terminate an obligor's duty of immediate performance, that duty is 15 if the event occurs. In *Lefkowitz*, the plaintiff 16 that the defendant refused to sell him a fur piece. The trial court 17 the plaintiff $138.50 as damages for breach of contract. The defendant then 18 for a new trial. The court, which did not agree that a new trial was necessary, 19 the defendant's motion. The court 20 authorities to the effect that the advertisement was an offer.

Chapter 3
Consideration

When a plaintiff files a law suit claiming that the defendant is in breach of contract, the plaintiff must **plead** and prove, among other things, that he gave the defendant consideration for her promise. In this way, the plaintiff proves that he paid for the defendant's promise and thus that the defendant is bound to perform, or pay for any losses the plaintiff suffers as a result of non-performance. The following cases revolve around determining whether the agreement in question is or is not supported by consideration.

A. Exclusive Dealership Contracts

Wood v. Lucy, Lady Duff-Gordon
222 N.Y. 88, 118 N.E. 214 (1917)

CARDOZO, J. The defendant styles herself "a creator of fashions." Her favor helps a sale. Manufacturers of dresses, millinery, and like articles are glad to pay for a
5   certificate of her approval. The things which she designs, fabrics, parasols, and what not, have a new value in the public mind when issued in her name. She employed the plaintiff to help her to turn this vogue into money. He was to have the exclusive right, subject always to her approval, to place her indorsements on the designs of others. He was also to have the exclusive right to place her own designs on sale, or to license
10   others to market them. In return she was to have one-half of "all profits and revenues" derived from any contracts he might make. The exclusive right was to last at least one year from April 1, 1915, and thereafter from year to year unless terminated by notice of 90 days. The plaintiff says that he kept the contract on his part, and that the defendant broke it. She placed her indorsement on fabrics, dresses, and
15   millinery without his knowledge, and withheld the profits. He sues her for the damages, and the case comes here on demurrer.

Questions on the Text

1 State the facts of the case in your own words.

2 What is the legal history of the case, as far as it can be discerned from this excerpt? What level court is considering the case here? If you do not understand the word **demurrer** (line 16), you will not understand the way in which the case reached this court. If you looked in *Black's Law Dictionary*, you would find the following definition of **demurrer**:

> ... The formal mode of disputing the sufficiency in law of the pleading of the other side. In effect it is an allegation that, even if the facts as stated in the pleading to which objection is taken be true, yet their legal consequences are not such as to put the demurring party to the necessity of answering them or proceeding further with the cause. An assertion that complaint does not set forth a cause of action upon which relief can be granted, and it admits, for purpose of testing sufficiency of complaint, all properly pleaded facts, but not conclusions of law.

As you may know from Unit II of *Einführung in die anglo-amerikanische Rechtssprache / Introduction to Anglo-American Law & Language*, a law suit is initiated when a plaintiff files a complaint with a court. The defendant is served process, meaning that he receives a copy of the complaint and a summons ordering him to appear and defend against the action. The defendant may file an answer to the complaint, in which he may 1) admit the truth of some of the facts the plaintiff has alleged (**admissions**), 2) **deny** the truth of some of the facts the plaintiff has alleged (**denials**), 3) raise **defenses** on his own behalf, such as the impossibility of performance defense to a claim of breach of contract and 4) raise **counterclaims**, which are legal claims he has against the plaintiff. The defendant, however, has another alternative. He may claim that the plaintiff's complaint is not supported by any legal foundation permitting the plaintiff to prevail over the defendant. This claim is referred to as a **demurrer**. The **demurrer** is a motion to the court to dismiss the complaint as being legally insufficient. The **demurrer** asks the judge to believe, for the sake of deciding on the demurrer alone, all of the facts the plaintiff has alleged. Still, the defendant argues, the plaintiff has no right to win the law suit against him. Accordingly, the demurrer does not raise any issue of fact. Indeed it agrees for the sake of argument that everything the plaintiff claims is true. Instead, it only raises an issue of law, namely is there any legal principle that would permit the plaintiff to win the law suit. If not, the complaint will be dismissed. The demurrer is a very important tool of civil procedure in a common law system, because it permits the parties to test the law before they actually have to go to trial, a procedure which can be time consuming and expensive particularly if a jury is used. The trial court judge confronted with a demurrer will have to decide first whether the plaintiff could prevail as a matter of law, assuming the plaintiff can prove the facts alleged, before actually hearing the case. The decision the judge reaches on the demurrer can, like any other trial court decision, be appealed, first to the intermediate appellate court and then possibly to the supreme court. Consequently, the demurrer permits the legal basis of the plaintiff's case to be tested in the highest court in the particular court system within which it was filed, thus enabling the parties to obtain a binding legal **precedent** for their case. Depending on the final outcome of the demurrer, the trial may never take place because the party against whom the precedent is established may agree to settle the dispute without a trial. In *Wood v. Lucy, Lady Duff-Gordon*, the defendant demurred to the plaintiff's complaint. The legal issue is whether the facts that you have just read do or do not state a cause of action for breach of contract. As you will see from the next excerpt, the defendant argued in the demurrer that the contract was not supported by consideration and thus was not binding on her. This question is a legal question and not a factual question. The demurrer went all the way to the highest court in the state of New York, the New York Court of Appeals, and it is this decision that you are reading.

[3] Does this agreement constitute a binding contract? What is the a) offer, b) acceptance and c) consideration for the agreement? Remember to analyze consideration as a *mutual* exchange, namely in light of the consideration moving from the plaintiff to the defendant and from the defendant to the plaintiff.

[4] Note that there is no patent law problem here, as sometimes is assumed, with the defendant placing her **indorsement** on the designs of others. As the opinion makes clear, fashion designers are even willing to pay for the defendant's indorsement. An indorsement (**endorsement**) as it is used here is a signature of approval or support. When you deposit a check in your bank account, you are also usually required to **endorse** the check on the back, meaning sign your name on the back of the check. Similarly, if a check is made out to you and you want to give the check to another person, you must make it payable to that other person and **endorse** it on the back.

Continue reading the case:

The agreement of employment is signed by both parties. It has a wealth of recitals. The defendant insists, however, that it lacks the elements of a contract. She says that the plaintiff does not bind himself to anything. It is true that he does not promise in
20   so many words that he will use reasonable efforts to place the defendant's indorsements and market her designs. We think, however, that such a promise is fairly to be implied. The law has outgrown its primitive stage of formalism when the precise word was the sovereign talisman, and every slip was fatal. It takes a broader view today. A promise may be lacking, and yet the whole writing may be "instinct with an
25   obligation," imperfectly expressed ... If that is so, there is a contract.

The implication of a promise here finds support in many circumstances. The defendant gave an exclusive privilege. She was to have no right for at least a year to place her own indorsements or market her own designs except through the agency of the plaintiff. The acceptance of the exclusive agency was an assumption of its duties ...

30   We are not to suppose that one party was to be placed at the mercy of the other ... Many other terms of the agreement point the same way. We are told at the outset by way of recital that:

"The said Otis F. Wood possesses a business organization adapted to the placing of such indorsements as the said Lucy, Lady Duff-Gordon, has approved."

35   The implication is that the plaintiff's business organization will be used for the purpose of which it is adapted. But the terms of the defendant's compensation are even more significant. Her sole compensation for the grant of an exclusive agency is to be one-half of all the profits resulting from the plaintiff's efforts. Unless he gave his efforts, she could never get anything. Without an implied promise, the transaction
40   cannot have such business "efficacy, as both parties must have intended that at all events it should have." ... But the contract does not stop there. The plaintiff goes on to promise that he will account monthly for all moneys received by him, and that he will take out all such patents and copyrights and trade-marks as may in his judgment be necessary to protect the rights and articles affected by the agreement. It is true, of
45   course, as the Appellate Division has said, that if he was under no duty to try to market designs or to place certificates of indorsement, his promise to account for profits or take out copyrights would be valueless. But in determining the intention of the parties the promise has a value. It helps to enforce the conclusion that the plaintiff had some duties. His promise to pay the defendant one-half of the profits and
50   revenues resulting from the exclusive agency and to render accounts monthly was a promise to use reasonable efforts to bring profits and revenues into existence. For this conclusion the authorities are ample ...

The judgment of the Appellate Division should be reversed, and the order of the Special Term affirmed, with costs in the Appellate Division and in this court.

55   CUDDEBACK, McLAUGHLIN, and ANDREWS, JJ., concur. HISCOCK, C.J., and CHASE and CRANE, JJ. dissent.

Order reversed.

Questions on the Text

[1] The court notes that the agreement has a "wealth of **recitals**" (line 17). **Recitals** are statements of purpose or reasons for adopting the document in which they are included. The court also refers to this agreement as an agreement of employment. Although a **principal** (here Lucy, Lady Duff-Gordon) "employs" the services of an **agent** (here Wood) in a very general sense, is this really a typical employment contract? Will Wood be paid if he makes no

sales? Will a regularly employed salesclerk in a boutique be paid wages even if he makes no sales?

[2] Did Wood actually promise to do anything under the contract? Suppose after this agreement was closed, Wood did nothing. Could Lucy, Lady Duff-Gordon sue him for breach of contract? What would she argue that he had obligated himself to do? What could she claim were her damages for breach of the "contract"?

[3] Notice the language in the recital quoted in lines 33–34: "The **said** Otis F. Wood ... as the **said** Lucy, Lady Duff-Gordon ... " This was typical legal language and merely means **the** Otis F. Wood referred to above in the agreement. Today the tendency is to avoid stilted constructions like this one when writing legal documents. Is there an equivalent to "the said Otis F. Wood" in your own language?

[4] The **Special Term** in line 54 refers to the trial court in this case, which in New York, confusingly enough, is usually called the **Supreme Court**. Which court is the **Appellate Division**?

[5] What is/are the issue(s) on appeal? What is the holding of the case? What is the ratio decidendi? Consider the following section of the *Uniform Commercial Code*:

Uniform Commercial Code § 2–306(2)

A lawful agreement by either the seller or the buyer for exclusive dealing in the kind of goods concerned imposes unless otherwise agreed an obligation by the seller to use best efforts to supply the goods and by the buyer to use best efforts to promote their sale.

The *U.C.C.* will be discussed in more depth in Chapter 5. Does this section of the *U.C.C.* contain the ratio decidendi of *Wood v. Lucy, Lady Duff-Gordon*?

[6] Does this section contain a rebuttable or irrebuttable presumption? How do you know? What language indicates the nature of the presumption as being rebuttable or irrebuttable?

B. Apparent Give-Aways

Maughs v. Porter
157 Va. 415, 161 S.E. 242 (1931)

PRENTIS, C.J. The record discloses that to the plaintiff's notice of motion for $461
5   the defendant filed a general demurrer, which was sustained. To that judgment plaintiff has been allowed a writ of error.

The motion is based upon these facts: The defendant inserted this advertisement in the "Daily Progress," a newspaper published in Charlottesville, Va.:

10

"New Model Ford Free

"At the auction fifty (50) beautiful residence lots Fry's Spring, Thursday, October 13, 1:30, on time. Every ... person over sixteen (16) years of age has an equal chance at the New Ford regardless of buying or bidding. Come to the auction of Oak Lawns."

15

Responding to that advertisement, the plaintiff, a ... person over sixteen years of age, attended the sale, and received from the defendant a slip of paper upon which, by direction of the auctioneer, she placed her name, and deposited it in a box held by the auctioneer. Upon the drawing of the slip from the box, she was adjudged the winner

20 of the automobile. In response to the auctioneer's demand, she paid him $5 for his services in drawing the lucky number. The defendant placed an order for the car with the Albemarle Motor Company, but refused to pay for it when it was ready for delivery, and has also refused the demand of the plaintiff that he pay her the value of the car, alleged to be $461.

25 The defendant demurred to the notice of motion, alleging two grounds, thus stated: (1) That the matters alleged in the plaintiff's notice of motion fail to show a sufficient consideration for defendant's promise, and that defendant's promise is nudum pactum, and hence unenforceable; (2) ...

Questions on the Text

[1] *Black's Law Dictionary* defines a **notice of motion** as:

> A notice in writing, entitled in a cause, stating that on a certain day designated, a motion will be made to the court for the purpose or object stated. Such notice is required to be served upon all parties.

Although the excerpt from the opinion here does not indicate what the plaintiff's object was in making the motion, presumably it was to have the court order the defendant to pay her $461. The defendant **demurred** to the **notice of motion,** meaning what? (Hint: a demurrer to a notice of motion is the same as a demurrer to a complaint). What would you argue in support of the demurrer? Remember, you may only make legal arguments and must assume that the above facts, as the plaintiff alleged, are true.

[2] The trial court sustained the defendant's demurrer and the plaintiff petitioned for a **writ of error,** which the appellate court granted. *Black's Law Dictionary* defines **writ of error** as follows:

> A writ issued from a court of appellate jurisdiction, directed to the judge or judges of a court of record, requiring them to remit to the appellate court the record of an action before them, in which a final judgment has been entered, in order that examination may be made of certain errors alleged to have been committed, and that the judgment may be reversed, corrected, or affirmed, as the case may require.

As you can see, the **writ of error** is somewhat similar to the **writ of certiorari** (see *Einführung in die anglo-amerikanische Rechtssprache*, Unit I, Chapter 2 for a full explanation) in that it is an order from a higher court directed to a lower court to send up the record in the case for appellate review. The writ of error has lost significance and the usual way of proceeding today is the appeal. In any event, this case is similar to *Wood v. Lucy, Lady Duff-Gordon* in that the plaintiff filed a complaint (here: **notice of motion**); the defendant **demurred** and the plaintiff has appealed the issue of law to the highest court in the State of Virginia. Again only a question of law is raised, namely was the contract supported by consideration?

3 To say that a promise is **nudum pactum** (lines 27-28) is the same as to say that it is not **supported by consideration**. Did the plaintiff here give the defendant consideration for the defendant's promise? Is the agreement binding? What is the offer? Is the offer for a unilateral or a bilateral contract? What is the acceptance? What is the consideration for the agreement?

Continue reading the case:

The questions then are: (1) Whether the alleged offer to make the gift can be enforced
30   as supported by a sufficient consideration; ...

First. In Spooner v. Hilbish ... we find this clear statement by Reily, J.: "A gift is a contract without a consideration, and, to be valid, must be executed. A valid gift is therefore a contract executed. It is to be executed by the actual delivery by the donor to the donee, or to some one for him, of the thing given, or by the delivery of the means
35   of obtaining the subject of the gift, without further act of the donor to enable the donee to reduce it to his own possession.' The intention to give must be accompanied by a delivery, and the delivery must be made with an intention to give.' Otherwise there is only an intention or promise to give, which, being gratuitous would be a mere nullity. Delivery of possession of the thing given, or of the means of obtaining it, so as to make
40   the disposal of it irrevocable, is indispensable to a valid gift." ...

In Gardner v. Moore's Adm'r ... we find this, the court speaking through Burks, J.: "Undoubtedly title to personal property of all kinds may be passed by gift, and, when so passed, it is as irrevocable as if passed by purchase; but in order to possess this quality the gift must be complete. The thing given must be delivered, else the gift is
45   incomplete. An agreement for future delivery is nothing more than a promise to make a gift. The delivery, however, may be actual, constructive, or symbolical, depending upon the nature of the thing given. But there must be delivery of some kind, else there is no gift ...

Questions on the Text

1. Can the plaintiff here rely on *Spooner v. Hilbish* and *Gardner v. Moore's Administrator* to her benefit? If the defendant's promise was a gratuitous promise, was it executed? Was there "actual, constructive, or symbolical" delivery under *Gardner*? **Constructive** delivery means that although there was no actual delivery, the courts will interpret from the defendant's conduct the intent to deliver and treat the case as if delivery had occurred. Did the defendant in this case do anything from which one could conclude that he intended to transfer the automobile? **Symbolical** delivery means that although there was no actual delivery of the subject of the gift, still something representing that subject was transferred. What could the defendant have done to transfer the automobile to the plaintiff symbolically? Did he do that?

2. At the beginning of this Unit you read that for a gratuitous promise to be binding it had to be notarized. What other method is available for making such a promise binding? Does your legal system also enforce gift contracts when the subject of the gift has been delivered?

Continue reading the case:

50 Clearly then the plaintiff, under the facts shown here, cannot recover, unless defendant is bound by a promise which is supported by a consideration sufficient to support the action.

It is often quite difficult to determine in such cases whether or not there is such a consideration. 1 Williston on Contracts, § 112, p. 232, thus illustrates the difficulty: "If a benevolent man says to a tramp: 'If you go around the corner to the clothing
55 shop there, you may purchase an overcoat on my credit,' no reasonable person would understand that the short walk was requested as the consideration for the promise, but that in the event of the tramp going to the shop the promisor would make him a gift. Yet the walk to the shop is in its nature capable of being consideration. It is a legal detriment to the tramp to make the walk, and the only reason why
60 the walk is not consideration is because on a reasonable construction it must be held that the walk was not requested as the price of the promise, but was merely a condition of a gratuitous promise. It is often difficult to determine whether words of condition in a promise indicate a request for consideration or state a mere condition in a gratuitous promise. An aid, though not a conclusive test in determining which
65 construction of the promise is more reasonable is an inquiry whether the happening of the condition will be a benefit to the promisor. If so, it is a fair inference that the happening was requested as a consideration. On the other hand, if, as in the case of the tramp stated above, the happening of the condition will be not only of no benefit to the promisor but is obviously merely for the purpose of enabling the promisee to
70 receive a gift, the happening of the event on which the promise is conditional, though brought about by the promisee in reliance on the promise, will not properly be

construed as consideration. In case of doubt where the promisee has incurred a
detriment on the faith of the promise, courts will naturally be loath to regard the
promise as a mere gratuity and the detriment incurred as merely a condition. But in
75 some cases it is so clear that a conditional gift was intended that even though the
promisee has incurred detriment, the promise has been held unenforceable."

Under the first ground of demurrer in this case it is contended for the defendant that
this was not a promise for a consideration, but, on the contrary, was a mere condition
of the proposed gift.

Questions on the Text

1 Was coming to the auction regardless of whether one bid on the residence
lots consideration for the defendant's promise or a mere condition for receiving a gift?

2 Williston proposes considering whether the promisor benefits from the happening of the condition. In the example you read in Chapter 1 in which A
promises D a mink coat if D abstains from using alcohol and tobacco products for one year, does A benefit from D's abstinence? Is the better way of
analyzing these cases to determine what the promisor was bargaining to
obtain? What could the defendant in *Maughs v. Porter* have been bargaining
to get?

Continue reading the case:

80 We conclude, however, that there was sufficient consideration to support the gift, ...
The object of the defendant unquestionably was to attract persons to the auction sale
with the hope of deriving benefit from the crowd so augmented. Even though persons attracted by the advertisement of the free automobile might attend only because
hoping to draw the automobile, and with the determination not to bid for any of the
85 lots, some of these even might nevertheless be induced to bid after reaching the place
of sale. So we conclude that the attendance of the plaintiff at the sale was a sufficient
consideration for the promise to give an automobile, which could be enforced if
otherwise legal.

Questions on the Text

1 Reanalyze the a) offer, b) acceptance and c) consideration in this case in light
of the court's decision.

2 The court states (lines 86–87) that "the attendance ... at the sale was a suffi-

cient consideration for the promise to give an automobile ... " Why is it that not everyone who attended the auction could sue the company to get the automobile? What is the legal relevance of having your ticket drawn from the lottery box? (Review §§ 224, 230 *Restatement (Second) Contracts*)

3 The court indicates (line 88) that the defendant's promise to give away an automobile could be enforced "if otherwise legal." In fact, in this case the plaintiff lost, not because no contract was closed, but because lotteries were illegal under the law of the State of Virginia. Do any of the laws of your own legal system prohibit this type of contract?

4 What relevance does paying the auctioneer $5 have to the case? Would it constitute sufficient consideration in this case, assuming that the auctioneer had the defendant's authority to act as agent? If so, when would the company have become bound? When is the company bound under the court's analysis of the case?

C. Detrimental Reliance

As a general rule a contract must be supported by consideration to be binding, but if the promisee has relied on the promisor's promise to his detriment, the courts may enforce the promise even if it does lack consideration. Consider the following case:

Allegheny College v. National Chautauqua County Bank
246 N.Y. 369, 159 N.E. 173 (1927)

CARDOZO, C.J. The plaintiff, Allegheny College, is an institution of liberal learn-
5 ing at Meadville, Pa. In June, 1921, a "drive" was in progress to secure for it an additional endowment of $1,250,000. An appeal to contribute to this fund was made to Mary Yates Johnston of Jamestown, New York. In response thereto, she signed and delivered on June 15, 1921, the following writing:

10   "Estate Pledge, Allegheny College Second Century Endowment

        "In consideration of my interest in Christian education, and in consideration of others subscribing, I hereby subscribe and will pay to the order of the Treasurer of Allegheny College, Meadville, Pennsylvania, the sum of five thousand dollars: $5,000.

15   "This obligation shall become due thirty days after my death, and I hereby

instruct my executor, or administrator, to pay the same out of my estate. This
pledge shall bear interest at the rate of – per cent per annum, payable an-
nually, from – till paid. The proceeds of this obligation shall be added to the
Endowment of said Institution, or expended in accordance with instructions
20   on reverse side of this pledge.

"Name: MARY YATES JOHNSTON,
"Address: 306 East 6th Street, Jamestown, N.Y.
"Dayton E. McClain, Witness,
"T.R. Courtis, Witness,
25   "To authentic signature."

On the reverse side of the writing is the following indorsement:

"In loving memory this gift shall be known as the Mary Yates Johnston
30   memorial fund, the proceeds from which shall be used to educate students
preparing for the ministry, either in the United States or in the Foreign Field.

"This pledge shall be valid only on the condition that the provisions of my
Will, now extant, shall be first met.

"MARY YATES JOHNSTON."

35

The subscription was not payable by its terms until thirty days after the death of the
promisor. The sum of $1,000 was paid, however, upon account in December, 1923,
while the promisor was alive. The college set the money aside to be held as a
scholarship fund for the benefit of students preparing for the ministry. Later, in July,
40   1924, the promisor gave notice to the college that she repudiated the promise. Upon
the expiration of thirty days following her death, this action was brought against the
executor of her will to recover the unpaid balance.

Questions on the Text

1️⃣ Did the promisor, Mary Johnston, and the plaintiff, Allegheny College, enter
into a binding contract? What was the a) offer, b) acceptance and c) consideration for the agreement? Is it a bilateral or unilateral contract? In the
alternative, does this instrument merely contain the promise to make a gift?

2️⃣ If the agreement was binding, was the promisor free to **repudiate** (line 40),
meaning to **revoke**, her offer? If the promise was gratuitous, would the
promisor be free to repudiate?

3️⃣ What effect could prepayment of $1000 on account have? What effect could
the college's acceptance of this prepayment have? The answers to these ques-

tions may or may not be totally clear to you at this stage, but attempt to analyze the issue on the basis of your knowledge of contract law.

4 In lines 32–33, the promisor indicates that the pledge "shall be valid only on the condition that the provisions of my Will, now extant, shall be first met." This statement means that Mary Johnston had already written her will at the time she made the pledge, because the will was then **extant** or in existence. Presumably the will left specified sums of money to other beneficiaries. This clause thus limits her executor's duty to pay the college by the requirement that the other beneficiaries be satisfied first. If the remaining sum of $4000 due the college is then still available, the executor would have the obligation to pay it. What kind of condition is contained in this clause?

5 Why did the college wait until the expiration of thirty days following her death to bring the action against her executor rather than sue her immediately in July 1924? If the agreement was binding, when did the college have a right to receive the money? Consider the following definition of **anticipatory repudiation** from *Black's Law Dictionary*:

> **Anticipatory breach of contract.** The assertion by a party to a contract that he or she will not perform a future obligation as required by the contract. Such occurs when a party to an executory contract manifests a definite and unequivocal intent prior to time fixed in contract that it will not render its performance under the contract when that time arrives, and in such a case the other party may treat the contract as ended ...

> The right of one party to a contract to sue for breach before the date set for performance when the other party conveys his intention not to perform ... Some jurisdictions require the aggrieved party to wait for the date for performance before commencing suit.

Consider the following case: A promises to deliver linoleum to B on January 18. B needs the linoleum for work he is doing under contract with C. On January 5, A discovers that B is the member of an organization A dislikes. On that same day, A informs B that she has no intention of delivering linoleum to anyone who is a member of such an organization. A's conduct is referred to as **anticipatory breach** of an **executory** contract. It is referred to as **anticipatory** because it occurs before A actually has any duty to perform under the contract (January 18), meaning it occurs in *anticipation* of the date of performance. An individual can breach only an **executory** contract **anticipatorily**. An **executory contract** is a contract relating to performance in the future, or to performance not yet rendered. If both parties have already performed their obligations under a contract, one says that the contract is **executed**. Once executed, a contract obviously can no longer be breached. The common law permits B, in our example, to treat A's conduct as a breach of contract immediately, or on January 5, rather than force B to wait until January 18. A's breach immediately releases B of any duties he has under the contract. Some jurisdictions permit B to file suit against A as of January 5, while others require B to wait until after January 18. In the *Allegheny College* case, Mary Johnston **anticipatorily** breached the contract she had with the college (assuming it was a binding contract) in July 1924. Assuming New York is not a jurisdiction which requires the non-breaching party to wait until performance is due before filing suit, what other reason is there for the college to wait? If you cannot answer this question refer back to question 4.

Continue reading the case:

The law of charitable subscriptions has been a prolific source of controversy in this state and elsewhere. We have held that a promise of that order is unenforceable like 45 any other if made without consideration ... On the other hand, though professing to apply to such subscriptions the general law of contract, we have found consideration present where the general law of contract, at least as then declared, would have said that it was absent ...

If A promises B to make him a gift, consideration may be lacking, though B has 50 renounced other opportunities for betterment in the faith that the promise will be kept.

The half truths of one generation tend at times to perpetuate themselves in the law as the whole truth of another, when constant repetition brings it about that qualifications, taken once for granted, are disregarded or forgotten. The doctrine of consider-55 ation has not escaped the common lot. As far back as 1881, Judge Holmes in his lectures on the Common Law ... separated the detriment which is merely a consequence of the promise from the detriment which is in truth the motive or inducement, and yet added that the courts "have gone far in obliterating this distinction." The tendency toward effacement has not lessened with the years. On the contrary, there 60 has grown up of recent days a doctrine that a substitute for consideration or an exception to its ordinary requirements can be found in what is styled "a promissory estoppel" ... Whether the exception has made its way in this State to such an extent as to permit us to say that the general law of consideration has been modified accordingly, we do not now attempt to say. Certain, at least, it is that we have 65 adopted the doctrine of promissory estoppel as the equivalent of consideration in connection with our law of charitable subscriptions. So long as those decisions stand, the question is not merely whether the enforcement of a charitable subscription can be squared with the doctrine of consideration in all its ancient rigor. The question may also be whether it can be squared with the doctrine of consideration as qualified 70 by the doctrine of promissory estoppel.

We have said that the cases in this State have recognized this exception, if exception it is thought to be. Thus, in Barnes v. Perine, 12 N.Y. 18, the subscription was made without request, express or implied, that the church do anything on the faith of it. Later the church did incur expense to the knowledge of the promisor, and in the 75 reasonable belief that the promise would be kept. We held the promise binding, though consideration there was none except upon the theory of a promissory estoppel ...

80 It is in this background of precedent that we are to view the problem now before us. The background helps to an understanding of the implications inherent in subscription and acceptance. This is so though we may find in the end that without recourse to the innovation of promissory estoppel the transaction can be fitted within the mould of consideration as established by tradition.

Analysis

The court refers here to the doctrine of **promissory estoppel**. Consider the following section of the *Restatement (Second) Contracts*:

§ 90. Promise Reasonably Inducing Action or Forbearance

(1) A promise which the promisor should reasonably expect to induce action or forbearance on the part of the promisee or a third person and which does induce such action or forbearance is binding if injustice can be avoided only by enforcement of the promise. The remedy granted for breach may be limited as justice requires ...

As the comment to this section goes on to point out, § 90 is often referred to as **promissory estoppel. Estoppel** is a principle of equity. The principle is applicable to cases in which an individual justifiably relies on a belief caused by another person's conduct. If in relying on the belief the individual changes his own position to his detriment, the person whose conduct caused that belief may not assert a right she otherwise would have had. **Promissory estoppel** is a doctrine of contract law intended to prevent injustice in cases in which a person promises something knowing that another person will rely on that promise and the other person in fact does rely on the promise to his detriment. As such the doctrine is a substitute for consideration, because enforcement of the promise depends on the other party's **detrimental reliance** on that promise and not on whether the promise was bargained for through promising to do, or doing, something in exchange. As you should see, however, from § 90, the doctrine of promissory estoppel, or detrimental reliance, is not generally applied, but rather only by way of exception: "if injustice can be avoided only by enforcement of the promise." One typical case in which promissory estoppel is applied is in the law of **charitable subscriptions,** or promises to make gifts to charities. Justice Cardozo indeed refers to promissory estoppel as being the "equivalent of consideration" (line 65). Still, this doctrine does not seem to dispose of the issue in the case, as Cardozo goes on to say "we may find in the end that without recourse to the innovation of promissory estoppel the transaction can be fitted within the mould of consideration as established by tradition." (lines 80–82). Cardozo's reluctance to rely completely on the doctrine of promissory estoppel also indicates that the doctrine is applied only exceptionally. Courts will be much happier enforcing a promise supported by consideration than substituting promissory estoppel for the consideration requirement. Can you make arguments that Mary Johnston's promise was supported by some consideration the college gave her in return?

Continue reading the case:

The promisor wished to have a memorial to perpetuate her name. She imposed a condition that the "gift" should "be known as the Mary Yates Johnston Memorial
85 Fund." The moment that the college accepted $1,000 as a payment on account, there was an assumption of a duty to do whatever acts were customary or reasonably necessary to maintain the memorial fairly and justly in the spirit of its creation. The college could not accept the money, and hold itself free thereafter from personal responsibility to give effect to the condition ... The purpose of the founder would be
90 unfairly thwarted or at least inadequately served if the college failed to communicate to the world, or in any event to applicants for the scholarship, the title of the memorial. By implication it undertook, when it accepted a portion of the "gift," that in its circulars of information and in other customary ways, when making announcement of this scholarship it would couple with the announcement the name of
95 the donor. The donor was not at liberty to gain the benefit of such an undertaking upon the payment of a part and disappoint the expectation that there would be payment of the residue. If the college had stated after receiving $1,000 upon account of the subscription, that it would apply the money to the prescribed use, but that in its circulars of information and when responding to prospective applicants it would
100 deal with the fund as an anonymous donation, there is little doubt that the subscriber would have been at liberty to treat this statement as the repudiation of a duty impliedly assumed, a repudiation justifying a refusal to make payments in the future. Obligation in such circumstances is correlative and mutual. A case much in point is New Jersey Hospital v. Wright, 94 N.J.L. 462, 464, 113 A. 144, where a subscription
105 for the maintenance of a bed in a hospital was held to be enforceable by virtue of an implied promise by the hospital that the bed should be maintained in the name of the subscriber ... A parallel situation might arise upon the endowment of a chair or a fellowship in a university by the aid of annual payments with the condition that it should commemorate the name of the founder or that of a member of his family. The
110 university would fail to live up to the fair meaning of its promise if it were to publish in its circulars of information and elsewhere the existence of a chair or a fellowship in the prescribed subject, and omit the benefactor's name ... . We do not need to measure the extent either of benefit to the promisor or of detriment to the promisee implicit in this duty. "If a person chooses to make an extravagant promise for an
115 inadequate consideration it is his own affair." ... It was long ago said that "when a thing is to be done by the plaintiff, be it never so small, this is a sufficient consideration to ground an action." ... The longing for posthumous remembrance is an emotion not so weak as to justify us in saying that its gratification is a negligible good.

Questions on the Text

1. In this excerpt, the court discusses a) anticipatory repudiation, b) the peppercorn theory, c) the difference between adequate and sufficient consideration. Can you find the passages where these topics are discussed?

2. Note that Cardozo again (as in *Wood v. Lucy, Lady Duff-Gordon*) finds an implied assumption of duty in the plaintiff's conduct. Do you find this assumption convincing? Did the college actually ever mention Mary Johnston's name in any of its circulars? Did it have a duty to do so that it impliedly assumed?

3. Suppose the college had refused to accept any further payment from Mary Johnston's executor, refused to establish the scholarship fund and returned the $1000 paid on account. Would the college have been in breach of contract?

Continue reading the case:

120 We think the duty assumed by the plaintiff to perpetuate the name of the founder of the memorial is sufficient in itself to give validity to the subscription within the rules that define consideration for a promise of that order. When the promisee subjected itself to such a duty at the implied request of the promisor, the result was the creation of a bilateral agreement ... There was a promise on the one side and on the other a
125 return promise, made it is true, by implication, but expressing an obligation that had been exacted as a condition of the payment. A bilateral agreement may exist though one of the mutual promises be a promise "implied in fact," an inference from conduct as opposed to an inference from words ... We think the fair inference to be drawn from the acceptance of a payment on account of the subscription is a promise
130 by the college to do what may be necessary on its part to make the scholarship effective. The plan conceived by the subscriber will be mutilated and distorted unless the sum to be accepted is adequate to the end in view. Moreover, the time to affix her name to the memorial will not arrive until the entire fund has been collected. The college may thus thwart the purpose of the payment on account if at liberty to reject
135 a tender of the residue ... Such must be the meaning of this transaction unless we are prepared to hold that the college may keep the payment on account, and thereafter nullify the scholarship which is to preserve the memory of the subscriber. The fair implication to be gathered from the whole transaction is assent to the condition and the assumption of a duty to go forward with performance ... The subscriber does not
140 say: I hand you $1,000, and you may make up your mind later, after my death, whether you will undertake to commemorate my name. What she says in effect is this: I hand you $1,000, and if you are unwilling to commemorate me, the time to speak is now.

The conclusion thus reached makes it needless to consider whether, aside from the
145 feature of a memorial, a promissory estoppel may result from the assumption of a duty to apply the fund, so far as already paid, to special purposes not mandatory under the provisions of the college charter (the support and education of students

preparing for the ministry) – an assumption induced by the belief that other payments sufficient in amount to make the scholarship effective would be added to the
150 fund thereafter upon the death of the subscriber ...

The judgment of the Appellate Division and that of the Trial Term should be
reversed, and judgment ordered for the plaintiff as prayed for in the complaint, with
costs in all courts.

Questions on the Text

1. If the transaction here was a gift, would the college have been permitted to
simply keep the $1000 and refuse to establish a scholarship in the donor's
name? Before answering this question, review the holding of *Spooner v. Hilbish* quoted in *Maughs v. Porter* in this Unit. If the $1000 was a gift, was it
executed? If so, can a donor require something in return from the donee? Or
is the donee free to do with the gift as he pleases? If he is not free, are we
really talking about a gift, or about a contract supported by consideration?

2. What is the legal history of this case? What is the holding? What parts of the
opinion contain dicta?

3. International Herald Tribune, January 4–5, 1997, p. 3:

**Most Americans of a certain age re-
call the series of rhyming signs the
Burma-Shave company** put along
rural roads as one of the most suc-
cessful campaigns of the time –
owing in large part to the sort of
gentle humor exemplified by this fa-
vorite:
WITHIN THIS VALE
OF TOIL
AND SIN
YOUR HEAD GROWS BALD
BUT NOT YOUR CHIN -
USE
BURMA-SHAVE.
But American History magazine re-
minds us of a time that Burma-
Shave was nearly too clever. A 1955
jingle promised:
FREE – FREE
A TRIP
TO MARS

FOR 900
EMPTY JARS
BURMA-SHAVE.
No one at the shaving-cream company's headquarters in Minneapolis
imagined the offer would be taken
seriously. But an enterprising Apple-
ton, Wisconsin, store manager
named Arliss French offered 15 cents
a jar and managed to accumulate
900. Burma-Shave, not wanting its
good name tarnished, was briefly
perplexed. Then someone suggested
sending Mr. French and his wife to
the German town of Moers, pro-
nounced something like Mars. In the
spirit of things, Mr. French showed
up in a silvery space suit. He and his
wife were treated as guests of honor
at a Moersfestival. And the day was
saved. Burma-Shave.

If Mr. French had brought suit against the Burma-Shave Co., what could he have argued on his behalf? What would the Burma-Shave Co. have argued?

Terminology

demurrer	motion, usually filed by a defendant in response to the plaintiff's complaint, asking the court to dismiss the complaint for legal insufficiency; test for whether the demurrer should be sustained is whether complaint states a cause of action, assuming that all facts plaintiff has claimed are true; raises purely a question of law (**Antrag auf Schlüssigkeitsprüfung**)
admissions	statements in a defendant's answer that indicate the defendant's agreement with certain facts the plaintiff has claimed in his complaint (**Geständnisse**)
denials	statements in a defendant's answer that indicate the defendant's disagreement with certain facts the plaintiff has claimed in his complaint (**Bestreiten von Klagebehauptungen**)
counterclaims	allegations of fact in the defendant's answer that would support a legal claim against the plaintiff (**Widerklage**)
recitals	statements of purpose or reasons given for why the document in which the recitals appear has been adopted by the parties (**einleitende Erklärungen**)
exclusive dealing agreement	an agreement whereby a seller grants a buyer a right to purchase goods for resale and the seller agrees not to sell the goods to anyone else other than the individual buyer with whom he has closed the agreement (**Alleinbezugsvertrag**)
indorsement/endorsement	signature of approval or support (**Indossament, Bestätigung, Zustimmung**)
civil procedure	body of rules governing the manner in which a private law dispute is carried out in the courts (**Zivilprozeßrecht**)
notice of motion	advance formal indication of intent to make a motion to a court for some specific purpose (**Vorankündigung eines Antrags**)
writ of error	order issued by a court of appellate jurisdiction directed to a lower court to have the lower court send up the record in a case for review because the party petitioning for the writ of error claims that the lower court has made a legal error in dealing with the case; although there are technical differences between an appeal and a hearing on a writ of error, for purposes of understanding the writ of error, one should consider it a form of appeal (**Beschluß, die Revision zuzulassen**)

plaintiff in error	party who petitioned for a writ of error (**Revisionskläger**)
defendant in error	party against whom a petition for a writ of error has been brought (**Revisionsbeklagter**)
nudum pactum	a "naked" agreement; the term is used to signify a contract that is not supported by consideration
constructive delivery	not actually transferring an object to another person, but acting in a manner that will be interpreted by a court to be the same as actually transferring or delivering the object (**Übergabesurrogat**)
symbolic delivery	not actually transferring an object to another person, but transferring something that is intended to represent the object; for the purpose of a valid gift, symbolic delivery is sufficient (**symbolische Übergabe**)
past consideration	consideration that has been given before any contract was closed; cannot support a conttract and make it binding (**Gegenleistung, die schon vor Vertragsabschluß erbracht worden ist**)
detrimental reliance	trusting in a promise or statement made by another person under circumstances that would lead reasonable people to trust in that promise or statement and suffering a loss as a result of this trust; as a principle of equity, detrimental reliance will in some cases be a reason for prohibiting the person who made the promise or statement from asserting a right he otherwise would have (**Haftung des Gefälligen für das Nichteinhalten einer Gefälligkeitsabrede**)
promissory estoppel	equitable doctrine of contract law which will bar a party from asserting a right he otherwise would have, such as refusing to keep his promise when a contract is not legally enforceable; doctrine applied if when making the promise the promisor knew that the promisee would rely on the promise and in fact the promisee did rely on the promise, changed his position, and would suffer a detriment if the promise were not kept (**Verwirkung von Rechten innerhalb einer Vertragsbeziehung**)
endowment	an amount of money given for a charitable purpose which is specified at the time of the gift (**Stiftung, Widmung von Stiftungskapital**)
estate pledge	promise to donate money or other assets from property that is left over after one's death (**Erbvertrag**)
anticipatory repudiation	indication of refusal to perform on a contract before performance is actually due under the contract; **repudiation** (**Weigerung, den Vertrag zu erfüllen**); **anticipatory repudiation** (**Weigerung, den Vertrag zu erfüllen, vor Fälligkeit der vereinbarten Leistung**)
aggrieved party	individual who has been harmed or injured; person who has been negatively affected (**Verletzter, Geschädigter**)

executory contract	a contract that has not yet been fully performed (**Vertrag, der noch nicht ganz erfüllt worden ist**)
executed contract	a contract that has been fully performed by all of the parties to the contract (**Vertrag, der bereits voll erfüllt worden ist**)
charitable subscription	promise to donate money to a charity (**Zusage, eine Spende für eine wohltätige Einrichtung zu geben**)
prayer for relief	formal request that the court grant the plaintiff a specified remedy; part of the complaint in which the plaintiff requests the court to order compensation for the wrong complained of (**Klageantrag**)

Terminology Review

to plead	to make a claim before a court; to file a complaint, answer or reply, which are referred to as the **pleadings**
pleadings (I.II.1)	documents filed at the initiation of a law suit; include plaintiff's **complaint** (**Klageschrift**), defendant's **answer** (**Klageerwiderung**), and possibly a **reply** by the plaintiff (**Replik**); also **preliminary pleading**
answer (I.1.1)	defendant's formal substantive response to the plaintiff's complaint (**Klageerwiderung**)
to sustain (I.I.1)	to uphold, to grant or support the validity of a formal request made by a lawyer during a trial; the opposite of **to overrule**; (**einem Antrag oder Einspruch stattgeben**)
precedent (I.I.1)	principle of law announced by court when reaching decision that binds that court and all lower courts when reaching decisions in future similar cases, thus **binding precedent**
jurisdiction (I.I.2)	authority of a court to hear and decide a case (**Zuständigkeit**); also the area over which a legal system is applicable, e.g. "the jurisdiction of California" means the State of California as a distinct legal system where California laws apply and are applied by California courts; or "a number of jurisdictions" means a number of legal systems
provision (I.I.1)	what the law **provides** (**vorsieht**), laws and parts of laws (**gesetzliche Bestimmung**); within the context of a will or testament meaning what that will specifies or provides (**testamentarische Bestimmung**)
writ of certiorari (I.I.2)	formal order issued by supreme court and addressed to lower court ordering lower court to certify record in a case and send it to supreme court for further judicial review (ca. **Zulassung der**

	Revision); if the supreme court agrees to hear a case it will: **grant the writ, grant certiorari, grant cert.**; if it decides not to hear the case it will: **deny the writ, deny certiorari, deny cert.**
to affirm (I.I.2)	to uphold, as an appellate court, the decision reached by a lower court (**die Entscheidung aufrechterhalten**)
to reverse (I.I.2)	to change, as an appellate court, the decision of a lower court in the same case (**aufheben**)
dissenting opinion (I.II.1)	the opinion of one or more judges in the minority of the court of judges hearing an appeal who do not agree on the holding the majority reached in the case (**Sondervotum, das eine im Ergebnis abweichende Meinung eines Richters enthält**)
title (I.II.2)	ownership right to property (**Eigentumsrecht** [and *not* **Titel**(!), meaning in German the right one acquires through a final judicial judgment in a case])

Vocabulary

to augment	to increase in size or amount
benevolent	well intended, showing goodwill, kind attitude toward others
to commemorate	to honor s.o., to establish a memorial to s.o.
correlative	mutual, reciprocal, going hand in hand
effacement	taking away significance of s.th.
extant	in existence
fatal	deathly, destroying effect of s.th.
to induce	to bring about, to cause
irrevocable	cannot be revoked, cannot be changed or withdrawn
liberal learning	education devoted to the seven liberal arts; refers to a college program rather than a professional school education
millinery	women's hats and other fashions to be worn on the head
ministry	profession of a minister, who is the person who leads church services in a Protestant church
to obliterate	to destroy, eradicate, efface
parasol	an umbrella against the sun's rays
pledge	a solemn promise to do or refrain from doing something
prolific	abundant, fruitful
to remit	to refer for consideration or further judgment

residence lot	a parcel of land on which a dwelling can be built
residue	remains, what is left over
to square with	to bring in agreement with, to align
to thwart	to frustrate

Language Exercises
Chapter 3

I. Fill in the blanks. Some may need more than one word:

The defendant 1 to the complaint, meaning he claimed the plaintiff's complaint failed to state a cause of action. Instead of doing that, he could have filed an 2 , containing 3 , or his agreement with some of the facts the plaintiff alleged in the complaint; 4 , or his disagreement with some of the facts alleged in the complaint; 5 or his claims that he had a good reasons for doing whatever the plaintiff is suing him for; and 6 , or his own reasons for suing the plaintiff.

An agreement to sell goods to only one person is called an 7 . Such an agreement appears not to be binding, because the buyer does not promise anything in return, but the courts interpret such agreements to mean that the buyer will 8 to 9 the sale of the goods. A contract that includes a list of statements of purpose or reasons for entering into the contract contains 10 . A person who represents the interests of another is called an 11 . The person whose interests are represented is the 12 .

A less common way of saying that a plaintiff has been permitted to appeal is to say that the plaintiff has been allowed a 13 . The plaintiff is then called the 14 and the other party the 15 . This procedure has some similarities to the 16 , an order issuing from a supreme court to a lower court to send up the 17 for the supreme court to 18 . To say that an agreement is nudum pactum means that the contract is not 19 , and thus is not binding. A promise to make a gift is called a 20 or 21 promise. To be binding it must be 22 , or, in the alternative, actually 23 , meaning that the donor has already delivered it to the donee. Delivery may not actually have taken place, but the court might interpret from the donor's conduct the intent to deliver and treat the case as if delivery had occurred, in which case we say there was 24 delivery. If the donor gives the donee something that represents the object to be given, then we say there was 25 delivery.

If an offeror indicates her refusal to perform on a binding contract before the date on which her performance is due, we say that she has 26 . Usually a contract is not binding without consideration. But if the person making the promise, the 27 , should reasonably expect that the person to whom the promise was made, the 28 , would rely on the promise, and in fact the 28 does rely on it, the promise is binding without consideration if injustice can only be avoided by enforcing the promise. This principle is referred to as the equitable principle of 29 . This principle is often applied in cases involving 30 , or promises to make donations to an organization which serves the common good. The reason for the injustice is that the person to whom the promise was made may have relied on the promise to his 31 , meaning he would otherwise suffer a loss. A solemn promise to donate money or other assets from property that is left after death is an 32 . Money held for a specified charitable purpose is an 33 . If a person dies without leaving a will, we say that person 34 . In such case the 35 will appoint an 36 or 37 to manage the decedent's assets until they are distributed to the decedent's lawful 38 . If an individual dies leaving a will, the individual is called the 39 or 40 , who will name an 41 or 42 to manage the assets. Contracts relating to future perform-ance, which have not as yet been performed, are called 43 contracts. Contracts that have already been fully performed are called 44 contracts.

II. Correct the following particularly common language mistakes. One sentence may have several mistakes:

1. I do not know the way how to approach the court on this issue.
2. The court based it's judgment on the evidences.
3. The court proofed if the contract was supported by consideration.
4. The question is, if the contract has already been executed.
5. The plaintiff considered the informations she had before filing her complaint.
6. The court held, that the defendant was liable for breaching the contract.
7. The parties expressively provided that acceptance was not effective until ac-tually communicated to the promisor.

Chapter 4
Defenses to Claims of Breach and Rights of Avoidance

If a party to a contract fails to fulfill her obligations under that contract, the promisee may sue for **breach of contract**. But in some cases the breaching party may have a **defense** to the action for breach. If the promisor has a good defense, the promisee's action will fail. Furthermore, **rights of avoidance**, meaning rights to have a contract declared void, are also recognized under the common law for cases in which one party's ability to contract was in some way negatively affected. In this Chapter we will discuss the defenses of **impossibility** and **frustration** and the rights of avoidance based on **mistake, fraud,** and **misrepresentation**.

A. Impossibility

Taylor and Another v. Caldwell and Another
32 L.J. Q.B. 164, [1861–73] All E.R. Rep. 24 (1863)

May 6, 1863. **BLACKBURN, J.,** read the following judgment. – In this case the
5   plaintiffs and defendants, on May 27, 1861, entered into a contract by which the defendants agreed to let the plaintiffs have the use of the Surrey Gardens and music hall on four days then to come, namely, June 17, July 15, Aug. 5 and Aug. 17, for the purpose of giving a series of four concerts and day and night fetes at the gardens and hall on those days, and the plaintiffs agreed to take the gardens and hall on those
10   days, and pay £100 for each day ...

After the making of the agreement, and before the first day on which a concert was to be given, the hall was destroyed by fire. This destruction, we must take it on the evidence, was without fault on either party, and was so complete that in consequence the concerts could not be given as intended; and the question we have to decide is
15   whether, under these circumstances, the loss which the plaintiffs have sustained is to fall upon the defendants. The parties, when framing their agreement, evidently had not present to their minds the possibility of such a disaster, and they made no express stipulation with reference to it, so that the answer to the question must depend on the general rules of law applicable to such a contract.

Questions on the Text

⒈ How would this case be decided under the laws of your own legal system? Is impossibility of performance always a good defense? What are the conditions of this defense in your system? In *Taylor v. Caldwell*, the plaintiffs "sought to recover the preliminary expenses of printing and advertising, and other expenses necessarily incidental to such an engagement," which the trial court found to be £58.

⒉ The law before *Taylor v. Caldwell* essentially rejected impossibility of performance as a defense. It was up to the parties to the contract to make provision in their agreement for such occurrences, and if they did not it was their problem. The courts began to recognize several exceptions, one of which is embodied in this decision, relating to the destruction of the subject matter of the contract. What cases does your legal system recognize?

⒊ Why should the law recognize impossibility as a defense? Remember, the alternative in this case would be to require the defendant to pay for the plaintiff's losses from not being able to hold the concerts. Why should the plaintiff bear the burden of the loss rather than the defendant whose concert hall burned? If a system is based on freedom of contract, why not require the defendant to pay for the loss since he included no clause in the contract excusing himself from performance if the hall burned?

Continue reading the case:

20   There seems no doubt that, where there is a positive contract to do a thing not in itself unlawful, the contractor must perform it or pay damages for not doing it, although, in consequence of unforeseen accident, the performance of his contract has become unexpectedly burdensome, or even impossible ... But this rule is only applicable when the contract is positive and absolute and not subject to any condition either
25   express or implied; and there are authorities which, as we think, establish the principle that where, from the nature of the contract, it appears that the parties must from the beginning have known that it could not be fulfilled unless, when the time for the fulfillment of the contract arrived, some particular specified thing continued to exist, so that when entering into the contract they must have contemplated such
30   continuing existence as the foundation of what was to be done; there, in the absence of any express or implied warranty that the thing shall exist, the contract is not to be construed as a positive contract, but as subject to an implied condition that the parties shall be excused in case, before breach, performance becomes impossible from the perishing of the thing without default of the contractor.

40   There seems little doubt that this implication tends to further the great object of making the legal construction such as to fulfill the intention of those who enter into the contract, for, in the course of affairs, men, in making such contracts, in general, would, if it were brought to their minds, say that there should be such a condition ...

45   There is a class of contracts in which a person binds himself to do something which
     requires to be performed by him in person, and such promises – for example,
     promises to marry ... , – are never in practice qualified by an express exception of the
     death of the party, and, therefore, in such cases, the contract is in terms broken if the
     promisor dies before fulfilment; yet it was very early determined that, if the perform-
     ance is personal, the executors are not liable ... 2 Williams on Executors 1353, where
50   a very apt illustration is given. The learned author says:

>   "Thus, if an author undertakes to compose a work and dies before complet-
>   ing it, his executors are discharged from the contract, for the undertaking is
>   merely personal in its nature, and by the intervention of the contractor's
>   death has become impossible to be performed." ...

55   These are instances where the implied condition is of the life of a human being, but
     there are others in which the same implication is made as to the continued existence
     of a thing. For example, where a contract of sale is made amounting to a bargain and
     sale, transferring presently the property in specific chattels, which are to be delivered
     by the vendor at a future day. There, if the chattels, without the fault of the vendor,
60   perished in the interval, the vendor is excused from performing his contract to
     deliver, which has thus become impossible ...

     In [*Williams v. Lloyd*], ... the count, which was in assumpsit, alleged that the plaintiff
     had delivered a horse to the defendant who promised to re-deliver it on request.
     Breach, that they requested to re-deliver the horse, he refused. Plea, that the horse
65   was sick and died, and the plaintiff made the request after its death; and, on demurrer
     it was held a good plea, as the bailee was discharged from his promise by the death
     of the horse without default or negligence on the part of the defendant ...

     It may, I think, be safely asserted to be now English law that in all contracts of loan
     of chattels or bailment, if the performance of the promise of the borrower or bailee
70   to return the thing lent or borrowed becomes impossible because it has perished, this
     impossibility, if not arising from the fault of the bailee, or from some risk which he
     has taken upon himself, excuses the borrower or bailee from the performance of his
     promise to re-deliver the chattel ... . The principle seems to us to be that in contracts
     in which the performance depends on the continued existence of a given person or
75   thing, a condition is implied that the impossibility of performance arising from the
     perishing of the person or thing shall excuse the performance. In none of these cases
     is the promise in words other than positive, nor is there any express stipulation that
     the destruction of the person or thing shall excuse the performance; that excuse is by
     law implied, because from the nature of the contract it is apparent that the parties
80   contracted on the basis of the continued existence of the particular person or chattel.

     In the present case, looking at the whole contract, we find that the parties contracted
     on the basis of the continued existence of the music hall at the time when the concerts
     were to be given, that being essential to their performance. We think, therefore, that
     the music hall having ceased to exist without fault of either party, both parties are
85   excused, the plaintiffs from taking the gardens and paying the money, the defendants
     from performing their promise to give the use of the hall and gardens, and other
     things. The rule must be made absolute to enter the verdict for the defendants.

Analysis

Notice the flow of the **argumentation by analogy** in the opinion. This type of argumentation is central to the common law, because lawyers and judges have to base their decisions on past **precedents**. These past precedents can be **extended** or **limited** in later cases. A court **extends a precedent** if it applies it in a new case to facts that are somewhat different from those in the former case in which the precedent was originally announced. After a precedent has been extended it applies in more types of cases than it did before it was extended. A court **limits a precedent** if it refuses to apply it in a new case based on somewhat different facts from those in the case in which the precedent was originally announced. After a precedent has been limited it does not apply at least to the types of cases in which the precedent was limited. In *Taylor v. Caldwell* the court **extends** past precedents to cover the **instant case.**

First the court concedes that **positive,** or absolutely binding, contracts can require the promisor to bear the risk of not being able to perform at the time performance is due. But the court limits these cases to ones in which the parties have expressly **allocated the risk** of impossibility to the promisor. In other cases, the court indicates that contractual obligations are subject to certain **implied conditions,** meaning conditions the parties did not express but which the courts will assume they meant to include in their agreement. The court goes on to consider past precedents where courts have recognized a defense of **impossibility** (lines 44–54). The first are those where the promisor has entered into a contract which only he can fulfill, such as a marriage contract or a **contract to compose a work,** such as a contract to paint a portrait. Since performance is personal in these cases, the promisor's death provides a good defense to an action for breach against the **executors** of the **decedent's estate.** As you may recall, an **executor** winds up the decedent's estate and distributes the assets to the decedent's heirs. If any individual has a good legal claim against the deceased, that claim can be made against the executor of the estate. If successful, the claimant will be awarded money damages, for example, out of the assets of the estate before they are distributed to the heirs. At the time *Taylor v. Caldwell* was decided, the courts and the scholarly literature already recognized the **defense of impossibility** for this limited group of cases in which the contract required personal performance.

The court in *Taylor v. Caldwell* proceeds to extend these precedents to cover the **case at bar.** It does so by considering cases in which the continued existence not of the promisor, but of an object, was contemplated by the contracting parties. The first case the court considers is one in which the vendor, or seller, of chattels is required to deliver them to the vendee, or buyer, at a date subsequent to the actual sale (lines 55–61). If the chattels are destroyed before the date of delivery, the vendor is excused from performance. The second case the court considers is one involving a **bailment** (lines 62–73). A **bailment** is a deposit of the **bailor**'s property with a **bailee**, either for the bailee simply to keep until the bailor requests redelivery of it or for the bailee to use in a certain specified manner. In the specific case the court considers, the owner of a horse, the **bailor**, delivered the horse to the **bailee** to keep until the bailor requested that the horse be returned. The bailee later refused to redeliver the horse and the bailor sued for breach (line 64) of the bailment contract. You can tell that this is a **breach of contract** case from line 62, where the court states that the **count** was **in assumpsit**. A **count** is an individual claim made in the complaint the plaintiff files to initiate the law suit. **Assumpsit** is the name given to a contract **cause of action** (see *Einführung in die anglo-ameri-kanische Rechtssprache / Introduction to Anglo-American Law & Language*, Unit I, Chapter 1 B. 3, for a detailed explanation of the common law causes of action). Accordingly, the plaintiff claimed in one **count** of the complaint that the defendant had breached a contract he had with the plaintiff. The bailee then answered the claim of breach by **pleading** the **defense of impossibility** (line 64). A **plea** is a formal request or claim presented to a court. Here it is the bailee's claim that he could not perform the contract because the horse he was supposed to redeliver had died through no fault of his own. The plaintiff then **demurred** to the defendant's **plea**. As you know from Chapter 3, a **demurrer** is a motion the defendant makes to the court claiming that the plaintiff's **complaint fails to state a cause of action**. In the case the court is discussing here, the plaintiff made the demurrer, but the principle is the same as when the defendant demurs. The plaintiff is claiming that the defense of impossibility is not a legally recognized defense to a claim of breach of contract. The plaintiff therefore is raising a purely legal and not any factual question. This demurrer requests the court to assume that the facts the defendant claims are true. Still the plaintiff argues, the defendant has no right to win the law suit as a matter of applicable law because he has no good defense to the breach of contract action. The court, however, denied the plaintiff's demurrer and held that the defendant had made a good plea (line 66). In other words, the court recognized the defense of impossibility to a breach of contract claim. *Nota bene:* The court has said nothing about whether indeed the horse died before the plaintiff requested the defendant to redeliver it, or about whether the defendant was or was not at fault for the horse's death. These are questions of fact and have to be determined at trial. The court is merely saying: Provided the facts the defendant claims are true, namely that the plaintiff made the request after the horse had died and that the defendant was not at fault for the death of the horse, then the defendant has a legally recognized defense to a contract cause of action. The effect of the court's denial of the plaintiff's demurrer is that the law suit will continue to trial, rather than being dismissed in the pretrial stage.

The court then draws its conclusion (lines 73–80) that when performance of a contract depends on either the continued existence of a person or thing, the discontinuation of the existence of that person or thing excuses the parties from performance of the contract. In the final line of the decision the court states that the **rule must be made absolute.** Consider the following definition from *Black's Law Dictionary*:

> *Rule absolute.* One which commands the subject-matter of the rule to be forthwith enforced. It is common, for example, when the party has failed to show sufficient cause against a rule *nisi*, to "make the rule absolute," i.e., imperative and final.

From the case excerpt you have, you cannot tell what kind of rule the court here means. But you do know that the rule involves **entering the verdict** for the defendants (line 87). The **rule nisi**, also known as a **rule to show cause**, discussed in *Black's Law Dictionary* is an order to a party to give a good reason, or as is the more common legal expression **to show cause**, why a court ruling should not become final. Presumably, at the end of the trial the defendant here made a **motion for a directed verdict** in his favor. A **motion for a directed verdict** is similar to a demurrer in that it only raises an issue of law and none of fact. It is made, however, not before, but rather during or at the end of the trial. The party who makes it requests the judge to look at the evidence presented at trial in a light most favorable to the *other* party. Still, the **moving party** claims that he has a right as a matter of law to win the law suit. The moving party thus is claiming that the case does not turn on a question of fact, because he is willing to accept the other party's evidence as true to the extent it is reasonable to do so. Instead he is urging the court to decide as a matter of law that he should win the case. The court would then give the other party an opportunity to respond to this motion. One way of doing that is to issue a **rule nisi** or a **rule to show cause** why the motion should not be granted. If the other party fails to make a good argument in response, then the **rule** would be made **absolute.**

Civil procedure in a common law system is extremely complex and any adequate treatment of it needs to be done in its own right and not merely in bits and pieces. It may help you to imagine a ping-pong match to understand it. The plaintiff hits the first ball by filing the complaint. The defendant hits it back by demurring. The plaintiff now has to justify the legal basis of the complaint. If he is successful the ball is shot back to the defendant. The defendant now has to answer the complaint. The ball goes back to the plaintiff who can return it by demurring to the answer. This back and forth of claims and rejections of the legal sufficiency of the claims is characteristic of the entire trial process.

Questions on the Text

1. In the first example the court uses of a thing perishing before the time of performance, the court states that the **property in specific chattels** was transferred at the time of the sale but that the chattels were to be delivered at a future day (lines 57–59). Who owned the chattels when they perished, the vendor or the vendee? Should that make a difference in deciding who should bear the burden of their accidental loss?

2. A bailor transfers possession but not any property or ownership rights when he delivers property to the bailee. Accordingly, who owned the horse in the court's second example of a thing perishing before the time of performance?

3. Reconsider the court's examples in support of the present decision. Do they place the risk of loss on the *owner* of the property rather than on the vendor or bailee? Is there any legal principle, other than impossibility as a defense to a claim of breach, that imposes the risk of loss of property on its owner in the absence of any person's fault? Can the court's cited precedents be explained by using this legal theory? If so, do they really stand for the principle that impossibility is a defense when the subject matter of the contract perishes?

4. Does the decision in *Taylor v. Caldwell* impose the risk of loss on the owner of the hall? If not, do the previous decisions really support this decision or are they different in a legally significant way? If your answer is yes, that does not mean the court in *Taylor v. Caldwell* was too dense to realize that as well, or that it made a mistake in deciding the way it did. This manner of arguing by analogy is the very essence of the common law development of precedents. The court had no other precedent on which to base its decision, so it took the closest thing it had available and extended it considerably to create the defense of impossibility of performance in the *Taylor v. Caldwell* type of case.

5. What is the law of **bailments** in your own legal system? Who bears the risk of loss, the **bailor** or the **bailee**?

6. Is the **impossibility defense** limited in your own system to bailments, or does it apply in other areas of law?

B. Frustration of Purpose

Krell v. Henry

72 L.J.K.B. 794, [1900–03] All E.R.Rep. 20 (1903)

The plaintiff, Paul Krell, sued the defendant, C.S. Henry, to recover £50, being the
5   balance of a sum of £75, at which price the defendant had agreed to hire from the
plaintiff some rooms at 56A, Pall Mall, London, of which the plaintiff was tenant, on
June 26 and 27, 1902, to view the processions which it had been intended to hold on
those days in connection with the coronation of His Majesty King Edward VII. The
defendant denied that he was liable to pay the £50, and counterclaimed for the return
10   of £25 which he had paid as a deposit, on the ground that, the processions not having
taken place owing to the illness of the King, there had been a total failure of consideration for the contract entered into by him. On August 11, 1902, the action came on
for trial before Darling, J., sitting without a jury, when the learned judge gave
judgment for the defendant on both claim and counterclaim. The plaintiff ap-
15   pealed ...

Aug. 11, 1903. **VAUGHAN WILLIAMS, L.J.**, read the following judgment. – The
real question in this case is the extent of the application in English law of the principle
of the Roman law which has been adopted and acted on in many English decisions,
20   and notably in *Taylor v. Caldwell* ...

I do not think that the principle of the civil law as introduced in the English law is
limited to cases in which the event causing the impossibility of performance is the
destruction or non-existence of some thing which is the subject-matter of the contract or of some condition or state of things expressly specified as a condition of it. I
25   think that you first have to ascertain, not necessarily from the terms of the contract,
but if necessary from necessary inferences, drawn from surrounding circumstances
recognised by both contracting parties, what is the substance of the contract, and
then to ask the question whether that substantial contract needs for its foundation
the assumption of the existence of a particular state of things. If it does, this will limit
30   the operation of the general words, and in such case if the contract becomes impossible of performance by reason of the non-existence of the state of things assumed
by both contracting parties, as the foundation of the contract, there will be no breach
of the contract thus limited.

What are the facts of the present case? The contract is contained in two letters of June
35   20, 1902, which passed between the defendant and the plaintiff's agent, Mr. Cecil
Bisgood. These letters do not mention the coronation, but speak merely of the taking
of Mr. Krell's chambers, or, rather, of the use of them, in the daytime of June 26 and
27, 1902, for the sum of £75, £25 then paid, balance £50 to be paid on the 24th. But
the affidavits, which by agreement between the parties are to be taken as stating the

40 facts of the case, show that the plaintiff exhibited on his premises, third floor, 56A
Pall Mall, an announcement to the effect that windows to view the royal coronation
processions were to be let, and that the defendant was induced by that announcement to apply to the housekeeper on the premises, who said that the owner
was willing to let the suite of rooms for the purpose of seeing the royal procession for
45 both days, but not nights, of June 26 and 27. In my judgment, the use of the rooms
was let and taken for the purpose of seeing the royal processions. It was not a demise
of the rooms or even an agreement to let and take the rooms. It was a licence to use
rooms for a particular purpose and none other. And in my judgment the taking place
of those processions on the days proclaimed along the proclaimed route, which
50 passed 56A, Pall Mall, was regarded by both contracting parties as the foundation of
the contract. I think that it cannot reasonably be supposed to have been in the
contemplation of the contracting parties, when the contract was made, that the
coronation would not be held on the proclaimed days, or the processions not take
place on those days along the proclaimed route; and I think that the words imposing
55 on the defendant the obligation to accept and pay for the use of the rooms for the
named days, although general and unconditional, were not used with reference to the
possibility of the particular contingency which afterwards occurred ... .

Each case must be judged by its own circumstances. In each case one must ask
oneself, first: What, having regard to all the circumstances, was the foundation of the
60 contract?; secondly: Was the performance of the contract prevented?; and thirdly:
Was the event which prevented the performance of the contract of such a character
that it cannot reasonably be said to have been in the contemplation of the parties at
the date of the contract? If all these questions are answered in the affirmative (as I
think they should be in this case), I think both parties are discharged from further
65 performance of the contract ... . The test seems to be, whether the event which causes
the impossibility was or might have been anticipated and guarded against. It seems
difficult to say, in a case where both parties anticipate the happening of an event,
which anticipation is the foundation of the contract, that either party must be taken
to have anticipated, and ought to have guarded against, the event which prevented
70 the performance of the contract ...

When once this is established, I see no difficulty whatever in the case. It is not
essential to the application of the principle of *Taylor v. Caldwell* that the direct
subject of the contract should perish or fail to be in existence at the date of performance of the contract. It is sufficient if a state of things or condition expressed in the
75 contract and essential to its performance perishes or fails to be in existence at that
time. In the present case the condition which fails and prevents the achievement of
that which was, in the contemplation of both parties, the foundation of the contract,
is not expressly mentioned either as a condition of the contract or the purpose of it,
but I think for the reasons which I have given that the principle of *Taylor v. Caldwell*
80 ought to be applied. This disposes of the plaintiff's claim for £50 unpaid balance of
the price agreed to be paid for the use of the rooms ... . I think this appeal ought to be
dismissed.

Questions on the Text

☐1 State the facts of this case in your own words. State the legal history of the case, which you should now easily understand from the opinion. What is the issue raised on appeal? Is it the same issue that was raised in *Taylor v. Caldwell*? How does this case differ from *Taylor v. Caldwell*? What is the holding in this case?

☐2 The court bases its opinion on *Taylor v. Caldwell*. Does *Krell v. Henry* limit, merely follow, or extend the precedent in *Taylor v. Caldwell*?

☐3 Although the court discusses this case in terms of **impossibility** of performance, today it is generally read to introduce a new type of defense to a claim of breach, namely the defense of **frustration**. Consider the following section of the *Restatement (Second) Contracts*:

> **§ 265. Discharge by Supervening Frustration**
>
> Where, after a contract is made, a party's principal purpose is substantially frustrated without his fault by the occurrence of an event the non-occurrence of which was a basic assumption on which the contract was made, his remaining duties to render performance are discharged, unless the language or the circumstances indicate the contrary.

Does your own law recognize the defense of frustration? Does your Civil Code include a section like the above section of the *Restatement*?

C. Mistake, Misrepresentation and Fraud

Wood v. Boynton
64 Wis. 265, 25 N.W. 42 (1885)

TAYLOR, J. This action was brought in the circuit court for Milwaukee county to
5   recover the possession of an uncut diamond of the alleged value of $1,000. The case was tried in the circuit court, and after hearing all the evidence in the case, the learned circuit judge directed the jury to find a verdict for the defendants. The plaintiff excepted to such instruction, and, after a verdict was rendered for the defendants, moved for a new trial upon the minutes of the judge. The motion was denied, and the
10 plaintiff duly excepted, and after judgment was entered in favor of the defendants, appealed to this court. The defendants are partners in the jewelry business. On the trial it appeared that on and before the twenty-eighth of December, 1883, the plaintiff was the owner of and in the possession of a small stone of the nature and value of which she was ignorant; that on that day she sold it to one of the defendants for the
15 sum of one dollar. Afterwards it was ascertained that the stone was a rough diamond,

and of the value of about $700. After hearing this fact the plaintiff tendered the defendants the one dollar, and ten cents as interest, and demanded a return of the stone to her. The defendants refused to deliver it, and therefore she commenced this action.

20   The plaintiff testified to the circumstances attending the sale of the stone to Mr. Samuel B. Boynton, as follows: "The first time Boynton saw that stone he was talking about buying the topaz, or whatever it is, in September or October. I went into the store to get a little pin mended, and I had it in a small box, – the pin, – a small ear-ring; ... this stone, and a broken sleeve-button were in the box. Mr. Boynton
25   turned to give me a check for my pin. I thought I would ask him what the stone was, and I took it out of the box and asked him to please tell me what that was. He took it in his hand and seemed some time looking at it. I told him I had been told it was a topaz, and he said it might be. He says, 'I would buy this; would you sell it?' I told him I did not know but what I would. What would it be worth? And he said he did
30   not know; he would give me a dollar and keep it as a specimen, and I told him I would not sell it; and it was certainly pretty to look at. He asked me where I found it, and I told him in Eagle. He asked about how far out, and I said right in the village, and I went out. Afterwards, and about the twenty-eighth of December, I needed money pretty badly, and thought every dollar would help, and I took it back to Mr. Boynton
35   and told him I had brought back the topaz and he says, 'Well, yes; what did I offer you for it?' and I says, 'One dollar'; and he stepped to the change drawer and gave me the dollar, and I went out." In another part of her testimony she says: "Before I sold the stone I had no knowledge whatever that it was a diamond. I told him that I had been advised that it was probably a topaz, and he said probably it was. The stone
40   was about the size of a canary bird's egg, nearly the shape of an egg, – worn pointed at one end; it was nearly straw color, – a little darker." She also testified that before this action was commenced she tendered the defendants $1.10, and demanded the return of the stone, which they refused. This is substantially all the evidence of what took place at and before the sale to the defendants, as testified to by the plaintiff
45   herself. She produced no other witness on that point.

The evidence on the part of the defendant is not very different from the version given by the plaintiff, and certainly is not more favorable to the plaintiff. Mr. Samuel B. Boynton, the defendant to whom the stone was sold, testified that at the time he bought this stone, he had never seen an uncut diamond; had seen cut diamonds, but
50   they are quite different from the uncut ones; "he had no idea this was a diamond, and it never entered his brain at the time." ...

Analysis

In lines 4–11 the court gives you the legal history of this case. Note the procedural moves taken by the plaintiff in this case. First the plaintiff filed a complaint in the state trial court, the circuit court for Milwaukee county (line 4). The trial took place, and at the end of the trial the trial court judge determined that the case should not go to the jury for determination. The trial court judge was of the opinion that, even believing the facts the plaintiff presented, no jury, as a matter of law, could reach a verdict in her favor. The judge thus intended to instruct the jury to find for the defendants, or to **direct the jury to find a verdict for the defendants** (line 7). The plaintiff **excepted**, meaning that she **objected** to this instruction (line 8), but the judge **overruled the objection** and **directed the verdict**. The plaintiff then made a **motion for a new trial**, which the judge denied (line 9). The plaintiff objected to the trial court's denial of her motion at the appropriate time for the objection, which is what the court here means when it says that the plaintiff **duly** excepted. Since the plaintiff raised an objection at the appropriate time during the trial, she could appeal with the argument that the trial court erred in **directing the verdict** and then **denying her a new trial**. A motion for a directed verdict can be made by either the plaintiff or the defendant, or the court, on its own initiative, can direct the verdict. In *Wood v. Boynton*, the idea behind the directed verdict is that the law does not permit the plaintiff to treat the contract as void for the type of mistake the parties made in this case. If the law does not provide a right of avoidance for this type of mistake, then the plaintiff must lose the law suit, even if all of her evidence is absolutely accurate. This type of motion, therefore, relates only to legal questions and not to factual questions. Thus, a jury, which acts only as the factfinder at trial, is not needed to deliberate on the verdict.

Questions on the Text

1. State in your own words the a) facts of the case; b) legal history of the case. What do you think the legal issue is on appeal?

2. How would the courts of your own state decide this case? Does Ms. Wood have a right to the return of the raw diamond? What criteria does your own legal system use to resolve this case? Give arguments for Ms. Wood and for Mr. Boynton under the rules of your own legal system.

3. Note in line 36 the grammatical mistake Ms. Wood makes in her sentence: " ... and I says, 'One dollar'" Courts usually record every statement made by witnesses during trial in the exact words used by the witness, including grammatical errors. What should Ms. Wood have said?

Continue reading the case:

   ... The only question in the case is whether there was anything in the sale which entitled the vendor (the appellant) to rescind the sale and so revest the title in her. The

only reasons we know of for rescinding a sale and revesting the title in the vendor so
55   that he may maintain an action at law for the recovery of possession against his
vendee are (1) that the vendee was guilty of some fraud in procuring a sale to be made
to him; (2) that there was a mistake made by the vendor in delivering an article which
was not the article sold, – a mistake in fact as to the identity of the thing sold with the
thing delivered upon the sale. This last is not in reality a rescission of the sale made,
60   as the thing delivered was not the thing sold, and no title ever passed to the vendee by
such delivery.

Analysis

Notice the way the issue raised on appeal is framed in lines 52–53. It is whether
a sale can be **rescinded** and **title** can **revest** in the seller. As you know, **title** means
an ownership right to property, which **vests** in a particular person, who is then
the owner of the property. When Ms. Wood sold and delivered the diamond to
Mr. Boynton, she **passed title** to him and the diamond became his property, or
title vested in him. In this case Ms. Wood wants to **rescind** the sale so that **title**
will **revest** in herself. Consider the following definition from *Black's Law Dictionary*:

> **Rescission of contract.** ... To declare a contract void in its inception and to put an end
> to it as though it never were ... A "rescission" amounts to the unmaking of a con-
> tract, or an undoing of it from the beginning, and not merely a termination, and it
> may be effected by mutual agreement of parties, or by one of the parties declaring
> rescission of contract without consent of other if a legally sufficient ground therefor
> exists, or by applying to courts for a decree of rescission ... It necessarily involves a
> repudiation of the contract and a refusal of the moving party to be further bound by
> it ...

As you know from Chapter 1, the typical remedy for breach of contract in a
common law system is money damages. This remedy puts the non-breaching
party in the position he would have been in had the contract been fully performed. The remedy of **rescission**, on the other hand, puts the **rescinding party**
back into the position he was in before the contract was ever closed. Before we
consider the exact difference between money damages and rescission, however,
let us first have a look at some of the reasons for rescinding a contract. In
particular the court mentions **fraud**. Similar to fraud is **material misrepresentation**. Consider the following definitions from *Black's Law Dictionary* and the
relevant provisions of the *Restatement (Second) Contracts*:

> **Fraud.** An intentional perversion of truth for the purpose of inducing another in
> reliance upon it to part with some valuable thing belonging to him or to surrender a
> legal right. A false representation of a matter of fact, whether by words or by

conduct, by false or misleading allegations, or by concealment of that which should have been disclosed, which deceives and is intended to deceive another so that he shall act upon it to his legal injury ...

Misrepresentation. Any manifestation by words or other conduct by one person to another that, under the circumstances, amounts to an assertion not in accordance with the facts. An untrue statement of fact ...

In a limited sense, an intentional false statement respecting a matter of fact, made by one of the parties to a contract, which is material to the contract and influential in producing it. A "misrepresentation," which justifies the rescission of a contract, is a false statement of a substantive fact, or any conduct which leads to a belief of a substantive fact material to proper understanding of the matter in hand, made with intent to deceive or mislead.

§ 164. When a Misrepresentation Makes a Contract Voidable

(1) If a party's manifestation of assent is induced by either a fraudulent or a material misrepresentation by the other party upon which the recipient is justified in relying, the contract is voidable by the recipient.

§ 162. When a Misrepresentation Is Fraudulent or Material

(1) A misrepresentation is fraudulent if the maker intends his assertion to induce a party to manifest his assent and the maker

(a) knows or believes that the assertion is not in accord with the facts, or

(b) does not have the confidence that he states or implies in the truth of the assertion, or

(c) knows that he does not have the basis that he states or implies for the assertion.

(2) A misrepresentation is material if it would be likely to induce a reasonable person to manifest his assent, or if the maker knows that it would be likely to induce the recipient to do so.

Now that we have this information we can consider two examples which clarify the difference between money damages and rescission. Assume that X contracts with Y for the purchase of 100 shares of the ABC Company. Y agrees to sell the shares for $50 per share, but breaches the contract by refusing to deliver. If the price of the shares at the time of the breach is $60 per share, X could sue Y for the difference between the originally agreed price and the market price of the shares at the time Y was required to deliver them to X. That would put X in the position he would have been in had Y performed the contract, and thus would represent the amount of money damages. Consider the alternative example of S who materially misrepresents the business activities of the ABC Company to T, who then purchases some shares in the company at $50 per share. If T purchases the shares and then discovers the truth about the company, she has the option of **avoiding,** or **repudiating,** the contract. A party who decides to exercise a **right of avoidance** can demand **rescission** of the contract. If the price of the shares has fallen to $10 per share, T will surely rescind the contract. She will then be put back into the position she was in before the contract was ever closed and therefore be entitled to a return of the $50 per share she paid. Of course if the price of the shares should increase to $60 per share, T will not rescind. Thus the fact that the contract is **voidable**, rather than **void**, gives the deceived party an advantage later in choosing whether to uphold the contract, or to rescind it.

Questions on the Text

[1] Was Mr. Boynton fraudulent in his dealings with Ms. Wood? Did he materially misrepresent any facts to her?

[2] The court also considers one particular type of mistake that could result in Ms. Wood recovering the diamond. This result would be reached not because she could rescind the sale, but because she still has title to the diamond, meaning title never really passed to Mr. Boynton on delivery. Can you give an example of what the court means here?

[3] What kind of mistakes does your legal system recognize as being a basis for declaring a contract void? Does your legal system draw a difference between money damages and rescission?

Continue reading the case:

In this case, upon the plaintiff's own evidence, there can be no just ground for alleging that she was induced to make the sale she did by any fraud or unfair dealings on the part of Mr. Boynton. Both were entirely ignorant at the time of the character
65   of the stone and of its intrinsic value. Mr. Boynton was not an expert in uncut diamonds, and had made no examination of the stone, except to take it in his hand and look at it before he made the offer of one dollar, which was refused at the time, and afterwards accepted without any comment or further examination made by Mr. Boynton. The appellant had the stone in her possession for a long time, and it
70   appears from her own statement that she had made some inquiry as to its nature and qualities. If she chose to sell it without further investigation as to its intrinsic value to a person who was guilty of no fraud or unfairness which induced her to sell it for a small sum, she cannot repudiate the sale because it is afterwards ascertained that she made a bad bargain ... There is no pretense of any mistake as to the identity of the
75   thing sold. It was produced by the plaintiff and exhibited to the vendee before the sale was made, and the thing sold was delivered to the vendee when the purchase price was paid ... Suppose the appellant had produced the stone, and said she had been told it was a diamond, and she believed it was, but had no knowledge herself as to its character or value, and Mr. Boynton had given her $500 for it, could he have
80   rescinded the sale if it had turned out to be a topaz or any other stone of very small value? Could Mr. Boynton have rescinded the sale on the ground of mistake? Clearly

not, ... nor could he rescind it on the ground of fraud, unless he could show that she falsely declared that she had been told it was a diamond, or, if she had been so told, still she knew it was not a diamond ...

85   It is urged, with a good deal of earnestness, on the part of the counsel for the appellant that, because it has turned out that the stone was immensely more valuable than the parties at the time of the sale supposed it was, such fact alone is a ground for the rescission of the sale, and that fact was evidence of fraud on the part of the vendee ... When this sale was made the value of the thing sold was open to the
90   investigation of both parties, neither knowing its intrinsic value, and, so far as the evidence in this case shows, both supposed that the price paid was adequate. How can fraud be predicated upon such a sale, even though after-investigation showed that the intrinsic value of the thing sold was hundreds of times greater than the price paid? It certainly shows no such fraud as would authorize the vendor to rescind the
95   contract and bring an action at law to recover the possession of the thing sold ...

We can find nothing in the evidence from which it could be justly inferred that Mr. Boynton, at the time he offered the plaintiff one dollar for the stone, had any knowledge of the real value of the stone, or that he entertained even a belief that the stone was a diamond. It cannot, therefore, be said that there was a suppression of
100 knowledge on the part of the defendant as to the value of the stone ... However unfortunate the plaintiff may have been in selling this valuable stone for a mere nominal sum, she has failed entirely to make out a case either of fraud or mistake in the sale such as will entitle her to a rescission of such sale so as to recover the property sold in an action at law.

105 The judgment of the circuit court is affirmed.

Analysis

Generally mistakes are categorized by the common law into those which are **mutual** or **common** on the one hand, and those which are **unilateral** on the other. Consider the treatment given to these two classes of mistakes by the *Restatement (Second) Contracts*. The first section (§ 152) relates to mutual or common mistakes. The second section (§ 153) relates to unilateral mistakes:

§ 152. When Mistake of Both Parties Makes a Contract Voidable

(1) Where a mistake of both parties at the time a contract was made as to a basic assumption on which the contract was made has a material effect on the agreed exchange of performances, the contract is voidable by the adversely affected party unless he bears the risk of the mistake under the rule stated in § 154 ...

Comment:

a. Rationale. Before making a contract, a party ordinarily evaluates the proposed exchange of performances on the basis of a variety of assumptions with respect to existing facts. Many of these assumptions are shared by the other party, in the sense that the other party is aware that they are made. The mere fact that both parties are mistaken with respect to such an assumption does not, of itself, afford a reason for avoidance of the contract by the adversely affected party. Relief is only appropriate in situations where a mistake of both parties has such a material effect on the agreed exchange of performances as to upset the very basis for the contract.

This Section applies to such situations. Under it, the contract is voidable by the adversely affected party if three conditions are met. First, the mistake must relate to a "basic assumption on which the contract was made." Second, the party seeking avoidance must show that the mistake has a material effect on the agreed exchange of performances. Third, the mistake must not be one as to which the party seeking relief bears the risk ... .

§ 153. When Mistake of One Party Makes a Contract Voidable

Where a mistake of one party at the time a contract was made as to a basic assumption on which he made the contract has a material effect on the agreed exchange of performances that is adverse to him, the contract is voidable by him if he does not bear the risk of the mistake under the rule stated in § 154, and

(a) the effect of the mistake is such that enforcement of the contract would be unconscionable, or

(b) the other party had reason to know of the mistake or his fault caused the mistake.

Comment:

a. Rationale. Courts have traditionally been reluctant to allow a party to avoid a contract on the ground of mistake, even as to a basic assumption, if the mistake was not shared by the other party. Nevertheless, relief has been granted where the other party actually knew ... or had reason to know of the mistake at the time the contract was made or where his fault caused the mistake. There has, in addition, been a growing willingness to allow avoidance where the consequences of the mistake are so grave that enforcement of the contract would be unconscionable. This Section states a rule that permits avoidance on this latter basis, as well as on the more traditional grounds ...

b. Similarity to rule where both are mistaken. In order for a party to have the power to avoid a contract for a mistake that he alone made, he must at least meet the same requirements that he would have had to meet had both parties been mistaken (§ 152). The mistake must be one as to a basic assumption on which the contract was made; it must have a material effect on the agreed exchange of performances; and the mistaken party must not bear the risk of the mistake ...

c. Additional requirement of unconscionability. Under Subparagraph (a), the mistaken party must in addition show that enforcement of the contract would be unconscionable. The reason for this additional requirement is that, if only one party was mistaken, avoidance of the contract will more clearly disappoint the expectations of the other party than if he too was mistaken ...

§ 154. When a Party Bears the Risk of a Mistake

A party bears the risk of a mistake when

(a) the risk is allocated to him by agreement of the parties, or

(b) he is aware, at the time the contract is made, that he has only limited knowledge with respect to the facts to which the mistake relates but treats his limited knowledge as sufficient, or

(c) the risk is allocated to him by the court on the ground that it is reasonable in the circumstances to do so.

Comment:

a. Rationale. Absent provision to the contrary, a contracting party takes the risk of most supervening changes in circumstances, even though they upset basic assumptions and unexpectedly affect the agreed exchange of performances, unless there is such extreme hardship as will justify relief on the ground of impracticability of performance or frustration of purpose. A party also bears the risk of many mistakes as to existing circumstances even though they upset basic assumptions and unexpectedly affect the agreed exchange of performances ...

Questions on the Text

1. Was Ms. Wood's mistake shared by Mr. Boynton? Which section of the *Restatement (Second) Contracts* then applies to this case?
2. Did Ms. Wood bear the risk of mistake in this case? What section of the *Restatement (Second) Contracts* gives you the answer?
3. If you purchase shares of stock on the stock exchange through your broker, are you in a position similar to Ms. Wood's position? Does the broker know whether the shares will increase or decrease in value over the next period of time? Do you know? Would all such contracts be voidable by the adversely affected party if *Wood v. Boynton* had been decided in Ms. Wood's favor?
4. The court considers the hypothetical that the parties in *Wood v. Boynton* thought the stone was a diamond and Mr. Boynton paid Ms. Wood $500 for it. Would Boynton in that hypothetical be able to avoid the contract under the provisions of the *Restatement*?

Terminology

impossibility	defense to a claim of breach of contract based on the promisor's inability to perform when performance is due (**Unmöglichkeit**); to be a good defense the promisor must not have been at fault for the circumstances giving rise to the impossibility

stipulation	provision, agreement or demand regarding a term in a contract, usually on what is to happen in the future or what is taken to be true (**Vertragsbedingung, Vereinbarung, Vertragsbestimmung**)
warranty	guarantee, promise that certain facts are true (**Zusicherung, Gewährleistung**); **warranties** can be **express** (**ausdrückliche Zusicherung**), meaning actually stated, or **implied** (**konkludente Gewährleistung**), meaning that one's conduct leads another person to conclude that the **warranty** was intended
count	individual claim against another individual; a **complaint** may include a variety of different claims, each based on a different legal theory and each of which would be one **count** (**Klagepunkt**)
bailment	deposit of goods with someone for safe keeping or for use for a specified purpose (**Besitzüberlassung an beweglichen Sachen auf Zeit, z.B. Hinterlegung, Verwahrung**)
bailor	one who deposits goods with another (**Hinterleger**)
bailee	one who holds another's goods in deposit (**Verwahrer**)
argumentation by analogy	arguing by comparing a case that has to be decided with other cases that have been decided in the past or to hypothetical cases where the correct solution seems intuitively clear; the purpose of this form of argumentation is convince s.o. of the appropriateness of one's own conclusion regarding the new case, because one claims that it is really no different from these other cases or hypotheticals (**Berufung auf eine Analogie**)
to extend a precedent	to take an already established precedent and apply it to a new case that is somewhat different in a legally relevant respect to the former case; after the precedent has been extended it applies in more cases than it did before it was extended (**den Anwendungsbereich eines Präzedenzurteils ausdehnen**)
to limit a precedent	to refuse to apply an already established precedent to a similar but still somewhat different case; after a precedent has been limited it does not apply to as many cases as one might previously have thought or argued (**den Anwendungsbereich eines Präzedenzurteils einschränken**)
allocation of risk	assignment to a certain person or persons of disadvantages that might materialize if some event occurs or facts become known (**Verteilung des Risikos**); also: division and distribution of goods, wealth, entitlements, benefits (**Verteilung von Gütern**)
express conditions	assumptions or stipulations that the parties actually state in their agreement (**ausdrückliche Bedingungen**)
implied conditions	assumptions or stipulations that are not actually stated but which a court will interpret into a contract based on the parties' behavior and expectations (**Bedingungen, die in einem Vertrag konkludent enthalten sind**)

contract to compose a work	agreement requiring one party to make, prepare or create s.th., such as a painting, musical score, book (ca. **Werkvertrag**)
rule absolute	final rule that is to take immediate effect, often because the person to whom it is directed has failed to **show cause**, or give a good reason, why the rule should not issue (**rechtskräftige richterliche Verfügung**)
to enter a verdict	to officially record a decision reached by the **factfinder** (either judge or jury) at trial; more often used in: **to enter judgment on the verdict**
to enter judgment on the verdict	to officially record, as a judge, the determination made at trial by the factfinder (**ein Urteil im Einklang mit dem Spruch der Geschworenen fällen**); entering judgment on the verdict gives legal effect to the verdict; if a jury is used and the judge is of the opinion that no reasonable jury could have reached the verdict the jury did reach, the judge may also **enter judgment notwithstanding the verdict**
judgment notwithstanding the verdict	a judge's official determination that the jury's verdict cannot be upheld as a matter of law; in order to be able to enter **judgment notwithstanding the verdict**, the judge must view the facts most favorably to the party for whom the verdict was reached and decide on the basis of that view of the facts that still the party should not have been successful in the law suit as a matter of law; either party to the law suit may make a motion at the end of the trial to have the judge **enter a judgment notwithstanding the verdict** (**ein Urteil nicht im Einklang mit dem Spruch der Geschworenen fällen**); a **judgment notwithstanding the verdict** permits the judge to override the jury's determination and thus ensure that the case is properly resolved; a **judgment notwithstanding the verdict** can*not* be reached if a jury in a criminal case finds the defendant not guilty; also called **judgment n.o.v.**, meaning **judgment *non obstante veredicto***
motion for a directed verdict	formal request addressed to the court which may be made by either the plaintiff or defendant and which asks the court to determine as a matter of law that the other party cannot win the law suit; if the **verdict is directed**, the jury does not deliberate, but rather the verdict is reached by the judge; the test for whether a party's motion for a directed verdict should be granted is whether a reasonable jury could reach a different result when applying the law correctly even if it viewed the facts in a light most favorable to the non-moving party; thus test is the same as for granting a **motion for a judgment notwithstanding the verdict**, but a **motion for a directed verdict** is made before the case is given to the jury for deliberation, whereas the **motion for a judgment notwithstanding the verdict** is made after the jury

	has deliberated and reached a verdict of its own (**Antrag auf Erlaß einer bindenden Weisung des Richters an die Geschworenen, ein bestimmtes Urteil zu fällen**)
frustration	defense to a claim of breach of contract based on a change in circumstances after the contract was closed that make one party's performance worthless to the other party (**Wegfall der Geschäftsgrundlage**)
demise	transfer of property for life or for a certain number of years
discharged from performance	released from the duty to perform according to the terms of a contract (**von einer Leistung befreit worden sein**)
to dismiss an appeal	(UK) to uphold the decision of a lower court in a case against appellate attack by a party dissatisfied with that decision (**die Revision zurückweisen**); opposite of **to allow an appeal** (**der Revision stattgeben**)
to vest	to become valid and effective, as in: **a right vests, title vests**; if s.th. **revests** it becomes effective or valid again, as in: **title revests in the seller if the contract is rescinded**
to pass title	to transfer ownership right in property (**Eigentum übertragen**)
rescission of contract	declaration that a contract is void from the beginning; may be made by a party or court (**Rücktritt vom Vertrag, Anfechtung**); if made by a party, that party is called the **rescinding party**
repudiation of a contract	treating a contract as if it were void and demanding to be restored to the position one had before the contract was performed (**Rücktritt vom Vertrag**); compare **anticipatory repudiation** (II.I.3), which is repudiation before performance under the contract is due
fraud	intentional deceit for the purpose of convincing another person to part with s.th. valuable (**arglistige Täuschung**; strafrechtlich: **Betrug**)
misrepresentation	intentional false statement (**vorsätzlich falsche Darstellung von Tatsachen**); if used to convince another person to agree to a contract it is a **material misrepresentation** (**rechtlich relevante, vorsätzlich falsche Darstellung von Tatsachen**)
void	empty of legal effect (**nichtig, unwirksam**); contrast to **voidable**
voidable	capable of being avoided at the discretion of an adversely affected party to a contract (**anfechtbar**); contrast to **void**, which means empty of effect regardless of the parties' intent or individual discretion
counsel	lawyer, attorney (**Rechtsanwalt**)
mutual mistake	mistake as to conditions relating to a contract that is shared by both parties; also called **common mistake** (**beiderseitiger Irrtum**)

unilateral mistake	mistake as to conditions relating to a contract that only one of the parties makes (**einseitiger Irrtum**)
unconscionable	in violation of good moral values, contrary to one's conscience (**gegen die guten Sitten**)

Terminology Review

instant case (I.III.2)	the case the court is considering at the moment; also: **the case at bar** (**der vorliegende Fall**)
case at bar (I.III.2)	the case the court is considering at the moment; also the **instant case** (**der vorliegende Fall**)
affidavit (I.III.1)	sworn statement of facts (ca. **eidesstattliche Erklärung**)
factfinder (I.I.2)	the person or body responsible for determining the facts of a case from the evidence presented at trial; it is the jury if a jury is used, otherwise the judge acts as the factfinder (**Richter oder Geschworenenbank, die für die Feststellung des Sachverhalts zuständig ist**)
assumpsit (I.I.1)	form of action for **damages** to compensate for the defendant's failure to perform as promised under a simple contract, whereby the promise may be implied by law (**general assumpsit**) or expressly made by the defendant (**special assumpsit**)
rule nisi (I.III.1)	order to give a good reason why a court ruling should not become final and enforced (ca. **Ladung mit Aufforderung, etwaige Einwendungen vorzubringen**)
rule to show cause (I.III.1)	order to give a good reason why a court ruling should not become final and enforced (ca. **Ladung mit Aufforderung, etwaige Einwendungen vorzubringen**)
verdict (I.I.2)	result of trial as jury determined; in a criminal case the verdict will be "guilty" or "not guilty;" in a private law dispute either "for the plaintiff in the amount of ... " or "for the defendant;" (ca. **Spruch der Geschworenen**); also referred to as a **general verdict** in contrast to a **special verdict**, which is merely a list of facts the jury believes are true to which the judge will apply the law in reaching the final judgment in a case; a **special verdict** is required when, for example, the judge feels the law is too complicated for the jury to apply correctly (ca. **Tatsacheninterlokut**)
to testify (I.I.2)	to tell what one knows relating to a law suit in a court of law (**aussagen**)

Vocabulary

to ascertain	to determine, to discover the truth of s.th.
contingency	s.th. that is not certain to happen, s.th. that is a matter of chance
inception	beginning
intrinsic	of the essential nature of s.th., inherent
to be predicated upon	to be based on
supervening	happening unexpectedly and materially changing the situation after one has already made a decision or started to act
suppression	hiding of s.th. from another person, concealment of facts

Language Exercises
Chapter 4

I. Fill in the blanks with one or more words:

Contract Law Terminology

If the parties to a contract actually state in the contract that performance depends on the occurrence of some event or the existence of some object, they have included an 1 in the contract. If they do not, but the court determines that they must have intended to make performance depend on the existence of an object or the occurrence of an event, then the contract is subject to an 2 . The seller of chattels is also referred to as the 3 and the buyer as the 4 . A person who deposits goods with someone else for safe keeping is the 5 . The person with whom he deposits them is the 6 . These two individuals then have entered into a 7 contract. The price the defendant paid for the stone was so insignificant that one would say it was a 8 . The effect of the mistake was such that it would be completely unfair, or 9 , to enforce the contract. Therefore the contract is 10 by the mistaken party. In other words the mistaken party has a right of 11 . Usually a contracting party takes the risk of 12 changes in circumstances, meaning unexpected and material changes occurring after the contract has been closed. The person who is harmed by a change in circumstances is the 13 , or the 14 , or the 15 party. If the promisor is unable to perform the contract and not a fault for his inability, he can claim the defense of 16 . An agreement to paint a portrait is one example of a 17 . If both parties to a contract share the same mistake, the mistake is 18 or 19 . However if only one party is mistaken, the mistake is 20 .

General Legal Expressions

The evidence included an 21 , which is a sworn statement of facts contained in a document. The plaintiff's complaint included three individual claims, also called 22 , each based on a different legal theory. If the judge follows the jury's verdict and officially records it, he enters 23 . On the other hand, if he disagrees with the verdict as a matter of law, he will enter 24 , or 25 . The lawyer for the appellant is the appellant's 26 or 27 . The case the court is currently considering is the 28 , or the 29 .

II. Fill in the appropriate verbs:

1. The defendant claimed that the plaintiff's complaint failed to state a cause of action. =
   The defendant ___ to the plaintiff's complaint.

2. The plaintiff suffered a loss. =
   The plaintiff <u>a</u> a loss. = The plaintiff <u>b</u> a loss.

3. The facts in the complaint are sufficient to withstand a demurrer. =
   The facts are sufficient ___ an action.

4. The judge upheld the plaintiff's objection. =
   The judge ___ the objection.

5. The parties formulated their agreement. =
   The parties ___ their agreement.

6. The parties expressly agreed that performance depended on the existence of the music hall. =
   The parties expressly <u>a</u> that performance depended on the existence of the music hall. =
   The parties expressly <u>b</u> that performance depended on the existence of the music hall.

7. The defendant was released from his duties under the contract. =
   The defendant ___ from the contract.

8. The defendant fulfilled his duties under the contract. =
   The defendant ___ the contract.

9. The contract assigned the risk of loss of the music hall to the plaintiff. =
   The contract ___ the risk of loss to the plaintiff.

10. The court applied a past precedent to new, somewhat different facts. =
    The court ___ the precedent.

11. The court refused to apply a past precedent to new, but very similar facts. =
    The court ___ the precedent.

12. The court ordered the defendant to give a good reason why the court ruling should not become final. =
    The court ordered the defendant ___ cause.

13. The court told the jury to reach a verdict for the defendant.
    The court ___ the verdict.

14. In his answer the defendant claimed he owed the plaintiff no money and claimed the plaintiff should be ordered to repay him the money he had already paid the plaintiff. = The defendant <u>a</u> that he was liable to the plaintiff and <u>b</u> for return of his own money.

15. The plaintiff held out money for the defendant to take. =
    The plaintiff ___ the defendant the money.

16. The plaintiff started a law suit. =
    The plaintiff <u>a</u> an action. = The plaintiff <u>b</u> an action. = The plaintiff <u>c</u> an action.

17. The plaintiff once again became the owner of the diamond. =
    Title to the diamond ___ in the plaintiff.

18. Each party to the contract is responsible for his own mistakes. =
    Each party to the contract ___ the risk of his own mistakes.

19. The defendant had to accept the loss. =
    The defendant ___ the burden of the loss.

20. The court interpreted the contract to contain an implied condition. =
    The court ___ the contract to contain an implied condition.

21. The mistaken party has to fulfill certain requirements in order to be able to treat the contract as non-binding.
    The mistaken party <u>a</u> certain requirements in order <u>b</u> the contract.

22. The seller transferred his ownership right in the property to the buyer. =
    The seller ___ title to the buyer.

23. The court declared the contract to be void from the beginning. =
    The court ___ the contract.

24. The promisor treated the contract as if it were void and demanded to be restored to the position he had before the contract was performed. =
    The promisor ___ the contract.

Chapter 5
Uniform Commercial Code

The *Uniform Commercial Code* represents an effort to codify the law of **commercial transactions** for the **sale of goods**. This effort was undertaken by the American Law Institute and the National Conference of Commissioners on Uniform State Laws. As you have already read in Chapter 1, the American Law Institute is responsible for the many *Restatements of the Law*, which are devoted to codifying the common law. These efforts to draft model codes that are uniform throughout the United States are in some sense eradicating one of the basic differences between a common law and a civil law system. The *Uniform Commercial Code*, however, cannot be seen as completely removed from the common law, because it expressly incorporates the principles of the common law and equity. Consider the following provision:

§ 1–103. Supplementary General Principles of Law Applicable.

Unless displaced by the particular provisions of this Act, the principles of law and equity, including the law merchant and the law relative to capacity to contract, principal and agent, estoppel, fraud, misrepresentation, duress, coercion, mistake, bankruptcy, or other validating or invalidating cause shall supplement its provisions.

Uniform Commercial Code (14th ed. 1995 Official Text, West Publishing Co. 1996)

In § 1–103, the particular provisions of this **Act** refers to the requirements of the *U.C.C.* itself, which if adopted by a state legislature would be **enacted**, or put into force as an **act** of the legislature. The **law merchant** refers to any other commonly accepted or uniform legislation on sales by **merchants**, or individuals in the business of selling goods. The law relative to **capacity to contract, principal and agent, estoppel, fraud, misrepresentation, duress, coercion**, and **mistake** is the law relating to circumstances that might **invalidate** an otherwise **valid** contract. As you know from the foregoing chapters, not every promise that is accepted is also binding on the parties under the law. The promise must be supported by consideration or formalized to be binding. Accordingly, consideration or formalization **validates** an otherwise invalid contract. Furthermore, valid contracts may be **avoided**, or **invalidated**, for example, because they were closed by an individual lacking the **capacity to contract**, or they were closed by someone who had no right to act as an **agent** on behalf of someone else, who is called the **principal**. Capacity to contract was discussed in Chapter 2 and the relationship between a principal and his agent in Chapter 1. In addition, principles of equity sometimes bar or **estop** an individual from exercising rights she would otherwise have under the common law of contracts. As you may recall, **estoppel** was discussed in Chapter 3. Finally, contracts may be void or voidable if they were closed under circumstances involving **fraud, misrepresentation, duress, coercion, or mistake**. In Chapter 4 we discussed these invalidating causes, with the exception of **duress** and **coercion**. Consider the following definitions from *Black's Law Dictionary* and *Restatement (Second) Contracts* §§ 174, 175 on **duress** and **coercion**:

> **Duress.** Any unlawful threat or coercion used by a person to induce another to act (or to refrain from acting) in a manner he or she otherwise would not (or would). Subjecting person to improper pressure which overcomes his will and coerces him to comply with demand to which he would not yield if acting as free agent ...
>
> A contract entered into under duress by physical compulsion is void. Also, if a party's manifestation of assent to a contract is induced by an improper threat by the other party that leaves the victim no reasonable alternative, the contract is voidable by the victim.
>
> **Coercion.** Compulsion; constraint; compelling by force or [*sic.* of] arms or threat.
>
> **§ 174. When Duress by Physical Compulsion Prevents Formation of a Contract**
>
> If conduct that appears to be a manifestation of assent by a party who does not intend to engage in that conduct is physically compelled by duress, the conduct is not effective as a manifestation of assent.
>
> **§ 175. When Duress by Threat Makes a Contract Voidable**
>
> (1) If a party's manifestation of assent is induced by an improper threat by the other party that leaves the victim no reasonable alternative, the contract is voidable by the victim.

Section 174 *Restatement* provides that the contract is **void**, because the agreement, as normally evidenced by the offeree's manifesting, or showing, his assent, was never closed for lack of that assent. It envisages a situation, for example, where the coerced party was physically forced to sign his name on a contract or to raise his hand at an auction as if to bid. Section 175 provides that the contract is **voidable** by the victim of an improper threat. It relates to threats, as opposed to physical coercion, which result in the victim's agreement out of fear created by the threat. Section 175 permits the aggrieved party to decide whether to uphold the contractual relationship or to repudiate it.

The main point of *U.C.C.* § 1–103 is to maintain the common law and principles of equity relating to such circumstances as these, which would render a contract **valid** or **invalid, void** or **voidable**.

A. Application of the *U.C.C.*

Within the United States, one of the benefits of the *Uniform Commercial Code* is that it makes the law of commercial transactions fairly uniform throughout the country. It has been adopted by every state, albeit sometimes in modified form, with the exception of Louisiana. Louisiana, unlike the other states in the United States has a civil law system, like the systems of continental Europe (see *Einführung in die anglo-amerikanische Rechtssprache / Introduction to Anglo-American Law & Language*, Unit I, Chapter 1 for a detailed discussion of the difference) That is because of the early French influence in Louisiana. As a result, Louisiana had its own commercial code, which it was unwilling to sacrifice in favor of the *U.C.C.* The other **jurisdictions**, however, readily adopted it and thus attained practical uniformity in the laws of the various states. Consequently, commercial transactions in **interstate commerce** (with the exception of those governed by the law of Louisiana) are all governed by the *U.C.C.* Furthermore, international sales of goods may be subject to the provisions of the *U.C.C.* if U.S. law applies to the particular case or if the parties so specify in their agreement. Consider the following section of the *U.C.C.*:

> § 1–105. **Territorial Application of the Act; Parties' Power to Choose Applicable Law.**
>
> (1) Except as provided hereafter in this section, when a transaction bears a reasonable relation to this state and also to another state or nation the parties may agree that the law either of this state or of such other state or nation shall govern their rights and duties. Failing such agreement this Act applies to transactions bearing an appropriate relation to this state ...

Official Comment

Purposes:

1. Subsection (1) states affirmatively the right of the parties to a multi-state transaction or a transaction involving foreign trade to choose their own law. That right ... is limited to jurisdictions to which the transaction bears a "reasonable relation." ... Ordinarily the law chosen must be that of a jurisdiction where a significant enough portion of the making or performance of the contract is to occur or occurs. But an agreement as to choice of law may sometimes take effect as a shorthand expression of the intent of the parties as to matters governed by their agreement, even though the transaction has no significant contact with the jurisdiction chosen.

2. Where there is no agreement as to the governing law, the Act is applicable to any transaction having an "appropriate" relation to any state which enacts it. Of course, the Act

applies to any transaction which takes place in its entirety in a state which has enacted the Act. But the mere fact that suit is brought in a state does not make it appropriate to apply the substantive law of that state. Cases where a relation to the enacting state is not "appropriate" include, for example, those where the parties have clearly contracted on the basis of some other law, as where the law of the place of contracting and the law of the place of contemplated performance are the same and are contrary to the law under the Code.

3. Where a transaction has significant contacts with a state which has enacted the Act and also with other jurisdictions, the question what relation is "appropriate" is left to judicial decision ... .

1. Choice of Law

This section of the *U.C.C.* contains a **choice-of law** provision. The **choice-of-law** provision permits the parties to choose what law shall apply to their agreement. As you may know, each state in the United States has its own statutory law and is a self-contained legal system (see *Einführung in die anglo-amerikanische Rechtsprache / Introduction to Anglo-American Law & Language*, Unit II for a detailed description of the federal and individual state legal systems). Assume that a merchant in Ohio enters into a contract for the sale of office furniture to a company with its headquarters in Louisiana, and branch offices in Oklahoma and Oregon. The furniture is to be delivered to all three of the buyer's office locations, and the invoice is to be sent to the buyer's headquarters. What law governs this transaction? The transaction bears a relation to four different states, each of which may have different **rules of civil procedure, statutes of limitation,** and, since the state of Louisiana is involved, also different substantive provisions on contract formation and the consequences of breach. Indeed, it may be that the state of Ohio has enacted the *U.C.C.* with some alterations in the original text, making Ohio commercial law slightly different from Oklahoma commercial law. Section 1–105 permits the parties to specify in their contract that Ohio law governs their transaction. The same is true for international agreements. Thus a French seller might agree to submit to the provisions of the *U.C.C.* as enacted in the buyer's home state of Nebraska.

2. Conflict of Laws

Section 1–105 also contains a **conflict-of-laws** provision. The **conflict-of-laws** provision tells the judge in a multi-state case whether to apply the law of one state or the other, assuming the parties have not effectively designated what law should apply to their agreement. Let us consider the case of a German company contracting to sell automotive parts to a German **subsidiary** of a U.S. **parent** company headquartered in New York. The automotive parts are to be delivered to the **subsidiary** in Germany. A **conflict-of-laws** problem does not arise until a law suit is filed with a particular court. Suppose a suit is filed in New York. New York has enacted the *U.C.C.*, so one might think the judge will apply New York law in this case. But as you read in § 1–105, the *U.C.C.* is only applicable if the transaction has an "appropriate relation" to New York. Essentially the New York judge will have to decide whether to apply New York law, and therefore the provisions of the *U.C.C.*, or to apply the law of Germany. Simply because the suit was initiated in New York is no reason to apply New York law. Indeed, the official comment to § 1–105 indicates that most likely German law will apply to this case because Germany is both the place of contracting and the place of contemplated performance. Conflict of laws is a rather complicated area of the law, however, and judges usually have a good deal of discretion in deciding whether to apply the law of the **forum state**, meaning the state where the court is located, or the law of some other state.

B. Scope of the *U.C.C.*

If you cast a glance in the table of contents of the *U.C.C.* you would find that it contains the following Articles:

Article 1. General Provisions	**Article 5. Letters of Credit**
Article 2. Sales	**Article 6. Bulk Sales**
Article 2A. Leases	**Article 7. Warehouse Receipts, Bills of Lading**
Article 3. Negotiable Instruments	**and Other Documents of Title**
Article 4. Bank Deposits and Collections	**Article 8. Investment Securities**
Article 4A. Funds Transfers	**Article 9. Secured Transactions; Sales of Accounts**
	and Chattel Paper

As you can see, a good deal other than contracts for the sale of goods (Article 2) is governed by the *U.C.C.* Still most of the legal areas it covers relate at least indirectly to sales contracts. Many of these areas of the law are relevant only for individuals engaged in larger business transactions, and not for the general consumer. Furthermore, although Article 2 covers contracts for the sale of goods, some of its provisions are expressly limited to contracts **between merchants**. A merchant is defined in the *Uniform Commercial Code* as follows:

§ 2–104. Definitions: "Merchant"; "Between Merchants"; ...

(1) "Merchant" means a person who deals in goods of the kind or otherwise by his occupation holds himself out as having knowledge or skill peculiar to the practices or goods involved in the transaction or to whom such knowledge or skill may be attributed by his employment of an agent or broker or other intermediary who by his occupation holds himself out as having such knowledge or skill ... .

(3) "Between merchants" means in any transaction with respect to which both parties are chargeable with the knowledge or skill of merchants.

Subsection (1) is somewhat difficult to read. Although it appears to contain only two alternatives joined by the disjunctive "or," it really contains three. To understand it you need to break the first half of the sentence into two alternatives: 1) "Merchant means a person who deals in goods of the kind ... involved in the transaction" and 2) "Merchant means a person who ... by his occupation holds himself out as having knowledge or skill peculiar to the practices or goods involved in the transaction." Adding the second half of the sentence to the definition, we also see: "Merchant means a person to whom ... knowledge or skill [peculiar to the practices or goods involved in the transaction] may be attributed by his employment of an agent or broker or other intermediary who by his occupation holds himself out as having such knowledge or skill." To state the three alternatives somewhat more clearly, "merchant" is either someone who actually deals in goods himself, or someone, such as an agent, who acts as if he had the skill of someone who deals in goods himself, or someone who will be treated as if he did have this skill because he employed an agent to deal in his name and the agent had this skill.

C. Modifications of the Requirements for Effective Acceptance of an Offer

Although the *U.C.C.* incorporates the common law, it has introduced significant changes regarding contracts for the sale of goods. In the following sections we will consider these changes in light of your current knowledge of the common law of contracts. Before moving on, however, it is important to note that a contract for the sale of **goods** does not mean a contract for the sale of land or provision of services. The *U.C.C.* therefore does not apply to sales contracts other than those for the sale of **movables** or **chattels**.

1. Demise of the Mirror-Image Rule

As you know from Chapter 2 B, an acceptance which varies the terms of an offer operates as a rejection of that offer and as a counter-offer, which the original offeree submits to the original offeror for acceptance. This common law rule, referred to as the **mirror-image rule**, requires a precise **meeting of the minds** before a contract is binding. The *U.C.C.* modifies this rule, particularly with respect to agreements **between merchants**. Consider the following *U.C.C.* provision:

§ 2–207 **Additional Terms in Acceptance or Confirmation.**

(1) A definite and seasonable expression of acceptance or a written confirmation which is sent within a reasonable time operates as an acceptance even though it states terms additional to or different from those offered or agreed upon, unless acceptance is expressly made conditional on assent to the additional or different terms.

(2) The additional terms are to be construed as proposals for addition to the contract. Between merchants such terms become part of the contract unless:

(a) the offer expressly limits acceptance to the terms of the offer;

(b) they materially alter it; or

(c) notification of objection to them has already been given or is given within a reasonable time after notice of them is received.

(3) Conduct by both parties which recognizes the existence of a contract is sufficient to establish a contract for sale although the writings of the parties do not otherwise establish a contract. In such case the terms of the particular contract consist of those terms on which the writings of the parties agree, together with any supplementary terms incorporated under any other provisions of this Act.

Official Comment

Purposes of Changes:

1. This section is intended to deal with two typical situations. The one is the written confirmation, where an agreement has been reached either orally or by informal correspondence between the parties and is followed by one or both of the parties sending formal memoranda embodying the terms so far as agreed upon and adding terms not discussed. The other situation is offer and acceptance, in which a wire or letter expressed and intended as an acceptance or the closing of an agreement adds further minor suggestions or proposals such as "ship by Tuesday," "rush," ... or the like. A frequent example of the second situation is the exchange of printed purchase order and acceptance (sometimes called "acknowledgement" forms). Because the forms are oriented to the thinking of the respective drafting parties, the terms contained in them often do not correspond. Often the seller's form contains terms different from or additional to those set forth in the buyer's

form. Nevertheless, the parties proceed with the transaction ...

3. Whether or not additional or different terms will become part of the agreement depends upon the provisions of subsection (2). If they are such as materially to alter the original bargain, they will not be included unless expressly agreed to by the other party. If, however, they are terms which would not so change the bargain they will be incorporated unless notice of objection to them has already been given or is given within a reasonable time ...

6. If no answer is received within a reasonable time after additional terms are proposed, it is both fair and commercially sound to assume that their inclusion has been assented to. Where clauses on confirming forms sent by both parties conflict each party must be assumed to object to a clause of the other conflicting with one on the confirmation sent by himself. As a result the requirement that there be notice of objection, which is found in sub-section (2), is satisfied and the conflicting terms do not become a part of the contract. The contract then consists of the terms originally expressly agreed to, terms on which the confirmations agree, and terms supplied by this Act, including subsection (2). The written confirmation is also subject to Section 2–201. Under that section a failure to respond permits enforcement of a prior oral agreement; under this section a failure to respond permits additional terms to become part of the agreement ...

7. In many cases, as where goods are shipped, accepted and paid for before any dispute arises, there is no question whether a contract has been made. In such cases, where the writings of the parties do not establish a contract, it is not necessary to determine which act or document constituted the offer and which the acceptance ... The only question is what terms are included in the contract, and subsection (3) furnishes the governing rule ...

Analysis

This section of the *U.C.C.* is designed to weaken the effect of the **mirror-image rule**. First, subsection (1) indicates that an acceptance is valid and thus closes the contract between the offeror and the offeree, even though it does not correspond to the original offer. As between a merchant and a consumer, any additional terms require the assent of the offeror. You can tell that from the first sentence of subsection (2), which provides that additional terms are proposals only. As between merchants, however, additional terms become part of the contract (subsection (2), second sentence), with certain exceptions as stated in subsections (2)(a), (b), and (c). The idea behind § 2–207 relates to the realities of the business world. Usually offers and acceptances are written on forms generally used by the particular company. These forms contain a whole list of **standard terms**. Standard terms, or clauses, relate the conditions under which a certain company has decided to do business generally. The problem arises when the standard terms

incorporated within the offeror company's offer differ from the standard terms
incorporated within the offeree company's acceptance. The same problem can
arise if one or both parties use **confirmation forms** to verify the terms of an
informal contract. This problem is commonly referred to as the **battle of the
forms**. If the common law mirror image rule were applied, most business relations would never ripen into a binding contract and each party would have an
easy way to relieve herself from the burdens the contract might prove to impose.
Consider the following text on § 2–207:

> It is a sad fact that many sales contracts are not fully bargained, not carefully drafted,
> and not understandingly signed or otherwise acknowledged by both parties. Often,
> here is what happens: underlings of seller and buyer each sit in their offices with a
> telephone and a stack of form contracts. Seller's lawyer has drafted seller's forms to
> give seller advantage. Buyer's lawyer has drafted buyer's forms to give buyer advant-
> age. The two sets of forms naturally diverge. They may diverge not only in substan-
> tive terms but also in permissible methods of contract formation.
>
> The process of "contracting" begins with underling telephoning underling or with
> the dispatch of a form. When the process ends, there will usually be two forms
> involved, seller's and buyer's. The deal will usually coincide with respect to the
> bargained terms such as price, quality, quantity and delivery terms. But on other
> terms, the forms will diverge in important respects. Frequently this will pose
> no problem, for the deal will go forward without breakdown. But sometimes the
> parties will fall into dispute even before the occasion for performance. More often,
> one or both will perform or start to perform and a dispute will break out. In all these
> cases the parties will haul out their forms and read them – perhaps for the first time –
> and they will find that their forms diverge. Is there a contract? If so, what are its
> terms?

J. White and R. Summers, *Uniform Commercial Code* (4th ed.) pp. 5–6, West
Publishing Co.

Questions on the Text

On request from the XYZ company, the ABC company, which is located in New
York, sends it an offer to sell a certain quantity and quality of computer chips at
a specified price. The ABC company uses its standard form in making the offer.
The XYZ company, which is located in Spain, responds to the offer with an
acceptance, also printed on one of its standard forms.

☐ On receipt of the goods, the XYZ company notices that the computer chips
do not conform to their description in the offer. The XYZ company files an

action in Madrid for breach of contract. What law will the court apply to this case? What do you need to know to answer that question?

2. Same facts as in no. 2 and assuming that the State of New York has adopted the *U.C.C.* in the same formulation as included in this Chapter: If the Spanish court decides that New York law applies to this case, does that mean that *U.C.C.* § 1–105 applies? What is the basic difference between § 1–105 and § 2–207? Are they both the same type of law?

3. Assuming the Spanish court decides that *U.C.C.* § 1–105 applies to this case, will it apply the substantive law of New York to determine the effect of non-conforming delivery?

4. Assume in addition to the original statement of facts the following: On the back of the ABC company's form, New York law is specified as governing the transaction. On the back of the XYZ company's form, the law of Spain is specified as governing the transaction. If the *U.C.C.* applies in this case, have the parties closed a binding contract?

5. If your answer to no. 4 is in the affirmative, what law applies to the case?

2. Method and Medium of Acceptance

As you know from Chapters 1 and 2, an offer for a unilateral contract requires an act, an offer for a bilateral contract a promise, as acceptance of the offer. Furthermore, the common law usually requires the offeree to communicate his acceptance by the same or a similar means as that selected by the offeror in order for the acceptance to be effective. The *U.C.C.* however obviates the difference between unilateral and bilateral contracts and permits acceptance by any reasonable means:

§ 2–206. Offer and Acceptance in Formation of Contract.

(1) Unless otherwise unambiguously indicated by the language or circumstances

(a) an offer to make a contract shall be construed as inviting acceptance in any manner and by any medium reasonable in the circumstances;

(b) an order or other offer to buy goods for prompt or current shipment shall be construed as inviting acceptance either by a prompt promise to ship or by the prompt or current shipment of conforming ... goods ...

(2) Where the beginning of a requested performance is a reasonable mode of acceptance an offeror who is not notified of acceptance within a reasonable time may treat the offer as having lapsed before acceptance.

Official Comment

1. Any reasonable manner of acceptance is intended to be regarded as available unless the offeror has made quite clear that it will not be acceptable. Former technical rules as to acceptance, such as requiring that telegraphic offers be accepted by telegraphed acceptance, etc., are rejected and a criterion that the acceptance be "in any manner and by any medium reasonable under the circumstances," is substituted. This section is intended to remain flexible and its applicability to be enlarged as new media of communication develop or as the more time-saving present day media come into general use.

2. Either shipment or a prompt promise to ship is made a proper means of acceptance of an offer looking to current shipment. In accordance with ordinary commercial understanding the section interprets an order looking to current shipment as allowing acceptance either by actual shipment or by a prompt promise to ship and rejects the artificial theory that only a single mode of acceptance is normally envisaged by an offer. This is true even though the language of the offer happens to be "ship at once" or the like ...

3. The beginning of performance by an offeree can be effective as acceptance so as to bind the offeror only if followed within a reasonable time by notice to the offeror ... For the protection of both parties it is essential that notice follow in due course to constitute acceptance. Nothing in this section however bars the possibility that under the common law performance begun may have an intermediate effect of temporarily barring revocation of the offer ...

Analysis

As you have just read, § 2–206(1)(a) creates a rebuttable presumption that acceptance can be made in any reasonable way and through the use of any reasonable means of communication. This presumption is rebutted if the language of the offer or the circumstances under which it was made indicate the offeror's insistence on one particular method of acceptance.

Section 2–206(1)(b) abolishes the unilateral-bilateral contract distinction, because the offeree may choose either to actually ship the goods ordered, as he would if the offer were an offer for a unilateral contract, or to promise to ship the goods, as he would if the offer were an offer for a bilateral contract. Either mode of acceptance binds the offeror, no matter how his offer was formulated. Section 2–206(2), however, requires the offeree to notify his acceptance to the offeror within a reasonable time. If the offeree fails to do so, the offeror is not bound by the contract.

Note in the last sentence of Comment 3, the *U.C.C.* expressly retains the option creating rule discussed in connection with *Petterson v. Pattburg* in Chapter 2 C.

Accordingly where the common law rule expressed in *Restatement (Second) Contracts* § 45 is applicable, beginning to perform in response to an offer for a unilateral contract still creates an option contract in favor of the offeree. If the common law rule does not apply, however, then beginning performance alone is insufficient to bind the offeror. Instead the offeree must also inform the offeror that he has accepted the offer. The common law rule would not apply, for example, if the offer is an offer for a bilateral contract. Simply beginning to perform in response to an offer for a bilateral contract does not constitute acceptance under the common law. It also does not create an option contract in favor of the offeree, because *Restatement* § 45 only applies to offers for unilateral contracts. Accordingly, an offeree who begins performing in response to an offer for a bilateral contract can only bind the offeror to his promise by notifying him within a reasonable time. Still *U.C.C.* § 2–206 does give the offeree some advantages he would not have under the common law. Since the offeree can bind the offeror by beginning to perform and within a reasonable time notifying the offeror, the offeror effectively loses his power to revoke the offer during that reasonable period of time.

Questions on the Text

1. A sends B a purchase order for 100 cases of champagne at $10 per bottle for immediate shipment. B starts picking the grapes for the champagne and sends A notification immediately that he accepts A's offer. Have A and B closed a binding contract under the *U.C.C.*? Under the common law?

2. On March 1, 1998, A, a Boston wine distributor, sends B, a French vineyard, a telefacsimile of a purchase order for 100 cases of champagne at $10 per bottle, stating "please respond by March 7, 1998." B immediately ships and sends A notification of acceptance by snail mail (ship, requiring 6 weeks for delivery, and not air) on March 6, 1998. Have A and B closed a binding contract under the *U.C.C.*? Under the common law?

3. Same facts as no. 2, but A's order states "please ship by March 7, 1998." Is A bound under the *U.C.C.*? Under the common law?

4. Same facts as no. 2, but B ships and sends A notification of acceptance by telefacsimile. The fax never arrives in Boston. Have A and B closed a binding contract under the *U.C.C.*? Under the common law?

3. Open Terms and Gap Fillers

Finally, the *U.C.C.* validates many agreements that would be invalid under the common law because the terms of the agreement are too indefinite. Consider the following section:

§ 2–204. Formation in General.

(1) A contract for sale of goods may be made in any manner sufficient to show agreement, including conduct by both parties which recognizes the existence of such a contract.

(2) An agreement sufficient to constitute a contract for sale may be found even though the moment of its making is undetermined.

(3) Even though one or more terms are left open a contract for sale does not fail for indefiniteness if the parties have intended to make a contract and there is a reasonably certain basis for giving an appropriate remedy.

Section 2–204 is aimed at confirming the existence of a binding contract between two parties even though many of the general formalities required for the creation of a contract have been omitted. Important is the determination that the parties intended to contract, regardless of whether they ever actually expressed an offer and an acceptance. Furthermore, it is not necessary to be able to pinpoint the actual time of closing the contract, and even contracts which leave out some relevant terms can be binding. Important is that the court has enough information to determine what remedy to award a non-breaching party if the other party breaches the contract. Of course, if contracts leave out relevant terms, the missing terms then have to be supplied, but the *U.C.C.* also provides so-called **gap fillers** for contracts with open terms. Consider the following **gap filler** to be used when a contract fails to specify the relevant price of the goods:

§ 2–305. Open Price Term.

(1) The parties if they so intend can conclude a contract for sale even though the price is not settled. In such case the price is a reasonable price at the time for delivery if

(a) nothing is said as to price; or

(b) the price is left to be agreed by the parties and they fail to agree; or

(c) the price is to be fixed in terms of some agreed market or other standard as set or recorded by a third person or agency and it is not so set or recorded.

(2) A price to be fixed by the seller or by the buyer means a price for him to fix in good faith.

(3) When a price left open to be fixed otherwise than by agreement of the parties fails to be fixed through fault of one party the other may at his option treat the contract as canceled or himself fix a reasonable price.

(4) Where, however, the parties intend not to be bound unless the price be fixed or agreed and it is not fixed or agreed there is no contract. In such a case the buyer must return any goods already received or if unable so to do must pay their reasonable value at the time of delivery and the seller must return any portion of the price paid on account.

Official Comment

1. This section applies when the price term is left open on the making of an agreement which is nevertheless intended by the parties to be a binding agreement. This Article rejects in these instances the formula that "an agreement to agree is unenforceable" if the case falls within subsection (1) of this section, and rejects also defeating such agreements on the ground of "indefiniteness". Instead this Article recognizes the dominant intention of the parties to have the deal continue to be binding upon both. As to future performance, ... there is usually a "reasonably certain basis for granting an appropriate remedy for breach" so that the contract need not fail for indefiniteness.

2. Under some circumstances the postponement of agreement on price will mean that no deal has really been concluded, and this is made express in the preamble of subsection (1) ("The parties *if they so intend*") and in subsection (4). Whether or not this is so is, in most cases, a question to be determined by the trier of fact.

3. Subsection (2), dealing with the situation where the price is to be fixed by one party, rejects the uncommercial idea that an agreement that the seller may fix the price means that he may fix any price he may wish by the express qualification that the price so fixed must be fixed in good faith. Good faith includes observance of reasonable commercial standards of fair dealing in the trade if the party is a merchant. (Section 2–103). But in the normal case a "posted price" or a future seller's or buyer's "given price," "price in ef-

fect," "market price," or the like satisfies the good faith requirement.

4. The section recognizes that there may be cases in which a particular person's judgment is not chosen merely as a barometer or index of a fair price but is an essential condition to the parties' intent to make any contract at all. For example, the case where a known and trusted expert is to "value" a particular painting for which there is no market standard differs sharply from the situation where a named expert is to determine the grade of cotton, and the difference would support a finding that in the one the parties did not intend to make a binding agreement if that expert were unavailable whereas in the other they did so intend. Other circumstances would of course affect the validity of such a finding.

5. Under subsection (3), wrongful interference by one party with any agreed machinery for price fixing in the contract may be treated by the other party as a repudiation justifying cancellation, or merely as a failure to take cooperative action thus shifting to the aggrieved party the reasonable leeway in fixing the price.

6. Throughout the entire section, the purpose is to give effect to the agreement which has been made. That effect, however, is always conditioned by the requirement of good faith action which is made an inherent part of all contracts within this Act. (Section 1–203).

Consider also the following text:

> Price gaps may be complete or partial. A "partial" gap arises when the parties have specified how the price is to be determined but the method fails. Section 2–305(1)(a) governs complete gaps. Section 2–305(1)(b) and (c) and 2–305(2) and (3) govern partial gaps.
>
> When there is a gap, 2–305 directs the court to determine "a reasonable price," provided the parties intended to contract. Note that the section says "a reasonable price" and not "fair market value of the goods." These two would not be identical. For example, evidence of a prior course of dealing between the parties might show a price below or above what is claimed to be the proper market [price]. Without more, a court could justifiably hold in these circumstances that the course of dealing price is the "reasonable price."
>
> A "partial gap" occurs when a price setting method fails. It is important to distinguish complete gap from partial gap cases, for what is a reasonable price in the two cases is not necessarily the same. In complete gap cases a court is on its own, and properly so. But in some partial gap cases, a reasonable price should be influenced to some extent by the price it thinks would have been set had the parties been successful with the method to which they agreed.
>
> Parties' price formulae are highly varied. First, parties may simply agree to agree on a price at a later date. Some courts invalidate these agreements as too indefinite. But the Code validates these – provided the parties intend to contract and there is a reasonably certain basis for granting an appropriate remedy. In these cases courts are to fill the gap with a reasonable price. Sometimes the parties will agree that one of them is to fix the price. Here the agreed method may fail for either of two quite different reasons. The appointed party may fail to set any price, or may set a price in bad faith. If the failure was owing to its own fault, 2–305 provides that the other party may "himself fix a reasonable price." But if the failure to fix a price was not the fault of either party, the Code empowers the court to fix a reasonable price. If the party who is to fix the price fixes it in bad faith, the court can substitute a reasonable price; 2–305(2) provides that a "price to be fixed by the seller or by the buyer means a price for him to fix in food faith."

J. White and R. Summers, *Uniform Commercial Code* (4th ed.) pp. 115–116, West Publishing Co.

Questions on the Text

1. A asks B to quote his best price for 100 cases of champagne for immediate shipment. B immediately ships the champagne accompanied by an invoice for 100 cases at $10 per bottle. Have A and B closed a binding contract under the *U.C.C.*?

2. Same fact as no. 1 but A pays B for the champagne. Immediately thereafter the price of this quality champagne drops on the world market by 50%. A informs B of his intent to reship the goods and demands return of the payment. Is the contract binding under the *U.C.C.*?

3. A regularly buys his champagne supply from B, who charges him according to a price list B publishes and mails to her buyers every six months. B's prices are generally 10% lower than the average price charged by the top ten suppliers of champagne on the world market. On June 30, 1997, A orders 100 cases of champagne from B. B has just changed her price list but not yet mailed the new list to A. B charges A a price per bottle that exceeds the average charged by the top ten suppliers by 30%. A refuses to pay that price and reships the champagne. Is A in breach of contract under the *U.C.C.*?

4. Same facts as in no. 3 but A pays B 10% below the average price per bottle charged by the top ten champagne suppliers on June 30, 1997. Is A in breach of contract under the *U.C.C.*?

D. Modification of the Consideration Requirement

The *U.C.C.* eliminates the requirement of consideration in two areas with which you are already familiar. One of them is that an offeror's promise to keep a price open for a certain period of time, a so-called **option contract**, does not have to be supported by consideration (§ 2–205). The other is that a binding contract may be modified through the agreement of both parties without being supported by some new consideration (§ 2–209). This second modification relates to the pre-existing legal duty rule.

1. Options

§ 2–205. Firm Offers

An offer by a merchant to buy or sell goods in a signed writing which by its terms gives assurance that it will be held open is not revocable, for lack of consideration, during the time stated or if no time is stated for a reasonable time, but in no event may such period of irrevocability exceed three months; but any such term of assurance on a form supplied by the offeree must be separately signed by the offeror.

Official Comment

Purpose of Changes:

1. This section is intended to modify the former rule which required that "firm offers" be sustained by consideration in order to bind, and to require instead that they must merely be characterized as such and expressed in signed writings.

2. The primary purpose of this section is to give effect to the deliberate intention of a merchant to make a current firm offer binding. The deliberation is shown in the case of an individualized document by the merchant's signature to the offer, and in the case of an offer included on a form supplied by the other party to the transaction by the separate signing of the particular clause which contains the offer ... .

3. This section is intended to apply to current "firm" offers and not to long term options, and an outside time limit of three months during which such offers remain irrevocable has been set ... A promise made for a longer period will operate under this section to bind the offeror only for the first three months of the period but may of course be renewed. If supported by consideration it may continue for as long as the parties specify. This section deals only with the offer which is not supported by consideration ... .

As you may recall from Chapter 2 C., the common law requires an offeree to give an offeror consideration for the offeror's promise to keep an offer open for a certain period of time. Contracts like these are called **options**, and are subject to the normal common law consideration requirement. As you can see from U.C.C. § 2–205, however, the consideration requirement has been eliminated for offers made by merchants if the offer is written and the offeror signs the writing giving assurance that the offer will be held open.

2. Pre-Existing Legal Duty Rule

§ 2–209. Modification, ...

(1) An agreement modifying a contract within this Article needs no consideration to be binding.

Official Comment

Purposes of Changes and New Matter:

1. This section seeks to protect and make effective all necessary and desirable modifications of sales contracts without regard to the technicalities which at present hamper such adjustments.

2. Subsection (1) provides that an agreement modifying a sales contract needs no consideration to be binding.
However, modifications made thereunder must meet the test of good faith imposed by this Act. The effective use of bad faith to escape performance on the original contract terms is barred, and the extortion of a "modification" without legitimate commercial reason is ineffective as a violation of the duty of good faith. Nor can a mere technical consideration support a modification made in bad faith.
The test of "good faith" between merchants or as against merchants includes "observance of reasonable commercial standards of fair dealing in the trade" (Section 2–103), and may in some situations require an objectively demonstrable reason for seeking a modification ...

As you may remember, in Chapter 2 C. you also read § 73 *Restatement (Second) Contracts* which provides that a pre-existing legal duty is not valid consideration for a new promise. Consequently, if A promises to deliver 2000 yards of silk fabric at $5 per yard to B on December 10, A may not then require B to pay $6 per yard in order to receive the silk on time. A has a pre-existing legal duty under the original contract to deliver the silk at $5 per yard. Even if B does promise to pay $6 per yard, the promise is unenforceable for lack of consideration. A has not given B anything B did not already have, namely A's promise to deliver, in exchange for B's promise to pay the higher price. As you can see from *U.C.C.* § 2–209, the pre-existing legal duty rule has been abandoned for modifications of contracts that have already been closed. Of course in the silk fabric example, B's promise to pay $6 would not be enforceable under the *U.C.C.* either, because the modification was not made in good faith. You may find examples of good faith modifications in the following text:

> Of course, a modifying agreement is one thing, an enforceable modifying agreement another. The Code reduces the formalities for a valid modification: under 2–209(1) consideration is unnecessary. Thus, the parties may modify free of any inflexibilities of the so-called preexisting duty rule. According to this common law rule, the

beneficiary of a modification must give or promise to give something beyond what one was under a duty to give under the original contract. Otherwise one can not enforce the prospective benefit. Reason and justice do not require this inflexible rule. Often it is neither unreasonable nor unjust to allow a party to benefit from a modification without paying anything further. For example, the parties may modify and set a date for contract performance earlier than in the prior agreement, and this may benefit one party without imposing any burden whatsoever on the other. When so, there is no reason why the beneficiary should have to pay for the change. The same is true with respect to some extensions of time for performance, some changes in place of performance, and many other possible types of modifications. Section 2–209(1) displaces the common law preexisting duty rule, and in effect permits the consideration given to support the original contract to serve also to support the modified contract.

J. White and R. Summers, *Uniform Commercial Code* (4th ed. 1995) p. 31, West Publishing Co. [footnotes omitted]

Questions on the Text

1. A, a fellow student of B's, offers to sell B his car for $3000. B tells A that she needs some time to think about the offer. A assures B that B can have two weeks to decide whether to accept the offer. Is A bound to his promise?
2. A, a car salesman, offers to sell B a new automobile for the sticker price minus 10%. B requests time to think about the offer. A promises to keep the offer open for two weeks. Is A bound?
3. On September 19, 1996, A, a dealer in Persian rugs, sends B a signed written offer to sell a particular rug for $25,000, the offer to remain open until December 31, 1996. On December 30, 1996, A sells the rug to C. On December 31, 1996, B telephones A to accept the offer. Is A in breach of contract?

Terminology

commercial transactions	trade, business of buying or selling goods (**Handelsgeschäfte**)
law merchant	body of law governing commercial transactions (**Handelsrecht**)
merchant	person in the business of buying or selling goods (**Kaufmann**)
duress	unlawful use of physical force or threats to cause an individual

	to act as he otherwise would not act in the absence of the force or threats (**Nötigungsnotstand**)
coercion	compulsion, force (**Nötigung, Zwang, Gewalt**)
validating causes	reasons for giving a contract legal effect (**Gesichtspunkte, die die bindende Wirkung eines Vertrages begründen**)
invalidating causes	reasons for canceling the legal effect of an otherwise valid contract (**Gesichtspunkte, die die bindende Wirkung eines Vertrages ausschließen**)
interstate commerce	sales of goods across state borders, trade or business conducted across state borders (**grenzüberschreitende Handelsbeziehungen**)
choice of law	determination by the parties to a contract that the law of a specified nation or state is to apply to their agreement (**Bestimmung des anzuwendenden Rechts**)
conflict of laws	area of law dealing with decision on which of two or more relevant legal systems to refer to in order to select the law that should be applied in a case with relevant connections to one or more states (**Kollisionsrecht, Internationales Privatrecht**)
parent	main company holding a controlling interest in another company (**Muttergesellschaft**), which is referred to as the parent's **subsidiary** (**Tochtergesellschaft**)
subsidiary	company the controlling interest of which is held by another company (**Tochtergesellschaft**), which is referred to as the subsidiary's **parent** (**Muttergesellschaft**)
negotiable instruments	"a written and signed unconditional promise or order to pay a specified sum of money on demand or at a definite time payable to order or bearer" *Black's Law Dictionary*; a check is an example of a negotiable instrument (**begebbare Wertpapiere**)
letter of credit	promise, usually made by a bank, to pay an amount of money to the person to whom it is issued when that person presents certain documents required in the letter of credit; arrangement undertaken to insure a seller that he will be paid for goods he delivers to a buyer regardless of the buyer's honesty or solvency (**Kreditbrief, Akkreditiv**)
bulk sales	sale of more than half of seller's inventory when seller has no intention to continue in the business of selling that type of inventory (**Gesamtverkauf**)
warehouse receipt	document of verification of having received goods, which is issued by a person who is in the business of storing goods in exchange for payment (**Lagerschein**)
bill of lading	document of verification of having received goods for shipment,

	which is issued by the transporter (**Frachtbrief, Seefrachtbrief, Konnossement**)
securities	documents indicating debt issued by an undertaking to an investor; shares of stock in a company are securities (**Wertpapiere, Effekten**)
secured transactions	agreements accompanied by the transfer of an interest in property, usually to a creditor, to ensure that the debtor pays back a loan; a loan accompanied by a mortgage is a secured transaction (**Geschäfte, die mit Sicherungsverträgen verbunden sind**)
chattel paper	"writing or writings which evidence both a monetary obligation and a security interest in or lease of specific goods" *U.C.C. § 9–105(1)(b)*; when an owner of property leases it to another or sells it on installment payments but retains a security interest in that property, the documents indicating the debt and the security interest are chattel paper (**Papiere, die eine Zahlungsverpflichtung und zugleich eine Sicherung dafür beurkunden**)
mirror-image rule	common law rule requiring the acceptance of an offer to exactly match the terms of the offer itself (**Regel, die die Entsprechung von Angebot und Annahme fordert**)
meeting of the minds	expression used to refer to complete agreement between two parties to a contract (**Einigung**)
standard terms	the conditions under which an individual generally does business (**allgemeine Geschäftsbedingungen, AGB**)
confirmation	written statement of terms of an agreement undertaken by the buyer or seller, or both, to verify an oral agreement, or an agreement that has been reached through the exchange of correspondence, also to give the agreement final form; usually contains list of standard terms used by the party writing the confirmation; also: **confirming form** (**Bestätigungsschreiben**)
battle of the forms	conflict between offeror's and offeree's standard terms as incorporated in their order forms or confirmations (**Kollision widersprechender AGB**)
open terms	conditions of an agreement that are not yet specified (**Vertragslücken**)
gap fillers	rules on how to determine what the conditions of an agreement are when those conditions have not been specified by the parties (**gesetzliche Auslegungsregeln**)
in good faith	honest and without effort to take advantage of another (**nach den Prinzipien von Treu und Glauben, bona fide**)
firm offer	an offer to contract that the offeror intends to keep open for a certain period of time (**festes Angebot**)

modifying agreement	an agreement by the parties to a contract to alter in some way the terms of that contract (**vertragsändernde Vereinbarung**)

Terminology Review

Act (I.I.1)	an enactment, a law that is in force (**Gesetz**)
to enact (I.I.1)	to formally adopt a law and put it into force (**verabschieden**)
statute of limitations (I.I.4)	(UK) **limitation period**: period within which a law suit may be initiated after a violation of rights has occurred (**Verjährungsfrist**)
forum state (I.II.2)	state in which a court is located

Vocabulary

albeit	although
to diverge	to differ
to envisage	to foresee, to conceive of, to have in mind
to eradicate	to destroy, to wipe out
to hamper	to hinder, to interfere with
to obviate	to dispose of, to get rid of
to pose	to present, to put forward; usually used in: **to pose a problem**
seasonable	timely

Suggested Reading

Randy Barnett, *Contracts. Cases and Doctrine*, Little, Brown and Co.: Boston/New York/Toronto/London (1995)

E. Allan Farnsworth, *Contracts* (2d ed.) Little Brown: Boston/Toronto (1990; 1994 supplement)

Charles Fried, *Contract as Promise*, Harvard University Press: Cambridge, Mass./London (1981)

Ferdinand Fromholzer, *Consideration*, Mohr Siebeck: Tübingen (1997)

Fuller and Eisenberg, *Contract Law* (6th ed.) West Publishing Co.: St. Paul, Minnesota (1996)

Grant Gilmore, *The Death of Contract*, Ohio State University Press: Columbus, Ohio (1974)

Franz J. Heidinger/Andrea Hubalek, *Anglo-amerikanische Rechtssprache*, Orac Verlag: Wien (1996)

Mathias Reimann, *Einführung in das US-amerikanische Privatrecht*, C.H. Beck Verlag: München (1997)

A.W. Brian Simpson, *Leading Cases in the Common Law*, Chapter 10: "Quackery and Contract Law: *Carlill v. Carbolic Smoke Ball Company*," Clarendon Press: Oxford (1995)

Michael H. Whincup, *Contract Law and Practice*, Kluwer: The Hague/London/Boston (1996)

James J. White and Robert S. Summers, *Uniform Commercial Code*, 4th ed., West Publishing Co.: St. Paul, Minnesota (1995)

Adams v. Lindsell, 106 Eng. Rep. 250 (K.B. 1818)

Oliver v. Campbell, 273 P.2d 15 (1954)

Sherwood v. Walker, 33 N.W. 919 (1887)

Ward v. Byham, [1956] 2 All E.R. 318

Web Sites

http://www.law.cornell.edu/topics/contracts.html

http://www.law.cornell.edu/ucc/ucc.table.html

http://www.findlaw.com/01topics/07contracts/index.html

http://crcse.business.pitt.edu/

http://www.kinseylaw.com/freestuff/FreeIndex.html

http://findlaw.com/16Forms/index.html

Language Exercises
Chapter 5

I. Fill in the blanks. Some could require more than one word:

A person who is in the business of selling goods is a 1 . The *U.C.C.* incorporates the common law and the 2 , or the law relating to 3 transactions. Another way of saying that one shows his agreement to something is to say that person 4 . A clause in a contract specifying what law is to apply to the parties' transaction is called a 5 . If the parties do not include such a clause, and the transaction 6 a reasonable relation to more than one state, the judge in the state where the complaint was filed, or the 7 , will decide what law to apply. In doing so the judge applies rules on 8 . These multi-state transactions can involve a main company, called the 9 , situated in one state and its 10 , or companies in which it has a controlling interest, situated in several other states. After two companies have reached an informal agreement they often send each other documents verifying the terms of the agreement called 11 . If the terms of these 11 diverge, we say there is a 12 , with each party insisting on his own terms. Sometimes the parties cannot or do not agree on some of the terms of the agreement, so they leave them 13 . The *U.C.C.*, however, provides 14 for such contracts, even permitting a judge to determine, for example, what price is to be paid for goods sold. Sometimes a contract will permit one of the parties to fix the price at a later date. If so, that party must fix it 15 . An offer which the offeror intends to leave open for a certain period of time is called a 16 .

II. Translate the following terms into English:

1. Antragender
2. Angebotsempfänger
3. Schuldner
4. Gläubiger
5. formgebundener Vertrag
6. Schenkungsvertrag
7. formfreier Vertrag
8. Angebot
9. Annahme
10. vertragstreuer Teil
11. ein Angebot widerrufen
12. aufschiebende Bedingung
13. auflösende Bedingung
14. widerlegliche Vermutung
15. unwiderlegliche Vermutung
16. Anfechtungsrecht

17. Minderjährige
18. Gegenangebot
19. Liegenschaften
20. Fahrnis
21. Alleinbezugsvertrag
22. Hinterleger
23. Verwahrer
24. ausdrückliche Bedingungen
25. Wegfall der Geschäftsgrundlage
26. Rücktritt vom Vertrag
27. beiderseitiger Irrtum
28. einseitiger Irrtum
29. Handelsgeschäfte
30. Muttergesellschaft
31. Tochtergesellschaft
32. begebbares Wertpapier
33. Kreditbrief
34. Konnossement
35. Nötigungsnotstand
36. Kaufmann
37. Wertpapiere
38. allgemeine Geschäftsbedingungen

Unit II
Torts

Tort law or **torts** is an area of the law dealing with injuries one person causes another for which the injured party may sue to obtain **damages**. The person causing the injury is referred to as the **tortfeasor**, or within the context of a private law action for damages, the **defendant**. The injured party is usually referred to as the **victim** or the **plaintiff**. The defendant's **liability**, or responsibility to pay for the damage, is either **liability based on fault** or **strict liability**. If liability is based on the defendant's fault in causing the tort, then the plaintiff has to prove that the defendant acted either **intentionally** or **negligently**. A typical example of an intentional tort is a **battery**, which involves the defendant's unlawful touching of the plaintiff, such as by intentionally punching him in the nose. (See *Einführung in die anglo-amerikanische Rechtssprache / Introduction to Anglo-American Law & Language*, Unit I, Chapter 1 B. 2. for two cases of **intentional torts**, *Ploof v. Putnam* and *Vincent v. Lake Erie*, both of which involved **trespasses** where one party intentionally used the property of another to save his own from destruction.) A common type of **negligent tort** occurs during an automobile accident. If liability is strict, the plaintiff does not have to prove that the defendant was at fault in causing the injury. A typical example of **strict liability** is liability for injuries caused by defective products, sometimes also referred to as **products liability**. This Unit contains three chapters, the first on intentional torts, the second on negligent torts and the third on products liability. You also will be confronted with a variety of issues relevant to the law of torts which arise in these cases and are discussed within their context.

Chapter 1
Intentional Torts

Examples of intentional torts are **battery, assault, trespass to land or chattels, false imprisonment,** and **defamation,** which can be either **libel** if written or **slander** if spoken. Since the vast majority of torts cases are based on negligence, this section on intentional torts will be confined to the torts of **battery** and **assault.**

A. Battery

Intentionally committed crimes of violence, such as murder, rape or robbery, are batteries, but an **action for battery can also be sustained** even when the plaintiff does not suffer physical injury, but instead actually experiences physical improvement. If a medical doctor, for example, administers treatment to which the patient has not **consent**ed, the doctor commits a battery even though the doctor's treatment is excellent and the patient's physical condition is significantly improved. The essence of a battery is a wrongful touching that is offensive to human dignity, whereby the offensiveness may be merely a violation of the plaintiff's personal autonomy. If the plaintiff has consented to the touching, then his personal autonomy has not been violated and **no action for battery may be had.** The defendant must have intended to come into physical contact with the plaintiff, although the defendant need not have intended to cause the plaintiff any real physical harm.

Consider the following two definitions of a battery in the *Restatement (Second) Torts* (American Law Institute Publishers: St. Paul, Minnesota (1965)). Like the *Restatement Contracts*, this *Restatement* represents the efforts of scholars and practitioners to codify the common law:

§ 13. Battery: Harmful Contact

An actor is subject to liability to another for battery if

(a) he acts intending to cause a harmful or offensive contact with the person of the other or a third person, or an imminent apprehension of such a contact, and

(b) a harmful contact with the person of the other directly or indirectly results.

§ 18. Battery: Offensive Contact

(1) An actor is subject to liability to another for battery if

(a) he acts intending to cause a harmful or offensive contact with the person of the other or a third person, or an imminent apprehension of such a contact, and

(b) an offensive contact with the person of the other directly or indirectly results.

(2) An act which is not done with the intention stated in Subsection (1, a) does not make the actor liable to the other for a mere offensive contact with the other's person although the act involves an unreasonable risk of inflicting it and, therefore, would be negligent or reckless if the risk threatened bodily harm.

Analysis

The difference between **harmful contact** and **offensive contact** is that the former actually causes the victim physical injury, whereas the latter infringes upon the victim's personal autonomy without causing any physical suffering. Still there must have been actual physical contact with the victim for the tortfeasor to be held liable for either type of battery. As you can see, the **intent requirement** for harmful-contact battery is the same as for offensive-contact battery (§ 13(a) and § 18(1)(a)). Four different states of mind are described in these subsections, any one of which is sufficient to fulfill the intent requirement. The actor could have 1) intended to cause harm to another person, or 2) he could have intended to cause offensive contact with another person, or 3) he could have intended to cause an imminent apprehension of harm to another person, or 4) he could have intended to cause an imminent apprehension of offensive contact with another person. An **imminent apprehension** of harmful or offensive contact is the antici-pation or awareness that such contact is about to occur. Furthermore you can tell from §§ 13(a) and 18(1)(a) that it is irrelevant whether the tortfeasor in-tended to cause the harmful or offensive contact with the victim ("the person of the other"), or with a third person. Accordingly, if John aims his fist at Anne, but actually hits Beatrice, then Beatrice will still be able to maintain an action in battery against John, even though John did not intend to harm her. The reason why that is so will be explained in Chapter 2 D. 1. on **transferred intent**.

Other than the difference between harmful and offensive contact, the major distinction between § 13 and § 18 is that if the actor did not act intentionally, he will still be **held liable in tort** for harmful contact if he acted **negligently** or **recklessly**, but will not be held liable in tort for offensive contact if he acted **negligently** or **recklessly**. Very generally stated, conduct is **negligent** if it falls below the standard of care that a **reasonable person** would take under the circumstances. Conduct is **reckless** if it exhibits a total disregard for the consequences that may ensue. Section 18(2) essentially excludes any form of tort liability for an offensive touching if it was not done intentionally. Section 13 does not include a parallel section, because the tortfeasor will be liable for a negligent tort if he inflicts actual harm on the victim.

Read the following case, which discusses most of the elements of the **tort of battery**:

Mink v. University of Chicago

460 F. Supp. 713 (N.D. Ill. 1978)

Grady, District Judge.

5

Plaintiffs have brought this action on behalf of themselves and some 1,000 women who were given diethylstilbestrol ("DES") as part of a medical experiment conducted by the defendants, University of Chicago and Eli Lilly & Company, between September 29, 1950, and November 20, 1952. The drug was administered to the
10 plaintiffs during their prenatal care at the University's Lying-In Hospital as part of a double blind study to determine the value of DES in preventing miscarriages. The women were not told they were part of an experiment, nor were they told that the pills administered to them were DES. Plaintiffs claim that as a result of their taking DES, their daughters have developed abnormal cervical cellular formations and are
15 exposed to an increased risk of vaginal or cervical cancer. Plaintiffs also allege that they and their sons have suffered reproductive tract and other abnormalities and have incurred an increased risk of cancer.

The complaint further alleges that the relationship between DES and cancer was known to the medical community as early as 1971, but that the defendants made no
20 effort to notify the plaintiffs of their participation in the DES experiment until late 1975 or 1976 when the University sent letters to the women in the experiment informing them of the possible relationship between the use of DES in pregnant women and abnormal conditions in the genital tracts of their offspring. The letter asked for information to enable the University to contact the sons and daughters of
25 the plaintiffs for medical examination.

The complaint seeks recovery on three causes of action. The first alleges that the defendants committed a series of batteries on the plaintiffs by conducting a medical experiment on them without their knowledge or consent. The administration of DES to the plaintiffs without their consent is alleged to be an "offensive invasion of their
30 persons" which has caused them "severe mental anxiety and emotional distress due to the increased risk to their children of contracting cancer and other abnormalities." ...

Both defendants have moved to dismiss the complaint for failure to state a claim. We
will deny the motions as to the first cause of action, …

35

Battery

We must determine whether the administration of a drug, DES, to the plaintiffs
without their knowledge or consent constitutes a battery under Illinois law. The
defendants argue that the plaintiffs' first count is really a "lack of informed consent"
40   case premised on negligence. Because the named plaintiffs have not alleged specific
physical injury to themselves, the defendants contend they have failed to state a claim
for negligence and the count should be dismissed. However, if we find the action to
be based on a battery theory, it may stand notwithstanding the lack of an allegation
of personal physical injury …

Analysis

The case starts by stating that the "Plaintiffs have brought this action on behalf
of themselves and some 1,000 women" (line 6). It then goes on to define the class
of women on whose behalf the action has been brought, namely all those women
who were given DES as part of a medical experiment the defendants conducted
between the years of 1950 and 1952. This language shows you that the case
involves a **class action**. A class action is a useful device for joining all possible
plaintiffs who have been harmed by the conduct of one or several defendants.
Since all possible plaintiffs are joined, only one trial has to be held. Accordingly,
the class action saves court costs and lawyer fees. Furthermore, the class action
is a good device for suing a defendant who has caused a large number of people
each a rather low amount of harm. Since the harm caused any one potential
plaintiff is low, it may not pay that individual to incur the costs of litigation to
recover damages. If the entire group of plaintiffs, however, is joined in one class
action, each plaintiff will benefit from one single law suit. In addition, the defendant will not be able to continue harming a large number of people without
fearing that he will have to compensate everyone he has harmed. Hence, the class
action is a good tool for correcting social injustice. Finally, the class action makes
any real case of unjust injury interesting for a lawyer to accept because his fee
will not be calculated on the basis of one plaintiff's insignificant amount of
damage but rather on the basis of the total amount of damage caused all of the
plaintiffs in the class. In *Mink*, the damage to any one plaintiff may have been
quite large. Consider the case, however, in which a company has been discrimi-
nating against its female employees by paying them $1.00 per hour less than its
male employees for the same work over the past year. Each woman employee
might have a valid claim for $8.00 per day multiplied by approximately 250

working days per year, or $2,000. Many women may decide that the expected rewards of filing suit are too insignificant. Many women may fear losing their jobs or being harassed if they file suit. Such an employer could easily continue to discriminate, paying off the few women who decide to do something about the situation and reaping the benefits from the majority who do not. Imagine, however, that the company employs 200 women. Filing the law suit as a class action will make it attractive for a very good lawyer to accept the case and spend a considerable amount of time working on it. All of the plaintiffs will receive compensation, rather than just a few, and the defendant company will not be permitted to continue discriminating. (As you may recall from *Einführung in die anglo-amerikanische Rechtssprache / Introduction to Anglo-American Law & Language*, Unit III, Chapter 2, *Brown v. Board of Education* was also brought as a class action. In that case the problem was not gathering enough plaintiffs together to make the suit financially interesting for a lawyer to file, but rather to ensure that all African-American children in the city of Topeka, Kansas would be admitted to the public schools on a non-segregated basis.) The class action does not exist in this form in Germany.

The defendants in this case **moved to dismiss for failure to state a claim** (line 33). The **motion to dismiss** is a formal request made to the court to reject the plaintiff's complaint for some legal deficiency. The legal deficiency may be that the court lacks jurisdiction, that the defendant was not served process or that the complaint fails to state a cause of action, or as is stated here **fails to state a claim**. As you should recall from Unit I, a **demurrer** is also the name for a motion to dismiss for failure to state a cause of action. In some states, both terms are still used, in which case the **motion to dismiss** is used to complain of procedural defects, such as the court's lack of jurisdiction, and the **demurrer** is used to complain of the legal insufficiency of the complaint. In the federal courts, the **motion to dismiss** is used to complain both of procedural defects and the legal insufficiency of the complaint. It thus includes the demurrer and the motion to dismiss under the one term **motion to dismiss**. The case you are reading here was decided by a federal court, namely the U.S. District Court for the Northern District of Illinois (see *Einführung in die anglo-amerikanische Rechtssprache / Introduction to Anglo-American Law & Language*, Appendix II for an explanation of case citations).

The issue on appeal is stated in lines 37-38, namely "whether the administration of a drug, DES, to the plaintiffs without their knowledge or consent constitutes a battery under Illinois law." As noted, the court hearing the case is the U.S. District Court for the Northern District of Illinois. Although this is a federal court, it must apply Illinois state law to the case. That is because the federal court does not have jurisdiction over the case because it raises a **federal question**, which would require the court to interpret and apply federal law, but rather because of

diversity of citizenship between the plaintiffs and the defendants. Citizenship here refers to being a citizen of Illinois as opposed to Georgia, or Massachusetts (see discussion of federal jurisdiction in *Einführung in die anglo-amerikanische Rechtssprache / Introduction to Anglo-American Law & Language*, Unit II, Chapter 2). Keep this fact in mind as you continue to read the case, and note the authorities cited by the court in its opinion. Are they all Illinois authorities? Could the fact that they are not indicate that a cause of action for battery is a common law cause of action and thus not dependent on individual peculiarities inherent to Illinois law?

The defendants here have argued that the plaintiffs have failed to state a cause of action and therefore the complaint should be dismissed. The gist of the argument is that the claim actually stated in the complaint is based on a negligence theory and that since the plaintiffs have not established that they themselves suffered any real damage, they cannot maintain an action for negligence. This discussion should tell you something about the requirements for maintaining a claim based on negligence as opposed to one based on battery, namely that for a negligence claim you have to prove actual personal injury, whereas for a battery claim you do not. Refer back to §§ 13 and 18 of the *Restatement* and the distinction between them. You may wonder why the allegations of personal injury are insufficient, but the court comments in a footnote as follows:

> We agree with the defendants that if the first cause of action is characterized as negligence, it fails to state a claim. With the exception of a conclusory statement of reproductive tract abnormalities in paragraph 1, the complaint does not allege any physical injury to the plaintiff class. There is no allegation of specific physical injury to any named plaintiff. The damage alleged in the first count is mental distress to the plaintiffs and an increased risk of cancer to the plaintiffs and their children. These allegations are insufficient to support a claim for negligence ...

Later in the opinion the court also points out:

> The plaintiffs argue that they have alleged personal physical injury in paragraph 1 [of their complaint], which states that DES "has or may cause reproductive tract and other abnormalities in themselves." There is no indication that any of the named plaintiffs have suffered any of these "abnormalities."

Continue reading the case:

45   True "informed consent" cases concern the duty of the physician to inform his patient of risks inherent in the surgery or treatment to which he has consented. While early cases treated lack of informed consent as vitiating the consent to treatment so there was liability for battery, the modern view "is that the action ... is in reality one for negligence in failing to conform to the proper standard, to be determined on the
50   basis of expert testimony as to what disclosure should be made." W. Prosser, *Law of Torts* § 32 at 165 (4th ed. 1971). Nonetheless, a battery action may still be appropri-

ate in certain circumstances. Where the patient has not consented to the treatment, it is meaningless to ask whether the doctor should have revealed certain risks necessary to make the consent an "informed" one. The distinction between battery and neg-
55 ligence is elucidated in *Trogun v. Fruchtman*, 58 Wis.2d 569, 596, 207 N.W.2d, 311-12 (1973):

> The courts of this country have recognized essentially two theories of liability for allegedly unauthorized medical treatment or therapy rendered by physi-
> cians to their patients. The first of these theories is the traditional intentional
60 tort of battery or assault and battery which is simply defined as the unautho-
> rized touching of the person of another. Underlying this theory of liability is, of course, the general feeling that a person of sound mind has a right to determine, even as against his physician, what is to be done to his body. Under this theory, liability is imposed upon a physician who has performed
65 non-emergency treatment upon a patient without his consent … .

> The second theory of liability, permitted by a majority of courts, is grounded upon negligence principles rather than on intentional tort … "[This] doctrine of 'informed consent' … concerns the duty of the physician or surgeon to inform the patient of the risk which may be involved in treatment or surgery."

70 As for the application of the distinction, we find the analysis of the court in *Cobbs v. Grant*, 8 Cal.3d 229, 104 Cal.Reptr. 505, 512, 502 P.2d 1, 8 (1972), persuasive:

> The battery theory should be reserved for those circumstances when a doctor performs an operation to which the patient has not consented. When the patient gives permission to perform one type of treatment and the doctor
75 performs another, the requisite element of deliberate intent to deviate from the consent given is present. However, when the patient consents to certain treatment and the doctor performs that treatment but an undisclosed inher-
> ent complication with a low probability occurs, no intentional deviation from the consent given appears; rather, the doctor in obtaining consent may
80 have failed to meet his due care duty to disclose pertinent information. In that situation the action should be pleaded in negligence.

Illinois courts have adopted the modern approach to true informed consent cases, and have treated them as negligence actions … . However, they have not overruled earlier cases which recognize a cause of action in battery for surgery performed
85 without a patient's consent … . Thus, it appears the two separate theories continue to exist in Illinois, and battery may be the proper cause of action in certain situations, for example, where there is a total lack of consent by the patient … . The question thus becomes whether the instant case is more akin to the performance of an unauthorized operation than to the failure to disclose the potential ramifications of an
90 agreed to treatment. We think the situation is closer to the former. The plaintiffs did not consent to DES treatment; they were not even aware that the drug was being administered to them. They were the subjects of an experiment whereby non-emergency treatment was performed upon them without their consent or knowledge.

Analysis

In this passage the court distinguishes between **informed consent cases** and the **tort of battery**. At one time, the court notes, **lack of informed consent** was treated as a battery. Accordingly, if a medical doctor failed to give a patient sufficient information on the risks involved in a certain treatment, and the patient then consented to treatment and finally suffered harm from one of the risks of which he was unaware, the doctor was held liable for a battery. This analysis seems rational, on the one hand, because the consent a patient gives to treatment justifies what would otherwise be an unlawful touching of the patient by the doctor. If the patient is not informed enough to effectively consent, the touching would not be justified and the doctor would be liable for the battery. On the other hand, as the court here points out, the more modern approach is to treat the doctor's failure to inform the patient adequately as raising a question of **negligence**. The inquiry then would be whether the doctor **breached** her **duty of care** toward the patient, which would be measured by the **standard of care** generally attained by similar doctors practicing in the same medical community. For that reason, the court points out the issue has to be resolved "on the basis of expert testimony as to what disclosure should be made" (line 50). Still, the court insists, some lack of informed consent cases can be batteries even under the more modern approach, namely those cases in which the plaintiff has not consented to the treatment at all. (Note again that it is essential for the plaintiffs in this case to base their claim on battery rather than negligence, because they have failed to show that they were actually harmed, a necessary requirement for a negligence cause of action).

Continue reading the case:

... Accordingly, we will analyze the plaintiffs' first cause of action under a battery
95 theory.

Battery is defined as the unauthorized touching of the person of another. To be liable for battery, the defendant must have done some affirmative act, intended to cause an unpermitted contact. "[I]t is enough that the defendant sets a force in motion which ultimately produces the result ...

100 "The gist of the action for battery is not the hostile intent of the defendant, but rather the absence of consent to the contact on the part of the plaintiff." [Prosser, *Law of Torts* § 9,] ... at 36. "The essence ... [of the] question in a battery case involving a physician is what did the patient agree with the physician to have done, and was the ultimate contact by the physician within the scope of the patient's consent." *Ca-*
105 *themer v. Hunter*, 27 Ariz.App. 780, 558 P.2d 975, 978 (1976). In sum, to state a cause of action for battery, the plaintiffs must allege intentional acts by the defendants resulting in offensive contact with the plaintiffs' persons, and the lack of consent to the defendants' conduct.

The administration of DES to the plaintiffs was clearly intentional. It was part of a
110 planned experiment conducted by the defendants. The requisite element of intent is
therefore met, since the plaintiffs need show only an intent to bring about the
contact; an intent to do harm is not essential to the action. *Prosser* at 36.

The act of administering the drug supplies the contact with the plaintiffs' persons. "It
is not necessary that the contact with the other's person be directly caused by some
115 act of the actor. All that is necessary is that the actor intend to cause the other, directly
or indirectly, to come in contact with a foreign substance in a manner which the other
will reasonably regard as offensive." *Restatement (Second) of Torts* § 18, Comment
c at 31 (1965). We find the administration of a drug without the patient's knowledge
comports with the meaning of offensive contact. Had the drug been administered by
120 means of a hypodermic needle, the element of physical contact would clearly be
sufficient. We believe that causing the patient to physically ingest a pill is indistin-
guishable in principle.

Analysis

In this passage, the court discusses two requirements of the tort of battery: 1)
intent and 2) physical contact. Regarding intent, the court is careful to point out
that the defendant need not intend to harm the plaintiff. It is sufficient that the
defendant merely intend to come into physical contact with the plaintiff (lines
111-112). In the well known case *Vosburg v. Putney*, 80 Wis. 523, 50 N.W. 403
(1891), the defendant, a twelve-year-old school boy, kicked a fourteen-year-old
classmate in the shin while school was in session. The plaintiff had previously
suffered an injury to the same leg and the defendant's kick aggravated that injury
with the result that the plaintiff became lame. The jury returned a **special verdict**
in which it found that the defendant had not intended to harm the plaintiff. Still,
the trial court **entered judgment on the special verdict** for the plaintiff. The
defendant appealed and the Wisconsin Supreme Court upheld the trial court's
decision. It was sufficient that the defendant intended to come into wrongful
physical contact with the plaintiff, regardless of whether he intended to do him
any actual physical harm. (See note below for an explanation of general and
special verdicts).

Secondly, the court considers whether the administration of medication can be
considered to be the type of physical contact required to maintain an action for
battery. The problem is that the plaintiffs were given the pills to take themselves,
so in some sense they were the ones who "voluntarily" brought about the contact
between the pills and their own bodies. On the other hand, they were unaware
that they were taking DES. Would that make any difference, especially since the
medical community did not know that DES was connected to cancer at the time

it was being given to the plaintiffs? Suppose the hospital had informed them that the pills they were taking were experimental and that their potential effect was as yet unknown? Does the fact that the plaintiffs did not understand the nature of what they were doing when taking the pills, namely participating in an experiment, give a good reason for considering the physical contact to be a product of the defendants' and not the plaintiffs' will? Does it make a difference that the plaintiffs were in a hospital where they could assume they were receiving proper medical treatment? Suppose A comes to his friend B's house with some pink pills and says to B "Take these, you'll like them." If B takes the pills under these circumstances and suffers physical harm, would B be able to argue that A wrongfully touched him within the meaning of the tort of battery?

The court answers the question of whether administration of the medication can be considered to be physical contact within the meaning of the tort of battery by analogizing the case to one where the medication was administered through injection. Mark F. Grady, a leading U.S.-American torts scholar, refers to this argument as the "epitome of legal reasoning." Courts will often consider hypothetical cases where everyone would agree on the appropriate result, or the result would be dictated by previous precedent. Then they analogize the case they are in the process of deciding to the hypothetical case, implying that the two clearly have to be treated the same. Since everyone agrees on the result to be attained in the hypothetical, then everyone would also have to agree with the court on the disposition of the **case at bar**, namely the case it is considering and has to resolve. Using the terms "intermediate facts" to mean those of the hypothetical, "past facts that have been litigated with a particular result" to mean the facts of a previous precedent and "actual facts at bar" to mean the facts of the case the court is trying to decide, Grady characterizes the argumentation process as follows:

> The steps are: (a) if the intermediate facts are not distinguishable from the past facts that have been litigated with a particular result and b) if the actual facts at bar are not distinguishable from the intermediate facts, then (c) the actual facts at bar are not distinguishable from the facts of past decided cases. The hypothetical facts are an intellectual bridge to help the analogy ...

Mark F. Grady, *Cases and Materials on Torts*, American Casebook Series, West Publishing Co.: St. Paul, Minn. (1994) 129.

If you recall *Marbury v. Madison*, in *Einführung in die anglo-amerikanische Rechtssprache / Introduction to Anglo-American Law & Language*, Unit III Chapter 1, and the argumentation process discussed in Unit I Chapter 4 on retroactivity of judicial precedents, you will understand the claim that this type of argument is the "epitome of legal reasoning."

Note on general and special verdicts: A **general verdict** contains the final resolution of a case. It is the result the jury reaches by applying the law as the judge explained it to the facts as the jury believes them to be true. A **general verdict** in a torts case would take the form: "We find the defendant liable in the amount of ... " or: "We find the defendant not liable." A **special verdict**, such as the one reached in *Vosburg v. Putney*, is not the final resolution of a case. It is merely a statement of the facts the jury believes to be true. The judge then will apply the law to those facts and reach a judgment in the case. In most cases, a jury returns a **general verdict,** but the judge may require the jury to return a **special verdict.** Judges will do so if they think the law is too complicated for the jury to apply without error.

Continue reading the case:

     Finally there is the question of consent. As previously stated, this is the real crux of the issue in cases involving a physician's treatment of his patient. If the patient has
125 assented to the doctor's treatment, he may not later maintain an action in battery. *Cathemer v. Hunter*, 558 P.2d at 978. The defendants argue that the plaintiffs consented to the treatment when they admitted themselves to the University's Lying-In Hospital for prenatal care. The scope of the plaintiffs' consent is crucial to their ultimate recovery in a battery action. The defendants' privilege is limited at least to
130 acts substantially similar to those to which the plaintiffs consented. If the defendants went beyond the consent given, to perform substantially different acts, they may be liable. The time, place and circumstances will affect the nature of the consent given. "It is ... possible that the consent given will be sufficiently general in its terms to cover the particular operation [or treatment], or that the surgeon may be authorized
135 with complete freedom to do whatever he thinks best to remedy whatever he finds, particularly where the patient has signed one of the written forms in common use in hospitals." *Prosser* at 104. These questions, however, are questions of fact which are to be determined by the jury, not by this court on a motion to dismiss. The plaintiffs have alleged sufficient lack of consent to the treatment involved to state a claim for
140 battery against both defendants.

Analysis

The final paragraph of the opinion discusses the issue of consent. As the court points out, consent to treatment makes physical contact "privileged" and undermines a claim for battery. There are three legally recognized forms of consent: **express consent, consent implied in fact** and **consent implied in law.** If the patients had signed "one of the written forms in common use in hospitals" in which was stated that women admitted to the hospital for problems with miscarriages agreed to take part in an experiment using the drug DES, the side-effects of which were completely unknown, they would have **expressly consented** to physical contact with the drug. If hospital personnel had informed patients that the red pills given them were possibly DES, an experimental drug the side-effects of which were unknown, and the plaintiffs voluntarily took them, their **consent would be implied in fact.** If a patient became unconscious and both the patient and her baby would have died unless the doctor gave her an injection of DES, then the patient's **consent would be implied in law,** assuming no other family member could be consulted in time to save the patient's life.

In lines 137-138, the court indicates that the question of whether the plaintiffs in *Mink* consented to taking DES is a "**question of fact … to be determined by the jury, not by this court on a motion to dismiss.**" As you may recall from Unit I Chapter 3, the standard for determining whether a **motion to dismiss** or a **demurrer** should be granted is whether the facts as the plaintiff alleged support all of the elements required for the cause of action. To determine whether to grant the motion, the judge hypothetically assumes that everything the plaintiff has alleged is true. Accordingly, the judge's determination on a demurrer is not a final resolution of the case, which is referred to as a **decision on the merits,** but rather a determination of the law applicable to the facts the plaintiff has alleged. To get a decision on the merits we need a jury to determine what the facts really were. Consequently, we do not know from reading the District Court's opinion here whether the *Mink* plaintiffs ultimately won or not. But we do know something about the law of consent in battery cases, namely that if the facts the plaintiffs alleged are indeed true, the defendants did commit a battery against them.

Questions on the Text

1. In your own words, state the facts of the case.
2. The legal history in this case is rather short. Has the case been to a lower court before it reached the U.S. District Court? What role does the District Court play in the federal court system? What court will hear the trial in this case? Has there already been a trial?
3. What issue(s) are raised? It is perhaps better to ask what main issue is raised and what subordinate issues are raised in this case?
4. What is the holding?
5. What is the ratio decidendi?

B. Assault

An assault is defined in the *Restatement (Second) Torts* as:

§ 21 Assault

(1) An actor is subject to liability to another for assault if

(a) he acts intending to cause a harmful or offensive contact with the person of the other or a third person, or an imminent apprehension of such a contact, and

(b) the other is thereby put in such imminent apprehension.

(2) An action which is not done with the intention stated in Subsection (1, a) does not make the actor liable to the other for an apprehension caused thereby although the act involves an unreasonable risk of causing it and, therefore, would be negligent or reckless if the risk threatened bodily harm.

Read the following passages on the tort of assault from one of the leading U.S.-American torts hornbooks:

§ 10. Assault

The interest in freedom from apprehension of a harmful or offensive contact with
5   the person, as distinguished from the contact itself, is protected by an action for the tort known as assault. No actual contact is necessary to it, and the plaintiff is protected against a purely mental disturbance
10   of this distinctive kind. This action, which developed very early as a form of trespass, is the first recognition of a mental, as distinct from a physical, injury. There is "a touching of the mind, if not of the
15   body." ...

Apprehension

Any act of such a nature as to excite an
20   apprehension of a battery may constitute an assault. It is an assault to shake a fist under another's nose, to aim or strike at another with a weapon, or to hold it in a threatening position, to rise or advance to
25   strike another, to surround another with a display of force, to chase another in a hostile manner, or to lean over a woman's bed and make indecent proposals, in such a way as to put her in fear.

Since the interest involved is the mental one of apprehension of contact, it should follow that the plaintiff must be aware of the threat of contact, and that it is not an assault to aim a gun at one who is unaware of it. Apprehension is not the same thing as fear, and the plaintiff is not deprived of an action merely because of being too courageous to be frightened or intimidated. It would seem, however, that the plaintiff need not be aware that the threatened danger proceeds from a hostile human being, and that if a concealed defendant sets off an explosion which puts the plaintiff in fear of life or safety, the same interest is invaded, and in substantially the same manner, as when a visible defendant shoots at the plaintiff with a gun ...

Intent

The intent element for assault is identical with that for battery. There is, properly
30 speaking, no such thing as a negligent assault. But the intent need not necessarily be to inflict physical injury, and it is enough that there is an intent to arouse apprehension. Thus it is an assault to fire
35 a gun, though not aimed at the plaintiff, for the purpose of frightening the plaintiff, or to point it at the plaintiff when the defendant knows that it is unloaded, and the plaintiff does not. Once apprehension
40 has been intentionally created, it is no defense that the defendant reconsidered and desisted or withdrew without doing physical harm. The tort is complete with the invasion of the plaintiff's mental
45 peace, and the failure to carry it through to battery will not prevent liability.

Assault and Battery

50 Assault and battery go together like ham and eggs. The difference between them is that between physical contact and the mere apprehension of it. One may exist without the other. It is a battery to strike a sleeping person, although the person struck does not discover it until afterward; it is an assault to shoot at, frighten, and miss a person. Except for this difference in the character of the invasion of the plaintiff's interests, the two are in all respects identical, ... In the ordinary case, both assault and battery are present; it is an assault when the defendant swings a fist to strike the plaintiff, and the plaintiff sees the movement; a battery when the fist comes in contact with the plaintiff's nose. The two terms are so closely associated in common usage that they are generally used together, or regarded as more or less synonymous. ... It is not accurate to say that "every battery includes an assault," but in practice the difference between the two is often entirely ignored.

Prosser & Keeton on *The Law of Torts*, West Publishing Co.: St. Paul, Minnesota (1984) pp. 43-46 [footnotes omitted]

Questions on the Text

1️⃣ The last sentence of the text points out that not every battery is an assault. Can you think of examples of batteries that could not be assaults? Did the defendants' conduct in *Mink* amount to an assault? Why, or why not? Can you point to something in the Prosser & Keeton text that indicates why or why not? What is the difference between a battery and an assault? Does the plaintiff have to have been aware of the threat of contact to maintain an action for battery? Does the plaintiff have to have been aware of the threat of contact to maintain an action for assault?

2️⃣ To constitute an assault, the defendant's act must "excite an apprehension of a battery." Consider the following hypothetical cases taken from the *Restatement (Second) Torts* and determine whether they involve assaults and/or batteries:

a) P receives threatening telephone calls from D. P's telephone number, but not her address, is listed in the telephone book. D does not know P's address and P does not think that D has her address. P becomes physically ill as a result of the telephone calls.

b) D says to P "If that policeman were not standing at the corner, I would knock your block off."

c) D is locked in a jail cell. When P walks by, D rattles the bars of the cell and threatens to kill P.

Terminology

tortfeasor	person who commits a tort (**Täter**)
liability based on fault	tortfeasor's legal responsibility to compensate for the harm he has caused the plaintiff which depends on whether the tortfeasor acted **intentionally, recklessly,** or **negligently** (**verschuldensabhängige Haftung**)
strict liability	principle of responsibility for a tort whereby the tortfeasor's legal responsibility to compensate for the harm he has caused the plaintiff does not depend on whether the tortfeasor was at fault in causing the harm (**verschuldensunabhängige Haftung, Gefährdungshaftung**)
recklessness	acting with a total disregard for the consequences of one's action; being aware that one's action creates a risk of harming another person and acting anyway (**bedingter Vorsatz und bewußte Fahrlässigkeit**)
negligence	failure to take adequate measures to avoid harming others; failure to act like a reasonable person would to avoid harming others; failure to see a risk of harm that a reasonable person would see (**Fahrlässigkeit**)
products liability	(UK) **product liability**: strict liability of a producer or seller of a product for any harm caused by that product if the harm resulted from a product defect, from the producer's or seller's failure to warn of potential risks involved in using the product, or from the producer's or seller's misrepresentation of the purpose for which the product can be used (**Produzentenhaftung**)
battery	tort of intentional harm or offensive contact with the person of another (**Körperverletzung**)
harmful contact battery	tort of inflicting physical harm with the intent to do so, or with the intent to offensively come into physical contact with the

	victim or to make the victim feel threatened with physical harm or offensive contact
offensive contact battery	tort of infringing on victim's personal autonomy with the intent to do so, or with the intent to come into harmful contact with the victim or to make him fear either harmful or offensive contact
to sustain / to maintain an action for battery	indicate that facts support a law suit for a battery; to allege facts sufficient to support a law suit for the tort of battery; usage, e.g. **an action / no action for battery can be sustained / maintained** (eine Klage auf Schadensersatz wegen Körperverletzung ist un/schlüssig)
no action for battery may be had	indicates that facts do not support a law suit for a battery; may also be used in the affirmative: **an action for battery may be had** (eine Klage auf Schadensersatz wegen Körperverletzung ist un/schlüssig)
an action for battery lies	indicates that facts support a law suit for a battery; may also be used in the negative: **no action for battery lies** (eine Klage auf Schadensersatz wegen Körperverletzung ist un/schlüssig)
trespass to land trespass to chattels	tort of unlawful interference with the real or personal property of another (**verbotene Eigenmacht**)
false imprisonment	tort of unlawful deprivation of the victim's personal liberty through detaining or confining him (**Freiheitsberaubung**)
defamation	"An intentional false communication, either published or publicly spoken, that injures another's reputation or good name. Holding up of a person to ridicule, scorn or contempt in a respectable and considerable part of the community; may be criminal as well as civil." (*Black's Law Dictionary*), (**üble Nachrede und Verleumdung**); includes both **libel** and **slander**.
libel	defamation in printed or written form (**schriftliche oder gedruckte Verleumdung bzw. üble Nachrede**)
slander	defamation in spoken form (**mündliche Verleumdung bzw. üble Nachrede**)
informed consent case	tort suit based on the defendant's negligent failure to adequately inform the tort victim of the dangers or risks of undertaking a certain act on the victim to which the victim has consented and as a result of which the victim suffers physical harm (**Klage wegen der Verletzung von Aufklärungspflichten**)
general verdict	conclusion reached by the jury on the final outcome of the case; includes the jury's application of the law, as instructed, to the facts the jury believes true to reach a final determination of the parties' rights (**Endurteil der Geschworenen**)
special verdict	conclusion of the jury on the facts only; list of facts the jury believes true without any application of the law to those facts to

	reach a final conclusion on the rights of the parties (**Urteil der Geschworenen, durch das der Tatbestand festgestellt wird**)
consent	agreement to what would otherwise be a wrongful touching of a person; can justify the commission of a battery (**Einwilligung; Einverständnis**)
express consent	actually saying or writing that one is in agreement with s.th. (**ausdrückliche Einwilligung**)
consent implied in fact	doing or saying s.th. from which a reasonable person would conclude that one is in agreement (**konkludente Einwilligung; stillschweigende Einwilligung**)
consent implied in law	circumstances from which one concludes as a matter of law that a person would be in agreement with s.th. (**mutmaßliche Einwilligung**)
motion to dismiss	formal request addressed to the court to declare the plaintiff's complaint deficient for lack of jurisdiction, defective service of process or other procedural flaws (**Rüge der Unzulässigkeit**); used in the federal courts to include also the demurrer, as in **motion to dismiss for failure to state a claim (Rüge der Unschlüssigkeit**)
assault	tort of intentionally causing the victim to fear that he will be harmfully or offensively touched physically on the instant occasion (**Bedrohung**)

Terminology Review

class action (I.III.2)	law suit filed by one or more plaintiffs on behalf of themselves and all individuals like them in the sense that they too have suffered from the same violation of their rights
demurrer (II.I.3)	motion, usually filed by a defendant in response to the plaintiff's complaint, asking the court to dismiss the complaint for legal insufficiency; test for whether the demurrer should be sustained is whether it states a cause of action, assuming that all facts plaintiff has claimed are true; raises purely a question of law (**Antrag auf Schlüssigkeitsprüfung**)
federal question jurisdiction (I.II.2)	power granted to the federal district courts to decide cases raising legal questions under the Constitution, laws or treaties of the United States (**Zuständigkeit eines Bundesgerichts, weil sich eine Rechtsfrage mit Bezug auf das Bundesrecht stellt**); cases raising such issues are referred to as **federal question cases**

case at bar (I.III.2)	the case the court is considering at the moment; also the **instant case** (**der vorliegende Fall**)
decision on the merits (I.I.4)	a judgment that resolves the substantive claims of the parties and not one based on some procedural defect, such as lack of jurisdiction (ca. **Sachurteil**)

Vocabulary

to aggravate	to irritate, to make worse
anxiety	overwhelming sense of fear, dread
apprehension	fear or anticipation of future harm
to arouse	to awaken, to give rise to
conclusory	drawing of a conclusion that is not supported by the facts
crucial	of central importance
crux	central point or idea
to deprive	(s.o. of s.th.) to refuse to give s.o. s.th. that is owed to him
to desist	to stop, to quit doing s.th.
to deviate	to depart from the normal course of action, to wander away from
double blind study	an experiment with medication in which neither the attending medical doctor nor the patient knows whether the patient is receiving the medication to be tested or a placebo such as a sugar pill
to elucidate	to clarify or explain, to cast light on
epitome	essence, central idea
gist	general or basic idea
hostile	having the characteristic of an enemy, unfriendly
imminent	about to happen, threateningly close
indecent	unrespectable, untoward
to ingest	to swallow, to consume, to absorb
miscarriage	loss of a fetus before birth
to be premised on	to be based on
ramification	consequence, result
to undermine	to take away the foundation for s.th.
to vitiate	to take away the significance of

Language Exercises
Chapter 1

I. Fill in the correct prepositions, prepositional phrases, or *conjunctions:* see pp. 127-134 for the original text

Plaintiffs have brought this action <u>1</u> themselves and some 1,000 women who were given DES <u>2</u> part <u>3</u> a medical experiment conducted <u>4</u> the defendants <u>5</u> September 29, 1950, and November 20, 1952. The drug was administered <u>6</u> the plaintiffs <u>7</u> their prenatal care <u>8</u> the University's Lying-In Hospital <u>9</u> part <u>10</u> a double-blind study to determine the value of DES <u>11</u> preventing miscarriages. The complaint alleges that the relationship <u>12</u> DES and cancer was know <u>13</u> the medical community <u>14</u> early <u>15</u> 1971, but that the defendants made no effort to notify the plaintiffs <u>16</u> late 1975 or 1976, when the University sent letters <u>17</u> them. The letter asked <u>18</u> information to enable the University to contact their children <u>19</u> medical examination. The complaint seeks recovery <u>20</u> three causes <u>21</u> action. Both defendants have moved to dismiss the complaint <u>22</u> failure to state a claim. We will deny the motions <u>23</u> the first cause of action. We must determine <u>24</u> the administration <u>25</u> a drug, DES, <u>26</u> the plaintiffs <u>27</u> their knowledge or consent constitutes a battery <u>28</u> Illinois law. The defendants contend that the plaintiffs have failed to state a claim <u>29</u> negligence and the count should be dismissed. However, if we find the action to be based <u>30</u> a battery theory, it may stand <u>31</u> the lack <u>32</u> an allegation <u>33</u> personal physical injury. <u>34</u> the other hand, if the doctor failed to meet his due-care duty to disclose pertinent information, the action should be pleaded <u>35</u> negligence.

II. Fill in the correct verbs: see pp. 127-138 for use in the original context

1. An action for battery ___ even when the plaintiff has suffered no physical injury.

2. If a plaintiff has consented to the touching, no action for battery ___.

3. An action for battery will ___, even though the defendant did not intend to harm the plaintiff.

4. Did the administration of DES to the plaintiffs ___ a battery under Illinois law?

5. In *Mink*, the plaintiffs ___ the action on behalf of themselves and some 1,000 other women.

6. The complaint ___ recovery on three causes of action.

7. The first cause of action <u>a</u> that the defendants <u>b</u> a series of batteries on the plaintiffs.

8. Both defendants <u>a</u> to dismiss the complaint for failure <u>b</u> a claim.

9. The court <u>a</u> the motions and <u>b</u> that the complaint <u>c</u> a cause of action.

10. Since the action <u>a</u> on a battery theory, it could <u>b</u> notwithstanding the lack of an allegation of personal physical injury.

11. *Mink*___ no federal question.

12. Early cases <u>a</u> lack of informed consent as <u>b</u> the consent to treatment.

13. Should the doctors in this case ___ certain risks to make the consent informed?

14. Under a battery theory, liability ___ upon a physician who has performed treatment without the patient's consent.

15. Illinois courts ___ the modern approach.

16. However, they have not ___ earlier cases supporting the less modern approach.

17. The defendants clearly ___ to administer DES to the plaintiffs.

III. Fill in the correct terminology: see pp. 127-139 for use in the original context

Torts

Ridiculing a person in public constitutes the tort of <u>1</u>, which if printed is <u>2</u> and if spoken is <u>3</u>. If an individual agrees to be touched by another, then that person <u>4</u> s to the potential battery. If the <u>4</u> is actually stated it is <u>5</u>. If one can conclude from the way a person acts that the person <u>4</u> ed, then the <u>4</u> is <u>6</u>. Regardless of whether a person <u>4</u> ed, still a judge may conclude that he did because under the circumstances any reasonable person would have. In such case we say the <u>4</u> was <u>7</u>. If A wrongfully locks B up, the A has committed the tort of <u>8</u>. If an individual's tort liability depends on his particular state of mind or blameworthiness, the liability is based on <u>9</u>. The states of mind that are relevant are <u>10</u>, meaning the <u>11</u> knew exactly what he was doing and wanted to bring about certain consequences, <u>12</u>, meaning that the <u>11</u> totally disregarded the risk of causing harm and the potential consequences for the victim, and <u>13</u>, meaning the <u>11</u> was not aware of the risk of causing harm but any reasonable person would have been aware of that type of risk. If liability is independent of any <u>9</u>, then the liability is <u>14</u>.

Legal System

A motion claiming that the plaintiff's complaint fails to state a cause of action is a _1_ . Another term for this motion, but one which also includes a claim that the complaint suffers from some procedural defect such as lack of correct jurisdiction is the _2_ . The jury handed down a _3_ , merely stating that it found in favor of the defendant. Sometimes a jury will hand down a _4_ , in which it lists the facts it believes to be true. The case the court is currently considering is the _5_ or the _6_ . When all potential plaintiffs bring one single law suit that suit is called a _7_ . The plaintiff claimed that an issue in the case had to be resolved under federal law and therefore that the U.S. District Court had _8_ over the matter. If a court delivers a judgment on the substantive issues in a law suit it delivers a _9_ .

Chapter 2
Negligent Torts

To maintain a tort cause of action based on negligence the plaintiff must prove that 1) the defendant owed the plaintiff a **duty of care**; 2) the defendant **breached this duty**; 3) the plaintiff suffered **damage**; 4) the breach of the defendant's duty of care was the **cause in fact** of the plaintiff's damage; 5) the breach of the defendant's duty of care was the **proximate cause** of the plaintiff's damage. These requirements are included in the *Restatement (Second) Torts* in a provision regarding what the plaintiff has to prove to maintain a cause of action for a negligent tort:

§ 328 A. Burden of Proof

In an action for negligence the plaintiff has the burden of proving

(a) facts which give rise to a legal duty on the part of the defendant to conform to the standard of conduct established by law for the protection of the plaintiff,

(b) failure of the defendant to conform to the standard of conduct,

(c) that such failure is the legal cause of the harm suffered by the plaintiff, and

(d) that the plaintiff has in fact suffered harm of a kind legally compensable by damages.

A. Duty of Care

Determining whether the defendant owed the plaintiff a duty of care raises a problem about which torts scholars disagree. One torts scholar has phrased the answer to this question as: "No better general statement can be made than that the courts will find a duty where, in general, reasonable persons would recognize it and agree that it exists." (Prosser & Keeton, *The Law of Torts*, West Publishing Co.: St. Paul, Minnesota (1984) 359). The United States District Court formulated the test as: "The court must balance the following factors when determining the existence of duty in each particular case: (1) foreseeability of harm to the plaintiff; (2) degree of certainty that plaintiff suffered injury; (3) closeness of connection between defendant's conduct and injury suffered; (4) moral blame attached to defendant's conduct; (5) policy of preventing future harm; (6) extent of burden to defendant and the consequences to the community of imposing a duty to exercise care with resulting liability for breach; and (7) availability, cost, and prevalence of insurance for the risk involved." (*Vu v. Singer Co.*, N.D. Cal. 1981, 538 F.Supp. 26, 29; cited by Prosser & Keeton on the *Law of Torts*, p. 359, fn. 24). A British torts authority wrote: "The current state of the law is uncertain, but it is abundantly clear that there are still areas and aspects in which no prima facie liability exists. As long as this is so the concept of duty-situation remains meaningful. One still needs to know the current state of the law to know whether there is prima facie liability in the given situation. If there is not, a defendant need not offer a defence; he need only raise a preliminary objection that the plaintiff has failed to make out a case." (Clerk & Lindsell, *Torts*, 16th ed., Sweet & Maxwell: London (1989) 434; Fourth Cumulative Supplement to the Sixteenth Edition (1994)). None of these answers is very helpful, however, when it comes to resolving the issue in a case with which one is confronted.

One could argue that individuals always have a duty to act in such a way as to prevent others from being harmed. But that principle is clearly too broad as a basis for tort liability, at least within the common law. In most states in the United States, for example, there is no **good Samaritan duty to render aid.** Accordingly, if the defendant merely sits back and watches the plaintiff's husband drown rather than throw him a rope and pull him to shore, the defendant will not be held liable for the plaintiff's loss. Similarly, the law does not impose a duty of care on individuals regarding every aspect of their contact with other individuals. The problem is figuring out when the law will impose such a duty. The *Restatement (Second) Torts* provides:

§ 314. Duty to Act for Protection of Others

The fact that the actor realizes or should realize that action on his part is necessary for another's aid or protection does not of itself impose upon him a duty to take such action.

A duty of care sufficient for tort liability arises, however, on the commission of an **affirmative act** that places the plaintiff in danger, such as driving an automobile. See, again, the *Restatement*:

§ 321. Duty to Act When Prior Conduct is Found to be Dangerous

1) If the actor does an act, and subsequently realizes or should realize that it has created an unreasonable risk of causing physical harm to another, he is under a duty to exercise reasonable care to prevent the risk from taking effect.

(2) The rule stated in Subsection (1) applies even though at the time of the act the actor has no reason to believe that it will involve such a risk.

§ 322. Duty to Aid Another Harmed by Actor's Conduct

If the actor knows or has reason to know that by his conduct, whether tortious or innocent, he has caused such bodily harm to another as to make him helpless and in danger of further harm, the actor is under a duty to exercise reasonable care to prevent such further harm.

A duty of care also arises when there is some **special relationship** between the plaintiff and the defendant, such as the relationship between a babysitter and the baby. A duty of care can arise from the defendant's express or implied **gratuitous undertaking**, such as an agreement the defendant makes to perform certain services for the plaintiff. Finally, a duty of care arises from the **occupation of land**, such as through ownership or possession of a house others may visit.

B. Breach of Duty

Once a court has determined that the defendant actually owed the plaintiff a duty of care, the question becomes how much care did the defendant owe him? The standard of care imposed will determine whether the defendant actually breached his duty to the plaintiff. Within the common law, the **reasonable person standard** prevails. The question is phrased as "What would a reasonable person have done under the circumstances?" This question is left to the jury, presumably a group of "reasonable" people. The jury decides in light of the evidence presented whether the defendant acted as a reasonable person would have. Of course, this standard is somewhat difficult to apply with any expectation of reaching much more than merely intuitive results. Consider Clerk & Lindsell's statement, which adds some body to the reasonableness standard:

It follows from what has been said that the standard of care varies with the circumstances. This means that reasonable conduct depends on the balance between, on the one hand, the degree of likelihood that harm will occur, and on the other hand, the cost and practicability of measures needed to avoid it, the seriousness of the consequences, the end to be achieved, including the importance and social utility of the activity in question, and the exigencies of an emergency, dilemma or sport.

Clerk & Lindsell, *Torts*, 16th ed., Sweet & Maxwell: London (1989) 493; Fourth Cumulative Supplement to the Sixteenth Edition (1994)

A similar approach has been taken at least in some negligence cases in the United States. The following case, which has become famous for its statement of the so-called **Learned Hand formula**, named after the judge who decided the case, develops a balancing test for the standard of care to be imposed on the defendant.

The case first discusses another aspect of tort law, namely the **liability of a master for the acts of his servant**. This type of liability is referred to as **vicarious liability**, which is the liability of one person for the acts of another. When the person who is liable is an employer and he is liable for the acts of his employee, the common law uses the rather antiquated term **master-servant relationship**. This aspect of the case will be discussed first. The second half of the opinion relates to the **breach-of-duty** issue within the framework of **contributory negligence**, which refers to the plaintiff's fault for at least some of his own damage. These two issues will be discussed at the end of the opinion.

The case is somewhat difficult to understand because four companies are involved: Conners Marine Co., Pennsylvania Railroad Company, the Grace Line, and Carroll Towing Co. The inter-relationship between these parties is as follows:

Conners Marine Co.	owner of barge "Anna C" employer of bargee on Anna C	chartered "Anna C" to Pennsylvania R.R., including services of bargee
Pennsylvania R.R. Co.	charterer of "Anna C"	loaded "Anna C" with cargo of U.S. flour and tied her to Pier 52
Carroll Towing Co.	owner of tug "Carroll" employer of "Carroll's" captain and deckhand	chartered "Carroll" to the Grace Line for purpose of moving a barge out from Public Pier
Grace Line	charterer of "Carroll" employed services of harbormaster to move a barge from Public Pier with the tug "Carroll" and her crew	hired "Carroll" to move a barge out from Public Pier, which was next to Pier 52 where "Anna C" was tied; barges at Public Pier and at Pier 52 were also tied together with one line running between the two piers

United States et al. v. Carroll Towing Co., Inc., et al.

159 F.2d 169 (2d Cir. 1947)

L. Hand, Circuit Judge.

5

These appeals concern the sinking of the barge, "Anna C," on January 4, 1944, off Pier 51, North River. The Conners Marine Co., Inc., was the owner of the barge, which the Pennsylvania Railroad Company had chartered; the Grace Line, Inc., was the charterer of the tug, "Carroll," of which the Carroll Towing Co., Inc., was the

10 owner. [The lower court's decree] held the Carroll Company liable to the United
States for the loss of the barge's cargo of flour, and to the Pennsylvania Railroad
Company, for expenses in salving the cargo and barge; and it held the Carroll
Company also liable to the Conners Company for one half the damage to the
barge; … [The lower court's decree] also held the Grace Line primarily liable for the
15 other half of the damage to the barge, … ; it also held the Pennsylvania Railroad
secondarily liable for the same amount that the Grace Line was liable. The Carroll
Company and the Pennsylvania Railroad Company have filed assignments of error.

The facts, as the judge found them, were as follows. On June 20, 1943, the Conners
Company chartered the barge, "Anna C," to the Pennsylvania Railroad Company at
20 a stated hire per diem, by a charter of the kind usual in the Harbor, which included
the services of a bargee, apparently limited to the hours 8 A.M. to 4 P.M. On January
2, 1944, the barge, which had lifted the cargo of flour, was … at Pier 52 [in a tier with
five other barges] … The Grace Line, which had chartered the tug, "Carroll," sent
her down to the locus in quo to "drill" out one of the barges which lay at the end of
25 the [next pier north, called the Public Pier]; and in order to do so it was necessary to
throw off [a line that connected the barges at the Public Pier to the barges at Pier 52.]
On board the "Carroll" at the time were not only her master, but a "harbormaster"
employed by the Grace Line … . The captain of the "Carroll" put a deckhand and the
"harbormaster" on the barges, told them to throw off the line … ; but before doing
30 so, to make sure that the tier [of barges] on Pier 52 was safely moored, as there was
a strong northerly wind blowing down the river. The "harbormaster" and the deckhand went aboard the barges and readjusted all the fasts to their satisfaction, including those from the "Anna C," to the pier.

After doing so, they threw off the line … and again boarded the "Carroll," which
35 backed away … She had only got about seventy-five feet away when the tier off Pier
52 broke adrift because the fasts from the "Anna C," either rendered, or carried
away. The tide and wind carried down the six barges, still holding together, until the
"Anna C" fetched up against a tanker, lying on the north side of the pier below …
whose propeller broke a hole in her at or near her bottom. Shortly thereafter: i.e., at
40 about 2:15 P.M., she careened, dumped her cargo of flour and sank. The tug,
"Grace," owned by the Grace Line, and the "Carroll," came to the help of the flotilla
after it broke loose; and, as both had syphon pumps on board, they could have kept
the "Anna C" afloat, had they learned of her condition; but the bargee had left her
on the evening before, and nobody was on board to observe that she was leaking.
45 The Grace Line wishes to exonerate itself from all liability because the "harbormaster" was not authorized to pass on the sufficiency of the fasts of the "Anna C" which
held the tier to Pier 52; the Carroll Company wishes to charge the Grace Line with
the entire liability because the "harbormaster" was given an over-all authority. Both
wish to charge the "Anna C" with a share of all her damages, or at least with so much
50 as resulted from her sinking …

Analysis

Nautical Vocabulary:

barge	long flat boat usually used to carry cargo
bargee	person who works a barge
tug	small boat with powerful engine used to move larger boats within a harbor
to salve	to cure, to heal, to remedy a problem
hire per diem	amount of money in daily rental payments for use of s.th.
pier	large dock, wooden platform extending into a harbor to which boats are tied
locus in quo	the relevant place
to drill out	to move a barge out away from other barges tied at a pier
to moor	to tie a boat to s.th., usually a dock or pier
fasts	ropes holding boat to dock
to render	to pass through a loop, loosen, slacken
to carry away	to break off
to fetch up against	to stop, to come to a standstill against s.th. else
tanker	large ship used for carrying liquids, such as oil
to careen	to sway, to tilt, to tip
flotilla	a small group of boats
syphon pumps	pumps to pull water into tubes of different heights for purpose of water removal

The statement of facts may seem somewhat difficult to understand because of the rather unusual vocabulary. A group, or flotilla, of barges was tied together in a line, or tier, at Pier 52. The "Anna C," with her load of flour, was one of these barges. Another line of barges was moored at the Public Pier. In addition, one rope connected the line of barges at Pier 52 to those at the Public Pier. Since the "Carroll" was supposed to remove one of the barges at the Public Pier, it was necessary to disconnect the barges at Pier 52 from those at the Public Pier and to disconnect the barge to be removed from the other barges tied at the Public Pier. To carry out this task, the Grace Line hired a harbormaster, who was assisted by the crew of the "Carroll." The harbormaster and the deckhand were not careful enough to be sure that the barges at Pier 52 were safely tied. As the "Carroll" backed up, pulling the barge away from the Public Pier, the barges tied to Pier 52 loosened and started to move downstream. The "Anna C" ran into a tanker and was torn open, which eventually resulted in her sinking and losing her cargo. Unfortunately no one realized in time that she had sprung a leak, because the bargee, who should have been on board, was gone.

The trial court, the U.S. District Court for the Eastern District of New York, determined the parties' liability as follows:

Carroll Co.	liable to	U.S.	for loss of cargo of flour
Carroll Co.	liable to	Pennsylvania R.R.	for costs of attempting to recover some of the flour and pulling up "Anna C" from river bed
Carroll Co.	liable to	Conners Co.	for 1/2 of damage to "Anna C"
Grace Line	liable to	Conners Co.	primarily liable for 1/2 of damage to "Anna C"
Pennsylvania Railroad	liable to	Conners Co.	secondarily for Grace Line's liability for 1/2 of damage to "Anna C"

To say that the Grace Line is **primarily liable** means that it is responsible to compensate for the damage caused. Only if the Grace Line cannot be forced to pay for some reason, such as **bankruptcy**, then the party **secondarily liable**, here Pennsylvania R.R., will have to pay for the damage. This form of liability is different from the **joint and several liability** sometimes imposed on **multiple or joint tortfeasors**. **Joint and several liability** is the duty each of two or more **joint tortfeasors** has to compensate the victim for the whole loss, both individually or together. Thus the victim can **execute judgment** against any one of the joint tortfeasors for the whole amount of that judgment, or he can execute it against them all.

The Carroll Co. and the Pennsylvania R.R. appealed, filing **assignments of error**. An **assignment of error** is a list of legal errors the appellant claims the trial court made in reaching its judgment. Thus it is the basis of the appeal, which can only raise issues of law and not of fact. What legal arguments can you make, based on the facts as found by the trial court, that the judgment was incorrect? Who would be liable for what damage under the rules of your own legal system?

In the excerpt that follows, Judge Hand first considers the Grace Line's **vicarious liability** for the acts of its employee, the harbormaster.

Continue reading the case:

    The first question is whether the Grace Line should be held liable at all for any part of the damages. The answer depends first upon how far the "harbormaster's" authority went, for concededly he was an employee of some sort. Although the judge made no other finding of fact than that he was an "employee," in his second conclu-
55 sion of law he held that the Grace Line was "responsible for his negligence." Since the facts on which he based this liability do not appear, we cannot give that weight to the conclusion which we should to a finding of fact; but it so happens that on cross-

examination the "harbormaster" showed that he was authorized to pass on the sufficiency of the fasts of the "Anna C." He said that it was part of his job to tie up
60 barges; that when he came "to tie up a barge" he had "to go in and look at the barges that are inside the barge" he was "handling"; that in such cases "most of the time" he went in "to see that the lines to the inside barges are strong enough to hold these barges"; and that "if they are not" he "put out sufficient other lines as are necessary." That does not, however, determine the other question: i.e., whether when the master
65 of the "Carroll" told him and the deckhand to go aboard the tier and look at the fasts, preparatory to casting off the line between the tiers, the tug master meant the "harbormaster" to exercise a joint authority with the deckhand. As to this the judge in his tenth finding said: "The captain of the Carroll then put the deckhand of the tug and the harbor master aboard the boats at the end of Pier 52 to throw off the line
70 between the two tiers of boats after first ascertaining if it would be safe to do so." Whatever doubts the testimony of the "harbormaster" might raise, this finding settles it for us that the master of the "Carroll" deputed the deckhand and the "harbormaster," jointly to pass upon the sufficiency of the "Anna C's" fasts to the pier. The case is stronger against the Grace Line than Rice v. The Marion A.C.
75 Meseck, [2 Cir., 148 F.2d 522] was against the tug there held liable, because the tug had only acted under the express orders of the "harbormaster." Here, although the relations were reversed, that makes no difference in principle; and the "harbormaster" was not instructed what he should do about the fasts, but was allowed to use his own judgment. The fact that the deckhand shared in this decision, did not exonerate
80 him, and there is no reason why both should not be held equally liable, as the judge held them.

1. The Master - Servant Relationship

As you have noticed from this case, the lower court held the Grace Line liable for the negligence of the harbormaster, a person the Grace Line had employed. On appeal, the Grace Line argued that the harbormaster was not authorized within the scope of his employment to determine whether the lines holding the "Anna C" to the pier were properly and tightly drawn. If not, then the Carroll Towing Co. would have been solely responsible for the "Anna C's" breaking away because of the conduct of its own employee, the deckhand of the tug "Carroll."

As indicated, a company is **vicariously liable** for the torts of its employee which were committed within the course of his employment. Read the following text on **vicarious liability** and the **master-servant relationship**:

§ 69. Vicarious Liability

A is negligent, B is not. "Imputed negligence" means that, by reason of some relation existing between A and B, the
5 negligence of A is to be charged against B, although B has played no part in it, has done nothing whatever to aid or encourage it, or indeed has done all that he possibly can to prevent it … [T]he result may
10 be that B, in C's action against him, becomes liable as a defendant for C's injuries, on the basis of A's negligence. This is sometimes called imputed negligence. More often it is called vicarious liability,
15 or the principle is given the Latin name of *respondeat superior*.

… The most familiar illustration, of course, is the liability of a master for the torts of his servant in the course of his
20 employment … .

A multitude of very ingenious reasons have been offered for the vicarious liability of a master: he has a more or less fictitious "control" over the behavior of
25 the servant; he has "set the whole thing in motion," and is therefore responsible for what has happened; he has selected the servant and trusted him, and so should suffer for his wrongs, rather than an inno-
30 cent stranger who has had no opportunity to protect himself; …

What has emerged as the modern justification for vicarious liability is a rule of policy, a deliberate allocation of a risk.
35 The losses caused by the torts of employees, which as a practical matter are sure to occur in the conduct of the employer's enterprise, are placed upon that enterprise itself, as a required cost of
40 doing business. They are placed upon the employer because, having engaged in an enterprise, which will on the basis of all past experience involve harm to others through the torts of employees, and
45 sought to profit by it, it is just that he,

rather than the innocent injured plaintiff, should bear them; and because he is better able to absorb them, and to distribute them, through prices, rates or liability insurance, to the public, and so to shift them to society, to the community at large.

§ 70. Servants

The traditional definition of a servant is that he is a person employed to perform services in the affairs of another, whose physical conduct in the performance of the service is controlled, or is subject to a right of control, by the other … .

Once it is determined that the man at work is a servant, the master becomes subject to vicarious liability for his torts … .But his vicarious liability, for conduct which is in no way his own, extends to any and all tortious conduct of the servant which is within the "scope of the employment." … [This phrase] refers to those acts which are so closely connected with what the servant is employed to do, and so fairly and reasonably incidental to it, that they may be regarded as methods, even though quite improper ones, of carrying out the objectives of the employment.

… It has been said that in general the servant's conduct is within the scope of his employment if it is of the kind which he is employed to perform, occurs substantially within the authorized limits of time and space, and is actuated, at least in part, by a purpose to serve the master.

Frolic and Detour

In 1834 Baron Parke [in Joel v. Morrison, 1834, 6 C. & P. 501, 172 Eng.Rep. 1338.] uttered the classic phrase, that a master is not liable for the torts of his servant who is not at all on his master's business, but is

"going on a frolic of his own." If the servant steps outside of his employment to
do some act for himself, not connected
with the master's business, there is no
50 more responsibility for what he does than
for the acts of any stranger ...

Intentional Torts

55 Early decisions, adhering to the fiction of
an "implied command" of the master, refused to hold him liable for intentional or
"willful" wrongdoing on the part of the
servant, on the ground that it could not be
60 implied that such conduct was ever authorized. Under modern theories of allocation of the risk of the servant's misbehav-
ior, however, it has been recognized that
even intentional torts may be so reason-

ably connected with the employment as to
be within its "scope," and the present
tendency is to extend the employer's responsibility for such conduct ... It may be
said, in general, that the master is held
liable for any intentional tort committed
by the servant where its purpose, however
misguided, is wholly or in part to further
the master's business.

Thus he will be held liable where his bus
driver crowds a competitor's bus into a
ditch, or assaults a trespasser to eject him
from the bus, or a salesman makes fraudulent statements about the products he is
selling, ...

Prosser & Keeton on *The Law of Torts*,
West Publishing Co.: St. Paul, Minnesota
(1984) pp. 43-46 [footnotes omitted]

Questions on the Text

1 What is the law in your own legal system on this issue? For the German legal
system compare § 831(1) with § 278 of the Civil Code. Do you think that
the common law has a doctrine comparable to the German "culpa in contrahendo"? Explain this doctrine in your own words. Consider the reason
why it was developed, then read the following:

By the time the BGB was drafted the idea of vicarious liability had gained some
ground, but ultimately it managed to establish itself only in the contractual context.
According to § 278 BGB, a debtor is responsible for the fault of those whom he
employs in performing his obligation, to the same extent as for his own fault. But
5   when it came to the law of delict, the forces of tradition largely had their way:
strongly supported - for obvious reasons - by lobbyists representing the interests of
trade, industry and agriculture. Nationalistic sentiments, strangely, also played their
role. The principle enunciated in art. 1384 code civil [imposing strict vicarious
liability on the master for the torts of his servant] was regarded as entirely alien to
10 traditional "German" notions of justice and fairness. The rather extensive way in
which the French courts applied their regime of vicarious liability did not inspire the
German observers with much confidence either. A master, horribile dictu, had even
been ordered to pay damages because his servant had sounded a trumpet at night and
thus disrupted the neighbours' tranquillity! In the end, liability for the unlawful acts
15 of employees under the BGB was thus made to hinge on culpa in eligendo vel
custodiendo vel inspiciendo; the less traditionally minded proponents of the French

system merely managed to achieve a reversal of the onus of proof. Despite this concession, § 831 BGB has turned out to be a major source of embarrassment. Countless ways have been developed by both courts and legal writers to bypass this
20   unsound rule: the rather extravagant encroachment of contractual remedies on the law of delict, for instance, a characteristic feature of the modern German law of obligations, is based largely on the desire to make available, for the benefit of the injured party, the stricter rule of § 278 BGB.

Reinhard Zimmermann, *The Law of Obligations. Roman Foundations of the Civilian Tradition*, Juta & Co. Ltd.: Cape Town, Wetton, Johannesburg (1990) pp. 1125-26

[2]   Do you agree with Reinhard Zimmermann, who is a professor of civil law, Roman law and historical comparative law at the University of Regensburg? What other reasons are there for a German lawyer to prefer to have a case decided under the principles applying to contracts rather than torts?

[3]   Returning to *United States v. Carroll Towing Co.*, note the distinction Judge Learned Hand draws between the lower court's findings of fact and conclusions of law. From your knowledge of the responsibilities of a trial court and an appellate court in a common law system, explain why Judge Hand states (in lines 56-57) "we cannot give that weight to the conclusion which we should to a finding of fact; ... " In line 68, Judge Hand refers to the trial court judge's "tenth finding." Do you think this was a finding of fact or a conclusion of law?

[4]   *Reasoning by analogy*: In lines 74-76, Judge Hand says that the case for vicarious liability against the Grace Line was even stronger than the case was against the tug held liable in *Rice v. The Marion A.C. Meseck*. In *Rice*, the tug had "acted under the express orders of the 'harbormaster,'" presumably not one of the tug's employees. Still the tug was held liable in *Rice*. In *Carroll Towing*, the harbormaster, an employee of the Grace Line had acted jointly with the deckhand, an employee of Carroll Towing. Judge Hand acknowledges that the two cases differ, but he states that makes no difference in principle. Can you make the argument why the precedent in *Rice* should determine the Grace Line's liability in *Carroll Towing*? Refer back to the hypodermic needle analogy in *Mink v. University of Chicago* to help you make your argument.

The last part of *U.S. v. Carroll Towing* relates to the question of the Conners Co.'s **contributory negligence**, and, within that framework, their own **breach of a duty of care**. These two issues will be discussed anon, but first continue reading the case:

We cannot, however, excuse the Conners Company for the bargee's failure to care for the barge, and we think that this prevents full recovery. First as to the facts. As we have said, the deckhand and the "harbormaster" jointly undertook to pass upon the
85 "Anna C's" fasts to the pier; and even though we assume that the bargee was responsible for his fasts after the other barges were added outside, there is not the slightest ground for saying that the deckhand and the "harbormaster" would have paid any attention to any protest which he might have made, had he been there. We do not therefore attribute it as in any degree a fault of the "Anna C" that the flotilla
90 broke adrift. Hence she may recover in full against the Carroll Company and the Grace Line for any injury she suffered from the contact with the tanker's propeller, which we shall speak of as the "collision damages." On the other hand, if the bargee had been on board, and had done his duty to his employer, he would have gone below at once, examined the injury, and called for help from the "Carroll" and the Grace
95 Line tug. Moreover, it is clear that these tugs could have kept the barge afloat, until they had safely beached her, and saved her cargo. This would have avoided what we shall call the "sinking damages." Thus, if it was a failure in the Conners Company's proper care of its own barge, for the bargee to be absent, the company can recover only one third of the "sinking" damages from the Carroll Company and one third
100 from the Grace Line. For this reason the question arises whether a barge owner is slack in the care of his barge if the bargee is absent ... .[The court then reviews a number of precedents on a barge owner's liability for damages attributable to a bargee's not being on board his barge].

105 It appears ... that there is no general rule to determine when the absence of a bargee or other attendant will make the owner of the barge liable for injuries to other vessels if she breaks away from her moorings. However, in any cases where he would be so liable for injuries to others, obviously he must reduce his damages proportionately, if the injury is to his own barge. It becomes apparent why there can be no such general
110 rule, when we consider the grounds for such a liability. Since there are occasions when every vessel will break from her moorings, and since, if she does, she becomes a menace to those about her; the owner's duty, as in other similar situations, to provide against resulting injuries is a function of three variables: (1) The probability that she will break away; (2) the gravity of the resulting injury, if she does; (3) the
115 burden of adequate precautions. Possibly it serves to bring this notion into relief to state it in algebraic terms: if the probability be called P; the injury, L; and the burden, B; liability depends upon whether B is less than L multiplied by P: i.e., whether $B < PL$. Applied to the situation at bar, the likelihood that a barge will break from her fasts and the damage she will do, vary with the place and time; for example, if a storm
120 threatens, the danger is greater; so it is, if she is in a crowded harbor where moored barges are constantly being shifted about. On the other hand, the barge must not be the bargee's prison, even though he lives aboard; he must go ashore at times. We need not say whether, even in such crowded waters as New York Harbor a bargee must be aboard at night at all; it may be that the custom is otherwise, ... ; and that, if so, the
125 situation is one where custom should control. We leave that question open; but we hold that it is not in all cases a sufficient answer to a bargee's absence without excuse, during working hours, that he has properly made fast his barge to a pier, when he leaves her. In the case at bar the bargee left at five o'clock in the afternoon of January

3rd, and the flotilla broke away at about two o'clock in the afternoon of the follow-
130 ing day, twenty-one hours afterwards. The bargee had been away all the time, and we
hold that his fabricated story was affirmative evidence that he had no excuse for his
absence. At the locus in quo - especially during the short January days and in the full
tide of war activity - barges were being constantly "drilled" in and out. Certainly it
was not beyond reasonable expectation that, with the inevitable haste and bustle, the
135 work might not be done with adequate care. In such circumstances we hold - and it
is all that we do hold - that it was a fair requirement that the Conners Company
should have a bargee aboard (unless he had some excuse for his absence), during the
working hours of daylight ...

Decrees reversed and cause remanded for further proceedings in accordance with the
140 foregoing.

2. Contributory and Comparative Negligence

This part of the opinion deals with Conners' partial responsibility for its own
damages. The original common law **defense of contributory negligence** was announced in *Butterfield v. Forrester*, 103 Eng.Rep. 926 (K.B. 1809). According to
the traditional rule, a plaintiff who was to any degree at fault in causing his own
injuries was completely barred from recovering any part of his damages from the
defendant. Since the rule works to the benefit of the defendant, freeing her from
liability, it is an example of a **defense** to an action in tort. Over time, courts and
legislatures found that acknowledging the **contributory negligence defense** often
wrought injustice. That was because the rule was too extreme and did not consider each party's share of responsibility for the harm caused. Consequently, they
began to develop and adopt modified versions of the defense. In England, the
Law Reform (Contributory Negligence) Act 1945 provides that the plaintiff's
damages will be apportioned according to each party's degree of fault. This
scheme corresponds to the German Civil Code § 254 provision on *Mitverschulden.*

The term **comparative negligence** is normally used in the United States for a rule
that apportions damages according to each party's degree of fault, as does the
English rule stated in the Law Reform (Contributory Negligence) Act 1945. The
English, however, still use the term **contributory negligence**, even though the rule
does not correspond to the original common law position on contributory negligence. In the United States, various forms of **comparative negligence** rules are
in operation. Read the following text on the nature of these rules:

There are basically three types of comparative negligence systems: pure, modified, and slight-gross.

5   Pure Comparative Negligence

Probably the simplest method of allocating damages is what is commonly called "pure" comparative negligence. In this
10   form, a plaintiff's contributory negligence does not operate to bar his recovery altogether, but does serve to reduce his damages in proportion to his fault ... Except for West Virginia, all of the states which
15   have adopted comparative negligence by judicial opinion have opted for the flexibility and relative simplicity of "pure" comparative negligence ... .

20   Modified Comparative Negligence

The most common legislative approach for apportioning fault is the modified or "50%" system, under which a plaintiff's
25   contributory negligence does not bar recovery so long as it remains below a specified proportion to the total fault. There are two varieties of the 50% comparative negligence approach. Under the "equal
30   fault bar" approach, the plaintiff cannot recover anything if his fault is *equal to* or greater than that of the defendant; he is allowed to recover, in other words only if his negligence is less than that of the defendant. Under the "greater fault bar" system, the plaintiff is prevented from all recovery only if his fault exceeds the defendant's; he is therefore allowed to recover if his negligence is equal to or less than that of the defendant ... Under both systems, the plaintiff's contributory negligence operates as a complete bar, and he takes nothing, if his fault exceeds the permitted threshold amount; if his negligence falls below that amount, his damages are reduced proportionately to his fault, just as if the pure system were to be applied ... .

Slight-Gross System

Two states, Nebraska and South Dakota, currently have statutes under which the plaintiff's contributory negligence is a bar to recovery unless his negligence is "slight," and the defendant's negligence by comparison is "gross." The plaintiff who meets this threshold criterion still has his damages reduced by the proportion of the total negligence that is attributable to him.

Prosser & Keeton on *The Law of Torts*, West Publishing Co.: St. Paul, Minnesota (1984) pp. 471-474 [footnotes omitted]

At the time *Carroll Towing* was decided, the United States Congress had already adopted its own rule of **comparative negligence** for **admiralty** or **maritime** cases, which are cases arising on navigable waters. According to U.S. law, damages were to be equally divided among the negligent parties, regardless of the exact share each party's negligence had in causing the harm. Since the court determined that Conners was contributorily negligent, it had to bear an equal share of the damages with Carroll Towing and Grace Line, or one-third. As you can see, the U.S. rule in 1947 was yet another variation on **comparative negligence**.

3. The Standard of Care

The question in the second part of the *Carroll Towing* decision is whether Conners, the owner of the barge "Anna C" was contributorily negligent by failing to have its bargee on board at the time of the accident. The answer to that question depends on the **standard of care** to be imposed on Conners for its own safety. Judge Hand announces his famous formula, B < PL, for making this determination and holds that the burden (B) of having the bargee on board was indeed less, particularly during his normal daytime working hours, than the probability (P) that a barge could break away from a pier in a crowded harbor where barges were constantly being shifted around, multiplied by the gravity of the resulting injury (L) should it occur. Assume that the sinking damage to a barge such as the "Anna C" is $1 million, that the cargo of flour costs $250,000 and that the probability of a barge adrift sinking is 5 percent. PL would equal $62,500. Suppose further that with a bargee on board, the probability of sinking is reduced to .5 percent. PL would then equal $6,250. Having a bargee on board all of the time, such as by hiring a second bargee to cover for the time when the first is absent, would reduce the cost of sinking damage by $56,250. One then could say that Conners breached its duty of care if the cost of hiring the second bargee is less than $56,250. That is because it would have been cheaper for Conners to pay for a substitute bargee than to take the risk that the barge would sink. This formula provides a theory of what conduct is **reasonable**, namely conduct that **minimizes total social costs**. Total social costs are the cost of taking a certain precaution plus the cost of an accident occurring at that level of precaution. Without the second bargee, total social costs would be $62,500. With a second bargee on board, total social costs would be $6,250 plus the cost of employing the second bargee. Learned Hand's formula recognizes that a defendant should not be required to take extremely costly precautions to avoid an accident that either is very unlikely to occur or is insignificantly costly if it does.

C. Cause in Fact

The **cause-in-fact** element of a tort claim based on the defendant's negligence requires that: *but for* the defendant's breach of duty the plaintiff would not have suffered damage. Accordingly, one also refers to a **cause in fact** as a **but-for cause**, which is what in Germany and the United States is referred to as the **conditio sine qua non**. If we remain within the frame of reference provided by the Learned Hand formula, the question can be phrased as whether taking a certain (reasonable = B < PL) precaution, such as having a bargee on board the Anna C, would have avoided the harm.

Read the following analysis of *Carroll Towing* on the **cause-in-fact issue** and its relation to **breach of duty**:

> Some writers have treated actual causation as a fact of nature, but this formulation ignores the plaintiff's creative role in specifying the breach of duty and the way in which the cause-in-fact issue depends on what breach-of-duty choice the plaintiff has made. While analysis of the breach-of-duty issue has an ex ante perspective, the test
> 5   of cause in fact is whether the same untaken precaution, viewed after the accident, would have prevented it.
>
> *Carroll Towing* itself illustrates how these two perspectives on the same untaken precaution can lead to one element being satisfied when the other is not. Under Hand's analysis, there were successive (that is, divisible) harms: the first, when the
> 10   barge *Anna C* broke away and collided with other boats in the harbor, and the second, when it sank. Surprisingly, given the way the case is commonly understood, Hand concluded that the absent bargee's employer was *not* liable for the collision damage that immediately followed the breakaway. True, his famous language established that there was a breach of duty with respect to collision risk, because the
> 15   burden of having a bargee aboard was less than the probability that the *Anna C* would break away multiplied by the gravity of resulting harm if she did. Nonetheless, as to the collision damage, there was no cause in fact because Hand concluded (in a little-heeded passage) that, if the bargee had been on board, the most he could have done would have been to protest to those who were moving the barges; there
> 20   was no evidence that these people would have paid any attention to him. Judge Hand appears to have inferred that the harbormaster and his helper were very strong-willed individuals. Ex post the accident, having a bargee on board could not be seen as preventing the breakaway, and therefore this untaken precaution was not a cause in fact of the damages to the barge that came from the initial impact.
>
> 25   The question for Hand then became whether the absence of the bargee was the cause in fact of the sinking. Here, the answer was yes, because if the bargee had been aboard at the time of collision, he would have realized that the barge had developed a hole below the water line. He both could and would have called for help, which was available and would have arrived in time to repair the barge before it sank.
>
> Mark F. Grady, "Untaken Precautions," *Journal of Legal Studies*, vol. XVIII (January 1989) 139-156

Questions on the Text

☐1☐ The author refers to the "plaintiff's creative role in specifying the breach of duty." How and when does a plaintiff specify the breach of duty?

☐2☐ Once the breach of duty has been specified, it must have been the cause in fact of the damage for the party to be held liable. Was the bargee's absence a cause in fact of the barge breaking away from the pier? Was it a cause in fact of the barge's sinking? If the Anna C had only collided with the tanker but not sank, would specifying the bargee's absence as the breach of duty been a wise move?

☐3☐ How would your own legal system deal with this case? Would it be seen as the basis for a cause of action in contract or tort?

☐4☐ What parts of the opinion contain dicta? What is the holding of the case? Point to the language in the opinion that tells you whether you are reading part of the holding or only dicta.

D. Proximate Cause

Although the defendant's **breach of a duty of care** he owed the plaintiff may have been a **cause in fact** of the plaintiff's injury, still the courts may hold that the defendant is not liable for the plaintiff's damage. That is true when the damage is too **remote**, or not **proximate** to the injury. Two ways of phrasing this problem are: 1) the plaintiff's injury was not the **direct consequence** of the defendant's breach of duty, or 2) the defendant could not have **reasonably foreseen** that his conduct could cause the damage it did.

The question of whether the plaintiff's injury is the **direct consequence** of the defendant's negligence is raised when some other cause intervenes between the defendant's negligent conduct and the plaintiff's injury. This **intervening cause** may be the product of human conduct, such as that of a third party or of the plaintiff himself, or an act of God, such as a sudden storm. In England the problem is addressed under the terminology **novus actus interveniens** or **nova causa interveniens**. In the United States we speak of **concurrent efficient causes** or **intervening causes**, meaning that the plaintiff's injury would not have occurred either if Cause$_1$ or Cause$_2$ had not occurred. Both Cause$_1$ and Cause$_2$ are **but-for causes** of the plaintiff's injury. There are a variety of considerations that go into determining whether the intervening cause will exonerate the defendant of tort liability. Was the intervening cause foreseeable under the circumstances?

Was it a purely voluntary and intentional act that had nothing to do with the defendant's former negligent conduct? Was it a lawful or an unlawful act?

The question of whether the plaintiff's injury was **reasonably foreseeable** causes some confusion. Consider the following texts on this question:

> [The requirements of the tort of negligence are] ... (3) A causal connection between the defendant's careless conduct and the damage. (4) Foreseeability that such conduct would have inflicted on the particular plaintiff the particular kind of damage of which he complains. Requirements (3) and (4) perform different functions and are determined by applying different tests. Requirement (3) ascribes causal responsibility to the *defendant*, whereas the function of requirement (4) is to limit actionability by the *plaintiff* by determining whether he should have an action against the defendant.

> Clerk & Lindsell on *Torts*, 16th ed., Sweet & Maxwell: London (1989) 434; Fourth Cumulative Supplement to the Sixteenth Edition (1994).

> Negligence, it must be repeated, is conduct which falls below the standard established by law for the protection of others against unreasonable risk. It necessarily involves a foreseeable risk, a threatened danger of injury, and conduct unreasonable in proportion to the danger. If one could not reasonably foresee any injury as the result of one's act, or if one's conduct was reasonable in the light of what one could anticipate, there would be no negligence, and no liability. But what if one does unreasonably fail to guard against harm which one should foresee, and consequences which one could in no way have anticipated in fact follow?

> Prosser & Keeton on *The Law of Torts*, West Publishing Co.: St. Paul, Minnesota (1984) 280 [footnotes omitted]

> The reasonable-foresight doctrine is addressed to multiple risks where the same set of precautions reduces two different risks. One would have been clearly foreseeable to a reasonable person in the position of the injurer prior to the accident. This will be called the "primary risk." The other would not have been clearly foreseeable. It is the "ancillary risk." The reasonable-foresight doctrine establishes the conditions under which an injurer who has breached a duty with respect to a primary risk will be liable for an actual harm that has arisen from an ancillary one.

> Mark F. Grady, *Cases and Materials on Torts*, American Casebook Series, West Publishing Co.: St. Paul, Minn. (1994) 655 [footnotes omitted]

Read the following case:

Palsgraf v. Long Island Railroad

248 N.Y. 339, 162 N.E. 99 (1928)

CARDOZO, C.J. Plaintiff was standing on a platform of defendant's railroad after
5   buying a ticket to go to Rockaway Beach. A train stopped at the station, bound for
another place. Two men ran forward to catch it. One of the men reached the platform
of the car without mishap, though the train was already moving. The other man,
carrying a package, jumped aboard the car, but seemed unsteady as if about to fall. A
guard on the car, who had held the door open, reached forward to help him in, and
10 another guard on the platform pushed him from behind. In this act, the package was
dislodged, and fell upon the rails. It was a package of small size, about fifteen inches
long, and was covered by a newspaper. In fact it contained fireworks but there was
nothing in its appearance to give notice of its contents. The fireworks when they fell
exploded. The shock of the explosion threw down some scales at the other end of the
15 platform many feet away. The scales struck the plaintiff, causing injuries for which
she sues.

Questions on the Text

1. Analyze this case under your own legal system's law of torts.

2. Analyze this case under the common law of torts. Did the defendant here
owe the plaintiff a duty of care? If so, what was the basis of this duty? Did
the defendant breach its duty of care to the plaintiff? If so, in what way? Was
the defendant's breach the cause in fact of Ms. Palsgraf's injury? Do you
think the defendant's breach was the proximate cause of Ms. Palsgraf's injury? Why or why not?

3. What "set of precautions" could the defendant have taken to avoid injury to
the passenger boarding the train? Would the same set of precautions have
avoided injury to Ms. Palsgraf? Which risk was the "primary risk" and
which the "ancillary risk" with respect to this set of precautions? Remember,
in the words of Mark Grady, the question the "reasonable-foresight doctrine" addresses is when "an injurer who has breached a duty with respect
to a primary risk will be liable for an actual harm that has arisen from an
ancillary one."

Continue reading the case:

The conduct of the defendant's guard, if a wrong in its relation to the holder of the package, was not a wrong in its relation to the plaintiff, standing far away. Relatively to her it was not negligence at all. Nothing in the situation gave notice that the falling
20   package had in it the potency of peril to persons thus removed. Negligence is not actionable unless it involves the invasion of a legally protected interest, the violation of a right. "Proof of negligence in the air, so to speak, will not do." ... The plaintiff as she stood upon the platform of the station might claim to be protected against intentional invasion of her bodily security. Such invasion is not charged. She might
25   claim to be protected against unintentional invasion by conduct involving in the thought of reasonable men an unreasonable hazard that such invasion would ensue. These, from the point of view of the law, were the bounds of her immunity, ... If no hazard was apparent to the eye of ordinary vigilance, an act innocent and harmless, at least to outward seeming, with reference to her, did not take to itself the quality of
30   a tort because it happened to be a wrong, though apparently not one involving the risk of bodily insecurity, with reference to someone else. "In every instance, before negligence can be predicated of a given act, back of the act must be sought and found a duty to the individual complaining, the observance of which would have averted or avoided the injury." ... "The ideas of negligence and duty are strictly correlative." ...
35   The plaintiff sues in her own right for a wrong personal to her, and not as the vicarious beneficiary of a breach of duty to another.

Questions on the Text

1. In line 17, the court refers to the "defendant's guard." What issue does this raise as to the liability of the Long Island Railroad? Would you say that the defendant in this case could be held liable for the conduct of its guards, the employees who tried to pull and push the passenger with the fatal package onto the moving train?

2. In lines 23-24, the court points out that Ms. Palsgraf could "claim to be protected against intentional invasion of her bodily security." Did Ms. Palsgraf claim that? If Ms. Palsgraf had claimed that, what tort would have been the basis of her action? What tort is the basis of the second alternative the court points out (lines 24-26)? Did Ms. Palsgraf base her claim on this alternative?

3. The court distinguishes Ms. Palsgraf's claim from the potential claim(s) of whom? Do you think the defendant was held liable to the other potential plaintiffs in this case? Who were they?

4. The court confuses the issue somewhat here, and in the remainder of the opinion, by insisting on discussing the issue of whether the defendant owed Ms. Palsgraf a duty of care. Do you think the problem here is whether a railroad owes passengers standing on its platforms a duty of care to protect

them from injury? Review the three texts above (Clerk & Lindsell, Prosser & Keeton and Grady) and formulate the central issue in *Palsgraf*.

Continue reading the case:

A different conclusion will involve us, and swiftly too, in a maze of contradictions. A guard stumbles over a package which has been left upon a platform. It seems to be a bundle of newspapers. It turns out to be a can of dynamite. To the eye of ordinary
40 vigilance, the bundle is abandoned waste, which may be kicked or trod on with impunity. Is a passenger at the other end of the platform protected by the law against the unsuspected hazard concealed beneath the waste? If not, is the result to be any different, so far as the distant passenger is concerned, when the guard stumbles over a valise which a truckman or a porter has left upon the walk? ... [T]he orbit of the
45 danger as disclosed to the eye of reasonable vigilance would be the orbit of the duty. One who jostles one's neighbor in a crowd does not invade the rights of others standing at the outer fringe when the unintended contact casts a bomb upon the ground. The wrongdoer as to them is the man who carries the bomb, not the one who explodes it without suspicion of the danger. Life will have to be made over, and
50 human nature transformed, before prevision so extravagant can be accepted as the norm of conduct, the customary standard to which behavior must conform.

The argument for the plaintiff is built upon the shifting meanings of such words as "wrong" and "wrongful," and shares their instability. What the plaintiff must show is "a wrong" to herself, i.e., a violation of her own right, and not merely a wrong to some
55 one else, nor conduct "wrongful" because unsocial, but not "a wrong" to any one. We are told that one who drives at reckless speed through a crowded city street is guilty of a negligent act and, therefore, of a wrongful one irrespective of the consequences. Negligent the act is, and wrongful in the sense that it is unsocial, but wrongful and unsocial in relation to other travelers, only because the eye of vigilance perceives the
60 risk of damage. If the same act were to be committed on a speedway or a race course, it would lose its wrongful quality. The risk reasonably to be perceived defines the duty to be obeyed, and risk imports relation; it is risk to another or to others within the range of apprehension ... This does not mean, of course, that one who launches a destructive force is always relieved of liability if the force, though known to be
65 destructive, pursues an unexpected path. "It was not necessary that the defendant should have had notice of the particular method in which an accident would occur, if the possibility of an accident was clear to the ordinarily prudent eye" ... . Some acts, such as shooting, are so imminently dangerous to any one who may come within reach of the missile, however unexpectedly, as to impose a duty of prevision not far from that
70 of an insurer ... . Under this head, it may be, fall certain cases of what is known as transferred intent, an act willfully dangerous to A resulting by misadventure in injury to B ... These cases aside, wrong is defined in terms of the natural or probable, at least when unintentional ... The range of reasonable apprehension is at times a question for the court, and at times, if varying inferences are possible, a question for the jury. Here,
75 by concession, there was nothing in the situation to suggest to the most cautious mind that the parcel wrapped in newspaper would spread wreckage through the station. If the guard had thrown it down knowingly and willfully, he would not have threatened

the plaintiff's safety, so far as appearances could warn him. His conduct would not have involved, even then, an unreasonable probability of invasion of her bodily
80 security. Liability can be no greater where the act is inadvertent.

1. Transferred Intent

In lines 71-72, the court refers to **transferred intent**. Read the following passage on this doctrine:

"Transferred" Intent

One definite area in which there is more extensive liability for intent than for negligence
5 is that covered by the curious surviving fiction of "transferred intent." The defendant who shoots or strikes at A, intending to wound or kill A, and unforeseeably hits B instead, is held liable to B for an intentional
10 tort. The intent to commit a battery upon A is pieced together with the resulting injury to B; it is "transferred" from A to B. "The intention follows the bullet."
This peculiar idea appeared first in crimi-
15 nal cases at a time when tort and crime were still merged in the old trespass form of action. It represents an established rule of the criminal law, in cases in which shooting, striking, throwing a missile or
20 poisoning has resulted in unexpected injury to the wrong person ... . But the same rule was applied to tort cases arising in trespass ... . It is quite probable ... that the persistence of the principle has been due to
25 a definite feeling that the defendant is at fault, and should make good the damage. The defendant's act is characterized as "wrongful," and the fault is regarded as absolute toward all the world, rather than
30 relative to any one person. Having departed from the social standard of conduct, the defendant is liable for the harm which follows from the act, although this harm was not intended.

The rule has been applied in a considerable number of American cases that have held the defendant liable for accidental battery to an unintended person by shooting, striking, or throwing, where the intent was to commit a battery upon a third person. It is not, however, limited to cases of intended or resulting battery. The principle extends at least to liability for battery on one person by an act intended to cause an assault on another, and liability for assault on one person by an act intended to cause a battery on another. Thus one who intended an assault, by shooting to frighten another, was held liable for battery when the bullet unexpectedly hit a stranger ...
[W]here the defendant's conduct is merely negligent, many courts refuse to hold the defendant liable unless the negligence can be found to be relative to the particular plaintiff, in the sense that the foreseeable risk of harm created extends to the plaintiff. The broader liability in the case of an intentional invasion of another's rights is an illustration of the general attitude of the courts as to the imposition of greater responsibility upon an intentional wrongdoer.

Prosser & Keeton on *The Law of Torts*, West Publishing Co.: St. Paul, Minnesota (1984) pp. 471-474 [footnotes omitted]

Note that the doctrine of **transferred intent** applies only when the tortfeasor acted intentionally and not negligently with respect to the initial conduct that ultimately brought about unforeseeable harm. If the original conduct was negligent, however, the question becomes whether the harm to the particular plaintiff was foreseeable or not. If it was, the breach of the duty of care toward the plaintiff will be considered to be the **proximate cause** of that plaintiff's injury.

2. The Domains of Judge and Jury in Negligence Cases

In lines 73-74, Judge Cardozo points out that whether the defendant could have reasonably foreseen that the plaintiff could be injured is sometimes a **question for the court,** and sometimes a **question for the jury.** As should already be clear from Unit I, the judge is responsible for questions of law and the jury for questions of fact. In a negligence case, the responsibilities of judge and jury are different regarding each of the elements of the plaintiff's prima facie case. Consider the *Restatement (Second) Torts* sections on the functions of the court and jury in a negligence case:

§ 328 B. Functions of Court

In an action for negligence the court determines

(a) whether the evidence as to the facts makes an issue upon which the jury may reasonably find the existence or non-existence of such facts;

(b) whether such facts give rise to any legal duty on the part of the defendant;

(c) the standard of conduct required of the defendant by his legal duty;

(d) whether the defendant has conformed to that standard, in any case in which the jury may not reasonably come to a different conclusion;

(e) the applicability of any rules of law determining whether the defendant's conduct is a legal cause of harm to the plaintiff; and

(f) whether the harm claimed to be suffered by the plaintiff is legally compensable.

§ 328 C. Functions of Jury

In an action for negligence the jury determines, in any case in which different conclusions may be reached on the issue:

(a) the facts,

(b) whether the defendant has conformed to the standard of conduct required by the law,

(c) whether the defendant's conduct is a legal cause of the harm to the plaintiff, and

(d) the amount of compensation for legally compensable harm.

The judge in a negligence case, as in any other case for which a jury is used, must first determine whether the evidence raises any factual issues justifying its submission to the jury [§ 328 B (a)]. If it does, then the jury is responsible for determining what the facts are [§ 328 C (a)]. In a negligence case, the judge is fully responsible for determining whether some reasonable version of the facts could indicate that the defendant owed the plaintiff a duty of care and if so, what the standard of conduct is for that duty, such as the reasonable person standard [§ 328 B (b) and (c)]. Again, the court also must decide whether the evidence raises any factual issue about which a reasonable jury could disagree regarding the defendant's failure to fulfill that standard. If the court decides in the affirmative, it must give the issue to the jury to decide [§ 328 B (d)] and the jury is then responsible for this determination [§ 328 C (b)]. The court instructs the jury on the applicable rules of law for resolving the cause-in-fact and proximate-cause issues [§ 328 B (e)] and the jury makes the final determination based on the evidence [§ 328 C (c)]. Finally, the court determines whether the law provides for compensation for the type of harm the plaintiff claims to have suffered [§ 328 B (f)]. If so, the jury determines the amount of damages the plaintiff will receive [§ 328 C (d)]

Questions on the Text

1. Point to passages in the text where Judge Cardozo engages in typical legal reasoning by analogizing the case at bar to hypothetical factual situations where the result is considered obvious.

2. Does the doctrine of transferred intent apply in *Palsgraf*? Why or why not? Did the railway employees intend to set off an explosion? If they had, would the doctrine of transferred intent have applied and provided a basis of liability toward Ms. Palsgraf? What if they had intended to throw the package on the ground, not knowing that it contained fireworks? Would the doctrine of transferred intent then apply, giving Ms. Palsgraf a cause of action?

3. Explain your own legal system's treatment of the transferred intent cases (aberratio ictus cases) in the field of: a) criminal law and b) tort law. Do you consider transferred intent to be a good doctrine?

4. Why does the court say "The range of reasonable apprehension [that an injury could occur] is at times a question for the court, and at times, if varying inferences are possible [regarding the facts] a question for the jury"? Can this statement be well justified with the rules set forth in the *Restatement*? What sections are applicable?

Continue reading the case:

> Negligence, like risk, is thus a term of relation. Negligence in the abstract, apart from things related, is surely not a tort, if indeed it is understandable at all ... Negligence is not a tort unless it results in the commission of a wrong, and the commission of a

wrong imports the violation of a right, in this case, we are told, the right to be
protected against interference with one's bodily security. But bodily security is protected, not against all forms of interference or aggression, but only against some.
One who seeks redress at law does not make out a cause of action by showing
85   without more that there has been damage to his person. If the harm was not willful,
he must show that the act as to him had possibilities of danger so many and apparent
as to entitle him to be protected against the doing of it though the harm was
unintended. Affront to personality is still the keynote of wrong. Confirmation of this
view will be found in the history and development of the action on the case. Neg-
90   ligence as a basis of civil liability was unknown to medieval law ... For damage to the
person, the sole remedy was trespass, and trespass did not lie in the absence of
aggression, and that direct and personal ... Liability for other damage, as where a
servant without orders from the master does or omits something to the damage of
another, is a plant of later growth ... When it emerged out of the legal soil, it was
95   thought of as a variant of trespass, an off-shoot of the parent stock. This appears in
the form of action, which was known as trespass on the case ... The victim does not
sue derivatively, or by right of subrogation, to vindicate an interest invaded in the
person of another. Thus to view his cause of action is to ignore the fundamental
difference between tort and crime ... He sues for breach of a duty owing to himself.

100   The law of causation, remote or proximate, is thus foreign to the case before us. The
question of liability is always anterior to the question of the measure of the consequences that go with liability. If there is no tort to be redressed, there is no occasion
to consider what damage might be recovered if there were a finding of a tort. We may
assume, without deciding, that negligence, not at large or in the abstract, but in
105   relation to the plaintiff, would entail liability for any and all consequences, however,
novel or extraordinary ... There is room for argument that a distinction is to be
drawn according to the diversity of interests invaded by the act, as where conduct
negligent in that it threatens an insignificant invasion of an interest in property
results in an unforeseeable invasion of an interest of another order, as, e.g., one of
110   bodily security. Perhaps other distinctions may be necessary. We do not go into the
question now. The consequences to be followed must first be rooted in a wrong.

The judgment of the Appellate Division and that of the Trial Term should be reversed
and the complaint dismissed, with costs in all courts.

[POUND, LEHMAN and KELLOGG, JJ., concur]

Analysis

Judge Cardozo's comments are somewhat obscure as regards the main issue in
the case, namely whether the defendant's breach of the duty of care he owed Ms.
Palsgraf was the proximate cause of her injuries. Judge Cardozo attempts to
shroud the issue with the question of whether the defendant owed Ms. Palsgraf

a duty of care at all. Yet there seems to be no doubt that a railway owes passengers a duty of care to protect them from being injured on platforms or in trains. The real issue is whether the type of harm Ms. Palsgraf suffered was the reasonably foreseeable consequence of helping a passenger carrying a package onto a moving train.

This passage of the text also creates some problems because of the rather metaphorical discussion of common law causes of action beginning in line 88. Cardozo discusses the action of **trespass** and the action of **trespass on the case**. Trespass would lie for direct injuries the defendant caused the plaintiff and is the basis for today's causes of action for intentional torts. Trespass on the case, a later development, could be sustained for the indirect injuries the defendant caused the plaintiff and is the basis of today's actions for negligent torts. The difference between direct and indirect injuries is the difference between injuries caused by the defendant's act alone and injuries caused by the defendant's act and some intervening cause. A common example to illustrate the difference is the defendant's tree falling directly on the plaintiff's head (trespass) as opposed to the defendant's tree falling on the street and the plaintiff's horse stumbling when trying to jump the tree resulting in the plaintiff's suffering head injuries (trespass on the case). See *Einführung in die anglo-amerikanische Rechtssprache / Introduction to Anglo-American Law & Language*, Unit I, Chapter 1, B, 3 for a detailed discussion of common law forms of action. In this passage, however, Cardozo is primarily concentrating on the difference between an intentional tort, where intent might be transferred, and a negligent tort, where it may not. If intent is transferred then the victim in some sense sues derivatively (line 97), meaning his right to sue for the intentional tort derives from the defendant's intent to harm another person. If the defendant did not intend to harm anyone, the plaintiff would have to show that the defendant breached a duty of care the defendant owed the plaintiff. Unfortunately the discussion is very misleading, even to students of the common law, because Cardozo keeps insisting that the issue here is not one of causation. *Palsgraf*, however, is one of the most famous proximate cause cases of the common law, so do not let yourself be confused.

Questions on the Text

1. Judge Cardozo refers to the master-servant relationship in line 93. Do you think, reconsidering the Prosser & Keeton text *supra* p. 156 that the railway guards in *Palsgraf* were acting within the scope of their employment? What if their employer had expressly forbidden them from helping passengers onto moving trains? What if the employer had simply instructed them al-

ways to exercise caution and not to take any risks when working? Would the master-servant relationship ever serve to hold an employer vicariously responsible for the torts of his employees if such instruction were sufficient to protect the employer from liability?

[2]   What is the legal history of this case? (You should be able to figure it out by the last statement of the majority opinion here.) Who won at the trial? Who won on appeal (the decision was 3-2)? The decision you have just read is the decision of the highest court in New York, namely the Court of Appeals. Here the decision was 4-3. What was the result in this case for Ms. Palsgraf? Suppose the defendant in this case had demurred to the complaint and Judge Cardozo had been the trial court judge. Would he have sustained the demurrer? What is the standard for sustaining it?

As noted, this case was close. Read the following opinion of the three dissenters. As you should understand, Judge Andrews wrote the dissenting opinion and was joined by Judges Crane and O'Brien, who **concurred** in Andrews' **dissent**:

ANDREWS, J. [with whom CRANE and O'BRIEN, JJ., concur] dissenting ... .Upon these facts may [Ms. Palsgraf] recover the damages she has suffered in an action brought against [the defendant]? The result we shall reach depends upon our theory as to the nature of negligence. Is it a relative concept - the breach of some duty owing
5   to a particular person or to particular persons? Or where there is an act which unreasonably threatens the safety of others, is the doer liable for all its proximate consequences, even where they result in injury to one who would generally be thought to be outside the radius of danger? This is not a mere dispute as to words. We might not believe that to the average mind the dropping of the bundle would seem to involve
10   the probability of harm to the plaintiff standing many feet away whatever might be the case as to the owner or to one so near as to be likely to be struck by its fall. If, however, we adopt the second hypothesis we have to inquire only as to the relation between cause and effect. We deal in terms of proximate cause, not of negligence ... .

But we are told that "there is no negligence unless there is in the particular case a legal
15   duty to take care, and this duty must be one which is owed to the plaintiff himself and not merely to others." ... This, I think too narrow a conception. Where there is the unreasonable act, and some right that may be affected there is negligence whether damage does or does not result. That is immaterial. Should we drive down Broadway at a reckless speed, we are negligent whether we strike an approaching car or miss it
20   by an inch. The act itself is wrongful. It is a wrong not only to those who happen to be within the radius of danger but to all who might have been there - a wrong to the public at large ...

It may well be that there is no such thing as negligence in the abstract ... In an empty world negligence would not exist. It does involve a relationship between man and his
25   fellows. But not merely a relationship between man and those whom he might reasonably expect his act would injure. Rather, a relationship between him and those whom he does in fact injure. If his act has a tendency to harm some one, it harms him a mile away as surely as it does those on the scene ...

... The proximate cause, involved as it may be with many other causes, must be, at
30   least, something without which the event would not happen. The court must ask
itself whether there was a natural and continuous sequence between cause and effect.
Was the one a substantial factor in producing the other? Was there a direct connection between them, without too many intervening causes? Is the effect of cause on
result not too attenuated? Is the cause likely, in the usual judgment of mankind, to
35   produce the result? Or by the exercise of prudent foresight could the result be
foreseen? Is the result too remote from the cause, and here we consider remoteness in
time and space ... Clearly we must so consider, for the greater the distance either in
time or space, the more surely do other causes intervene to affect the result. When a
lantern is overturned the firing of a shed is a fairly direct consequence. Many things
40   contribute to the spread of the conflagration - the force of the wind, the direction and
width of streets, the character of intervening structures, other factors. We draw an
uncertain and wavering line, but draw it we must as best we can ...

... The act upon which defendant's liability rests is knocking an apparently harmless
package onto the platform. The act was negligent. For its proximate consequences
45   the defendant is liable. If its contents were broken, to the owner; if it fell upon and
crushed a passenger's foot, then to him. If it exploded and injured one in the immediate vicinity to him also ... Mrs. Palsgraf was standing some distance away. How far
cannot be told from the record - apparently twenty-five or thirty feet. Perhaps less.
Except for the explosion, she would not have been injured. We are told by the
50   appellant in his brief "it can not be denied that the explosion was the direct cause of
the plaintiff's injuries." So it was a substantial factor in producing the result - there
was here a natural and continuous sequence - direct connection. The only intervening cause was that instead of blowing her to the ground the concussion smashed the
weighing machine which in turn fell upon her. There was no remoteness in time, little
55   in space. And surely, given such an explosion as here it needed no great foresight to
predict that the natural result would be to injure one on the platform at no greater
distance from its scene than was the plaintiff. Just how no one might be able to
predict. Whether by flying fragments, by broken glass, by wreckage of machines or
structures no one could say. But injury in some form was most probable.

60   Under these circumstances I cannot say as a matter of law that the plaintiff's injuries
were not the proximate result of the negligence. That is all we have before us. The
court refused to so charge. No request was made to submit the matter to the jury as
a question of fact, even would that have been proper upon the record before us.

The judgment appealed from should be affirmed, with costs.

Consider the following analysis of the majority and dissenting opinions in
Palsgraf. Note the strategic approach the author takes in considering how
Ms. Palsgraf's story could have been told to possibly increase her chances of
success:

There are really two doctrines of proximate cause in the common law: the direct-consequences doctrine and the reasonable-foresight doctrine. The concept of the untaken precaution is the key to understanding both. Under the first interpretation of

proximate cause (the Andrews position in *Palsgraf*), harm is regarded as direct if
5   between the time of the defendant's untaken precaution and the time of the plaintiff's
harm, there was no intervening cause. We can think of an intervening cause as an
opportunity by a third party to take some precaution that would have prevented the
loss. When harm is not direct but consequential, events take the following sequence:
at T_1 there is negligence by the defendant, at T_2 there is an opportunity for some third
10   party to prevent the impending harm, and at T_3 there is actual harm to the plaintiff.
Under the direct-consequences rule, the plaintiff's best strategy is to assign an untaken precaution to the defendant that leaves no T_2. Ideally, the defendant's untaken
precaution and the plaintiff's harm should be simultaneous, because then there will
be no possibility of an intervening cause ...

15   While direct-consequences proximate cause has an ex post orientation (much like
cause in fact), the reasonable-foresight doctrine (like breach of duty) has an ex ante
orientation. Looking from the vantage point of the relevant untaken precaution,
could the defendant have reasonably foreseen the type of harm that the plaintiff
sustained? Different possible untaken precautions create different ex ante perspec-
20   tives for the same accidental loss.

Consider the *Palsgraf* case. The untaken precaution on which the plaintiff relied was
the railroad's failure to be more careful in assisting a passenger who was trying to
board a moving train while he was carrying a package. When the package dropped
and exploded (unbeknownst to the conductor the package contained fireworks), the
25   concussion shook the train platform and toppled scales onto the plaintiff. In holding
for the defendant, Justice Cardozo emphasized the distance between the place where
the plaintiff was harmed and the site of the untaken precaution (the tracks). He said:
"Nothing in the situation gave notice that the falling package had in it the potency of
peril to persons thus removed."

30   Mrs. Palsgraf might have had a better chance to recover if she had relied on a
different untaken precaution to set up her case in proximate cause. If scales topple
onto bystanders when the platform shakes, then the scales are not very stable. Heavy
equipment and heavy cargo are so common in a train depot that vibrations on the
platform must be relatively frequent. If her attorney had alleged that the railroad
35   failed to ensure that the scales would stay upright when the platform is shaken, Mrs.
Palsgraf would not have lost on the proximate cause issue. From the vantage point of
this untaken precaution, the harm to Mrs. Palsgraf would have been quite foreseeable.

Of course, if Mrs. Palsgraf's lawyer had said the scales should have been fixed, there
40   is no guarantee that she would have won on the breach-of-duty (or cause-in-fact)
issue. If the concussion from the fireworks was unusually sharp, so that the burden
of an adequate precaution was great, or if nothing gave the railroad notice that the
scales were wobbly, then Mrs. Palsgraf might have lost her case anyway. As it should
now be clear, formulating a winning untaken precaution can be like threading a
45   needle, and in many cases no untaken precaution will pass muster under all of the
different tests - which is doubtless as it should be. Nonetheless, the plaintiff in many
cases will be able to improve the odds of success by choosing the right untaken
precaution. Likewise, a defendant who is sensitive to the issue may be able to prevail

50 by showing a fatal discontinuity between the elements of breach, cause in fact, and
proximate causation in the plaintiff's case.

Mark F. Grady, "Untaken Precautions," *Journal of Legal Studies*, vol. XVIII
(January 1989) 139, 151-53

Questions on the Text

1. Review the Grady text in the section on cause in fact. Note that the author
is giving lawyers advice on how to formulate their pleading to improve their
chances of success. He suggests that Ms. Palsgraf could have improved her
chances of winning on the proximate cause issue if she had claimed that the
defendant's breach of duty was its failure to attach the scales to the platform
more securely. But the author notes, if she had done that, she might have lost
on the breach-of-duty issue. Why is that? Use the Learned Hand formula
(B < PL) for determining when there is a breach of duty in this case. Note the
comment in lines 41-42 of the text.

2. How does your own legal system approach the proximate cause issue? Does
it take the direct-consequences approach, or the reasonable-foresight approach?

3. *Are the following statements true or false:*
   a) The intent element for assault is identical with that for battery.
   b) The intent to commit an assault is the intent to inflict physical injury.
   c) To maintain an action for battery, the plaintiff must allege specific physical
      injury to himself.
   d) If John aims a loaded gun at Harry but Harry does not see John doing so,
      John has still committed an assault.
   e) If Sally slips George's orange juice with vodka, but tells him the drink
      contains no alcohol, Sally has committed a battery on George if George
      actually drinks the juice.
   f) If Sally slips George's orange juice with vodka, but tells him the drink
      contains no alcohol, Sally has committed an assault on George even
      though the drink tips over and George never drinks it.
   g) If a medical doctor fails to inform his patient of one very unlikely risk
      involved in surgery and in fact the patient suffers because that risk materi-
      alized, the doctor is liable for negligence regardless of whether other doc-
      tors in the medical community would have informed their patients of that
      type of risk or not.
   h) On the way home from work, Fred decides to rob a woman because he

feels that his employer is not paying him enough. The employer is liable for Fred's tort.

Terminology

duty of care	obligation to take precautions to avoid harming another person (**Sorgfaltspflicht**)
good Samaritan duty to render aid	general obligation imposed by law to assist people who are in a dangerous situation in order to avoid their being harmed (**allgemeine Hilfeleistungspflicht**)
affirmative act	basis for the law to impose a duty of care on the actor; used to refer to an act that places s.o. else in danger and thus gives a good reason for requiring the person who committed the act to take measures to protect the potential victim (ca. **Ingerenz**)
special relationship	basis for the law to impose a duty of care; refers to a relationship in which one party has undertaken a responsibility to care for another; exists between a doctor and his patient, a babysitter and the baby (**Schutzverhältnis**)
gratuitous undertaking	basis for the law to impose a duty of care; refers to a situation in which an individual enters into a non-contractual relationship to render services for s.o. else (**Auftragsverhältnis**)
occupation of land	basis for the law to impose a duty of care; refers to the responsibility the owner or possessor of real property has to keep the property in a condition that others will not injure themselves when they are on the property (**Grundlage einer Verkehrssicherungspflicht**)
breach of duty	failure to meet up to the standard of care imposed by law on a person who has a duty of care to another individual (**Sorgfaltspflichtverletzung**)
standard of care	the norm established by law for determining whether an individual has fulfilled a duty of care (**Sorgfaltsmaßstab**)
reasonable person standard	one way of expressing the standard of care applicable to torts of negligence; measures defendant against the average person in the community (**die im Verkehr erforderliche Sorgfalt**)
Learned Hand formula	one way of expressing the standard of care applicable to torts of negligence; determines the defendant's obligation by comparing the burden of his taking a certain precaution against the probability that harm will occur if the precaution is not taken multiplied by the seriousness of that harm if it does occur; if the burden of taking the

	precaution is less that the probability times the harm, then the defendant has not met the standard of care (B < PL)
damage	harm caused the victim of a tort (**Schaden**)
damages	remedy in money to compensate for the injury caused a tort victim, as in: **money damages (Schadensersatz)**
cause in fact but-for cause	test of causation whereby one determines whether A caused B by asking whether if A had not occurred, B would have occurred; if not then A was the **cause in fact** or the **but-for cause** of B (**conditio sine qua non; äquivalente Verursachung**)
untaken precaution	a measure of care a defendant to a tort claim could have taken but did not take; question for tort liability is whether this untaken precaution was the **cause in fact** and **proximate cause** of the plaintiff's injury; resolving this issue still does not resolve the issue of whether the defendant breached a duty of care to the plaintiff by not taking the precaution, since it may be that the defendant had no duty to take the precaution, e.g. under the Learned Hand formula
proximate cause	test of causation from the point of view of remoteness of result; for a breach of a duty of care to be actionable, it must have been the proximate cause of the plaintiff's injuries (**Einschränkung der Äquivalenztheorie der Kausalität**; vergleichbar der **Adäquanztheorie der Kausalität** oder der **Theorie der objektiven Zurechnung**)
direct consequence	one method of formulating the question of proximate causation; focuses on whether causes other than the defendant's act intervened before the plaintiff was injured (**unmittelbare Folge**)
intervening cause	a cause in fact of the plaintiff's injury that happened after the defendant's act (**dazwischentretende Ursache**)
concurrent efficient cause	another term for an intervening cause (**kumulative Kausalität**)
novus actus interveniens	(UK) intervening act which was also a but-for cause of the plaintiff's injury
nova causa interveniens	(UK) intervening cause
foreseeability of the risk	a method of formulating the question of proximate cause; focuses on whether normal people would have realized ex ante that conduct such as the defendant's would cause a certain kind of harm (**Voraussehbarkeit der Gefahr**)
reasonable foresight doctrine	determines the conditions under which tort liability will be imposed on a defendant who could not clearly foresee a secondary risk of his conduct
master-servant relation	relationship of employer to employee; is a basis for imposing strict tort liability on the employer for the torts of his employee which were committed within the scope of the employment relationship (**Dienstverhältnis, Arbeitsverhältnis**)

vicarious liability	liability of one person for the torts of another, such as the employer for the torts of the employee (**Haftung für zurechenbares Drittverschulden**)
imputed negligence	attributing the negligence of one person to another because of the relationship between the two (**Zurechnung eines Drittverschuldens**)
respondeat superior	another name for the principle of imposing liability vicariously
contributory negligence	(US) refers to original English doctrine that barred a plaintiff from collecting any damages whatsoever from a defendant if the plaintiff was at all at fault for his own injuries (**Ausschluß des Anspruchs bei Mitverschulden**); (UK) term used today to mean that plaintiff may collect only the amount of damages necessary to compensate for the defendant's share of fault in causing the plaintiff harm (**Mitverschulden**)
comparative negligence	(US) refers to principle of sharing responsibility for harm caused by a tort; damages are apportioned between the plaintiff and the defendant depending on each party's degree of fault (**Mitverschulden**)
pure comparative negligence	apportions damages according to each party's fault in causing harm (**Mitverschulden**)
modified comparative negligence	apportions damages between plaintiff and defendant but imposes a 50% limit on the plaintiff's own fault for the plaintiff to recover any damages (**Mitverschulden, das Schadensersatzansprüche proportional mindert und bei einer mehr als 50%igen Selbstverschuldung des Klägers sogar ausschließt**)
equal fault bar	modified comparative negligence rule which bars the plaintiff from recovering any damages from the defendant if the plaintiff's negligence accounts for 50% or more of his own harm; if it is less than 50%, the rule of pure comparative negligence applies
greater fault bar	modified comparative negligence rule which bars the plaintiff from recovering any damages from the defendant if the plaintiff's negligence accounts for more than 50% of his own harm; if it is 50% or less, the rule of pure comparative negligence applies
slight-gross system	bars plaintiff from recovering any damages from defendant if the plaintiff's negligence was not insignificant in comparison to the defendant's negligence; if it was insignificant, the damages are still apportioned according to each party's share of responsibility for the harm
primary liability	full responsibility for harm caused through one's tort which is backed up by s.o. else's secondary liability for the damages in case of default by the party primarily liable (**Haftung des Hauptschuldners**)
secondary liability	liability to pay the tort damages for s.o. who is primarily liable

	in case that person defaults and cannot be forced to pay (**Ausfallhaftung**)
joint and several liability	duty each of two **joint tortfeasors (Gesamtschuldner)** has to compensate the victim for the total loss, both individually or together; the victim can execute judgment against either one of the joint tortfeasors for the whole amount of that judgment, or he can execute it against them both (**gesamtschuldnerische Haftung**)
joint tortfeasors	two or more persons who act together in committing a tort (**Gesamtschuldner**)
assignments of error	list of legal errors appellant claims a lower court, whose judgment the appellant is appealing, made (**Revisionsrüge**)
onus of proof **burden of proof**	obligation to provide enough evidence to prove legal claim (**Beweislast**)
law of delict	another term for tort law (**Deliktsrecht**)
actionability	the ability to maintain a law suit in the sense that the law supports the particular claim (**Einklagbarkeit**)
transferred intent	doctrine of English law, applicable today in England and the U.S., which imputes the intent to cause prohibited harm to s.o. who in fact was only negligent with respect to causing that harm, because the actor intentionally attempted to cause a different type of harm, or the same type of harm to a different victim, and as a result negligently caused the harm in question
right of subrogation	"The substitution of one person in the place of another with reference to a lawful claim, demand or right, so that he who is substituted succeeds to the rights of the other in relation to the debt or claim and its rights, remedies, or securities." *Black's Law Dictionary* (**gesetzlicher Forderungsübergang** bzw. **Anspruch auf Forderungsabtretung**)
trespass does not lie	expression indicating that the facts do not support a legal claim of trespass
punitive damages	damages awarded to punish tortfeasor (**Zivilstrafe im Gewand von Schadensersatz**)

Terminology Review

to remand (I.I.2)	to send back case, as an appellate court, to lower court for some specified treatment of case (**zurückverweisen**), such as **to remand for further proceedings not inconsistent with this opinion**, meaning lower court has to deal with case as directed in decision of higher appellate court

admiralty jurisdiction (I.II.2)	case that arose on the high seas, great lakes, or other navigable bodies of water; also: **maritime jurisdiction (ca. Seegerichtsbarkeit)**
trespass (I.I.1)	a tort at common law involving direct injury to s.o. committed either intentionally or negligently for which the injured party could sue for compensation; form of action to recover damages to compensate for injury caused by the defendant's unlawful interference with the plaintiff's person, property or rights
trespass on the case (I.I.1)	form of action to recover **damages** to compensate for injury resulting from the defendant's wrongful act which was not an act of direct or immediate force (**trespass**) but instead which caused the harm indirectly or as a secondary consequence; generally referred to simply as **case**

Vocabulary

to actuate	to put into motion, to put into action
allocation	assignment of parts of s.th. to various individuals as their share of the whole
ancillary	additional, extra
anon	soon, in the near future
bustle	busy activity
concession	giving in to s.o., giving up s.th.
concussion	shock or effect from a heavy blow
discontinuity	inconsistency, not fitting together well
to dislodge	to loosen, to force out of a fixed position
encroachment	a gradual take over of rights or possession of property
ex ante	from before, viewpoint taken before s.th. happens
exigency	demands, requirements
ex post	from afterwards, viewpoint taken after s.th. happens
to exonerate	to relieve from blame
fabricated	made up, invented, not corresponding to fact
fringe	edge, outermost part of s.th.
haste	hurry, speed, swiftness
hazard	danger

to hinge on	to depend on, to turn on
to import	to mean, to signify
impending	about to happen
impunity	without punishment, with no bad consequences
inadvertent	unintended, accidental
to infer	to conclude (logically), to deduce
ingenious	clever
to intervene	to come between, to occur between two other events
lame	partial inability to use one's leg
maze	confusing network, s.th. of extreme complication and confusion
mishap	accident
muster	review, close inspection (**to pass muster**: to withstand careful consideration)
odds	chance, probability
to opt for	to decide in favor of
potency	power, strength
to be predicated on	to be based on (normally used with "on" and not with "of" as in text
proximate	close to s.th., not remote, not far away
to bring into relief	to make three dimensional and thus add depth to
remote	far away, not proximate
to shroud	to cover and thus to give a false appearance to s.th.
slight	small, minimal
threshold	gate, entrance, level which must be overcome before s.th. occurs
tier	row, layer
to trod on	to step on with one's feet
valise	travel bag
vantage point	point of view that is particularly beneficial for gaining an overview
vicarious	through s.o. else rather than directly
vigilance	watchfulness with respect to avoiding danger
to vindicate	to free from error or blame, to avenge
to waver	to sway back and forth
to wreak	to cause (**wreak, wrought, wrought**)

Language Exercises
Chapter 2

I. Fill in the blanks with the correct terminology: see pp. 148-177 for use in the original context

The elements of a negligent tort are: 1 ; 2 ; 3 ; 4 ; 5 . A person who commits a tort is called a 6 . The victim of a tort may sue the person who committed the tort and then he (the victim) is referred to in court as the 7 and the other party as the 8 . In most states in the U.S., individuals are not required to act to protect others because there is no 9 imposed by law. In order to have a duty of care, one must be in a 10 with the plaintiff, as is, for example, a babysitter to the baby. A duty of care may also arise from the defendant's 11 , such as his rendering services to the plaintiff for free. A duty of care also arises from the 12 , through ownership or simply possession of the premises; or because the defendant did something to put the plaintiff in danger through his 13 . The standard of care relevant in tort cases is called the 14 . In *Carroll Towing* the issue was raised as to whether an employer is responsible for the torts of his employee. The somewhat antiquated term used for this relationship in the common law is the 15 relationship, which in Latin is called the principle of 16 . It is just one example of 17 , which is the liability one person has for the acts of another. If more than one person is responsible for a tort, we call them 18 . 19 is the responsibility of each of two 18 to compensate the victim for the whole loss, both individually and together. If one party is liable for damages, but a second party is required to pay in case of the first party's default, we say the first party is 20 , whereas the second is 21 . Under the old English doctrine of 22 , the plaintiff was barred from any recovery if he was at all responsible for his own injury. This doctrine has been abandoned and now the doctrine of 23 applies, which reduces the plaintiff's recovery by the percentage his injury resulted from his own fault. The 24 announced in *Carroll Towing* is determined by applying the Learned Hand formula, B < PL. The conditio sine qua non is also referred to as the 25 or as the 26 cause of the plaintiff's harm. Even if the defendant's conduct was the 25 of the plaintiff's injury, it may have been too remote and therefore not the 27 cause of that injury. One way of formulating this test of causation is to ask whether the plaintiff's injury was the 28 of the defendant's negligence. Another way of formulating it is to ask whether the defendant could have <u>29</u> that his conduct would cause the damage it did. If A intends to hit B, but actually hits C, then the doctrine of <u>30</u> will make A liable to C for the intentional <u>31</u> .

II. Fill in the blanks:

In an <u>1</u> for negligence the <u>2</u> has the <u>3</u> of proving facts which give rise to a legal <u>4</u> on the part of the <u>5</u> to conform to the <u>6</u> of conduct established by law for the protection of the <u>2</u> , failure of the <u>5</u> to conform to the <u>6</u> of conduct, that such failure is the <u>7</u> of the harm <u>8</u> by the <u>2</u> , and that the <u>2</u> has in fact <u>8</u> harm of a kind legally compensable by <u>9</u> . If the actor knows or <u>10</u> to know that by his conduct, whether tortious or innocent, he has caused such bodily <u>11</u> to another as to make him helpless and in <u>12</u> of further harm, the actor is under a <u>13</u> to exercise <u>14</u> care to prevent such further harm. In an <u>1</u> for negligence the court determines <u>15</u> the <u>16</u> as to the facts makes an issue upon which the <u>17</u> may reasonably find the existence or non-existence of such facts; <u>15</u> such facts give <u>18</u> to any legal duty on the <u>19</u> of the defendant; the standard of <u>20</u> required of the defendant by his legal duty; <u>15</u> the defendant has conformed to that standard, in any <u>21</u> in which the jury may not <u>22</u> come to a different conclusion; the <u>23</u> of any rules of <u>24</u> determining <u>15</u> the defendant's <u>20</u> is a legal <u>25</u> of harm to the plaintiff; and <u>15</u> the harm claimed to be <u>8</u> by the plaintiff is legally <u>26</u>

Chapter 3
Products Liability

Products liability cases are usually divided into three major groups: 1) cases involving **manufacturing** or **construction defects,** 2) cases involving **design defects,** and 3) cases involving **failure to warn** of an inherent danger. A **manufacturing defect** is a defect that affects only one or a few products of a whole product line. Section A deals with one of the exploding bottle cases, which involve manufacturing defects. Only a few of all the bottles produced leave the assembly line with unnoticed defects, either because of a flaw in the glass or because the bottle has been too highly charged with carbonation. Generally it can be said that courts will always impose a **strict liability standard** in **construction defect** cases. A **design defect** is a defect in all of the products of a product line. It does not arise because a worker failed to be careful constructing the product as it passed through the assembly line, but rather because the way the product was made in general was defective. Section B examines a case involving a home workshop machine that had inadequate screws to hold the wood it was supposed to hold while the machine was in operation. Here all of these machines were essentially the same and all of them had inadequate screws for doing the job they were supposed to do. Design defect cases are more complex than construction defect cases, because the imposition of **strict product liability** depends on a number of factors. A **failure to warn** is a failure to give consumers notice that a product can be dangerous if incorrectly used, or that a product is dangerous but cannot be made any safer in light of the current state of the art. Section C will discuss a failure to warn case in the pharmaceutical industry where the inherent danger in taking a medication was unknown to the manufacturer at the time the drug was marketed. Failure to warn cases present problems similar to design defect cases, because the failure to warn of a danger inherent to a product is often analyzed as being the same as a defect in the design of the product. Accordingly, the case in Section C has been selected not so much for its character as a failure to warn case, but rather because it presents an interesting issue of causation and the burden of proof.

A. Construction Defects

Escola v. Coca Cola Bottling Co.
24 Cal. 2d 453, 150 P.2d 436 (1944)

GIBSON, CHIEF JUSTICE. Plaintiff, a waitress in a restaurant, was injured when a
5   bottle of Coca Cola broke in her hand. She alleged that defendant company, which
had bottled and delivered the alleged defective bottle to her employer, was negligent
in selling "bottles containing said beverage which on account of excessive pressure
of gas or by reason of some defect in the bottle was dangerous ... and likely to
explode." This appeal is from a judgment upon a jury verdict in favor of plaintiff.

10   Defendant's driver delivered several cases of Coca Cola to the restaurant, placing
them on the floor, one on top of the other, under and behind the counter, where they
remained at least thirty-six hours. Immediately before the accident, plaintiff picked
up the top case and set it upon a near-by ice cream cabinet in front of and about three
feet from the refrigerator. She then proceeded to take the bottles from the case with
15   her right hand, one at a time, and put them into the refrigerator. Plaintiff testified that
after she had placed three bottles in the refrigerator and had moved the fourth bottle
about 18 inches from the case 'it exploded in my hand.' The bottle broke into two
jagged pieces and inflicted a deep five-inch cut, severing blood vessels, nerves and
muscles of the thumb and palm of the hand ... A fellow employee, on the opposite
20   side of the counter, testified that plaintiff "had the bottle, I should judge, waist high,
and I know that it didn't bang either the case or the door or another bottle ... when
it popped. It sounded just like a fruit jar would blow up ... The witness further
testified that the contents of the bottle "flew all over herself and myself and the walls
and one thing and another."

25   The top portion of the bottle, with the cap, remained in plaintiff's hand, and the
lower portion fell to the floor but did not break. The broken bottle was not produced
at the trial, the pieces having been thrown away by an employee of the restaurant
shortly after the accident. Plaintiff, however, described the broken pieces, and a
diagram of the bottle was made showing the location of the 'fracture line' where the
30   bottle broke in two.

One of the defendant's drivers, called as a witness by plaintiff, testified that he had
seen other bottles of Coca Cola in the past explode and had found broken bottles in
the warehouse when he took the cases out, but that he did not know what made them
blow up.

35   Plaintiff then rested her case, having announced to the court that being unable to
show any specific acts of negligence she relied completely on the doctrine of res ipsa
loquitur.

Analysis

At the time *Escola* was decided, strict product liability had not yet been adopted either by courts or by the legislatures of the various states. Generally plaintiffs who had been injured by a defective product based their claims on one or more different contract or tort causes of action. The most predominantly employed causes of action were: 1) breach of an **express warranty**, 2) breach of an **implied warranty**, or 3) **negligence**.

An **express warranty** claim was based on a contract closed by the plaintiff and defendant in which the defendant had guaranteed his product. If the product did not perform as guaranteed, the plaintiff could sue for damages for breach of contract. Since this cause of action was contractual, the plaintiff had to show that he was in **privity of contract** with the defendant in order to win the suit. Only the actual parties to a contract are in **privity** of contract. Accordingly, if a consumer purchased a product from a **retailer** who had purchased that product from the manufacturer, the consumer and the manufacturer were not in privity of contract. Consequently, the consumer could only sue the retailer and that only if the consumer had negotiated for an express warranty from the retailer.

Of course, one problem with the express warranty claim was that the buyer had to negotiate to get the warranty at the time he entered into the contract. As products came to be mass produced, the consumer lost contact with the manufacturer of the products she was purchasing. If the manufacturer did not automatically supply an express warranty with the product, the consumer had no warranty claim. To protect buyers, courts began to interpret a warranty into the sales contract running from the seller to the buyer. Consequently, the mere sale of a product implied that the seller was guaranteeing the product for the general purposes for which it was sold. Some disagreement existed in the courts regarding whether a law suit filed on the basis of breach of an **implied warranty** was an action in tort or in contract. If the action was **delictual**, then the buyer would have to prove that the defendant was negligent, but not that he was in privity of any contract with the defendant. If, on the other hand, the action was contractual, the buyer had to be in privity of contract with the defendant to the suit, but did not have to prove that the defendant had acted negligently. Both of these interpretations had their own advantages and disadvantages. The tort cause of action permitted the consumer to sue the manufacturer of the product, but imposed on him the burden of proof of the manufacturer's negligence. The contract cause of action required no proof of the defendant's negligence, but did not permit a consumer who had purchased a product from a retailer to sue the manufacturer of that product, because the consumer was not in privity of contract with him.

As you have just read in *Escola*, the plaintiff based her claim on the defendant's negligence, or on a tort cause of action. Since a restaurant employee had thrown away the bottle that exploded in the plaintiff's hand, the plaintiff had no direct proof that the accident was caused by the defendant's negligence. As you can see (lines 7-8) the plaintiff alleged alternative possible breaches of duty the defendant could have been responsible for, namely using defective bottles, or putting too much carbonation in the beverage. But since she could not prove what precaution the defendant failed to take, she could not carry her **burden of proof** in a negligence action. Accordingly, she relied on the **doctrine of res ipsa loquitur** (line 36). Consider the following section from the *Restatement (Second) Torts* on this doctrine:

§ 328 D. Res Ipsa Loquitur

(1) It may be inferred that harm suffered by the plaintiff is caused by negligence of the defendant when

(a) the event is of a kind which ordinarily does not occur in the absence of negligence;

(b) other responsible causes, including the conduct of the plaintiff and third persons, are sufficiently eliminated by the evidence; and

(c) the indicated negligence is within the scope of the defendant's duty to the plaintiff ...

The doctrine of res ipsa loquitur, meaning the thing speaks for itself, operates to shift the burden of proof from the plaintiff to the defendant in certain types of cases. It assumes that if the accident was the type that normally would not happen in the absence of negligence, and the defendant had total control over the instrumentality which caused the harm, then one can conclude that the defendant was negligent. Of course the plaintiff has to prove that the defendant had a duty of care to the plaintiff and that other causes of the accident can be eliminated. When plaintiff has proved that, the burden of proof on the fault issue shifts to the defendant. This doctrine was used in products liability cases before the strict liability standard replaced it.

Continue reading the case:

Defendant contends that the doctrine of res ipsa loquitur does not apply in this case, and that the evidence is insufficient to support the judgment ... .

40 Res ipsa loquitur does not apply unless (1) defendant had exclusive control of the thing causing the injury and (2) the accident is of such a nature that it ordinarily would not occur in the absence of negligence by the defendant ...

Many authorities state that the happening of the accident does not speak for itself where it took place some time after defendant had relinquished control of the in-
45 strumentality causing the injury. Under the more logical view, however, the doctrine may be applied upon the theory that the defendant had control at the time of the

alleged negligent act, although not at the time of the accident, *provided* plaintiff first proves that the condition of the instrumentality had not been changed after it left the defendant's possession ...

50   Upon an examination of the record, the evidence appears sufficient to support a reasonable inference by defendant. It follows, therefore, that the bottle was in some manner defective at the time defendant relinquished control, because sound and properly prepared bottles of carbonated liquids do not ordinarily explode when carefully handled.

55   The next question, then, is whether plaintiff may rely upon the doctrine of res ipsa loquitur to supply an inference that defendant's negligence was responsible for the defective condition of the bottle at the time it was delivered to the restaurant. Under the general rules pertaining to the doctrine, as set forth above, it must appear that bottles of carbonated liquid are not ordinarily defective without negligence by the
60   bottling company ... .

An explosion such as took place here might have been caused by an excessive internal pressure in a sound bottle, by a defect in the glass of a bottle containing a safe pressure, or by a combination of these two possible causes. The question is whether under the evidence there was a probability that defendant was negligent in any of
65   these respects. If so, the doctrine of res ipsa loquitur applies.

The bottle was admittedly charged with gas under pressure, and the charging of the bottles was within the exclusive control of defendant. As it is a matter of common knowledge that an overcharge would not ordinarily result without negligence, it follows under the doctrine of res ipsa loquitur that if the bottle was in fact excessively
70   charged an inference of defendant's negligence would arise. If the explosion resulted from a defective bottle containing a safe pressure, the defendant would be liable if it negligently failed to discover such flaw. If the defect were visible, an inference of negligence would arise from the failure of defendant to discover it. Where defects are discoverable, it may be assumed that they will not ordinarily escape detection if a
75   reasonable inspection is made, and if such a defect is overlooked an inference arises that a proper inspection was not made. A difficult problem is presented where the defect is unknown and consequently might have been one not discoverable by a reasonable, practicable inspection ...

A chemical engineer for the Owens-Illinois Glass Company and its Pacific Coast
80   subsidiary, maker of Coca Cola bottles, explained how glass is manufactured and the methods used in testing and inspecting bottles. He testified that his company is the largest manufacturer of glass containers in the United States, and that it uses the standard methods for testing bottles recommended by the glass containers association. A pressure test is made by taking a sample from each mold every three hours
85   -- approximately one out of every 600 bottles -- and subjecting the sample to an internal pressure of 450 pounds per square inch, which is sustained for one minute. (The normal pressure in Coca Cola bottles is less than 50 pounds per square inch). The sample bottles are also subjected to the standard thermal shock test. The witness stated that these tests are "pretty near" infallible.

90   It thus appears that there is available to the industry a commonly-used method of

testing bottles for defects not apparent to the eye, which is almost infallible. Since Coca Cola bottles are subjected to these tests by the manufacturer, it is not likely that they contain defects when delivered to the bottler which are not discoverable by visual inspection. Both new and used bottles are filled and distributed by defendant.

95 The used bottles are not again subjected to the tests referred to above, and it may be inferred that defects not discoverable by visual inspection do not develop in bottles after they are manufactured. Obviously, if such defects do occur in used bottles there is a duty upon the bottler to make appropriate tests before they are refilled, and if such tests are not commercially practicable the bottles should not be re-used. This

100 would seem to be particularly true where a charged liquid is placed in the bottle. It follows that a defect which would make the bottle unsound could be discovered by reasonable and practicable tests.

105 Although it is not clear in this case whether the explosion was caused by an excessive charge or a defect in the glass there is a sufficient showing that neither cause would ordinarily have been present if due care had been used. Further, defendant had exclusive control over both the charging and inspection of the bottles. Accordingly, all the requirements necessary to entitle plaintiff to rely on the doctrine of res ipsa

110 loquitur to supply an inference of negligence are present.

It is true that defendant presented evidence tending to show that it exercised considerable precaution by carefully regulating and checking the pressure in the bottles and by making visual inspections for defects in the glass at several stages during the bottling process. It is well settled, however, that when a defendant produces evidence

115 to rebut the inference of negligence which arises upon application of the doctrine of res ipsa loquitur, it is ordinarily a question of fact for the jury to determine whether the inference has been dispelled ...

The judgment is affirmed.

SHENK, CURTIS, CARTER, and SCHAUER, JJ., concurred.

Questions on the Text

☐1 This case extends the doctrine of res ipsa loquitur beyond its original scope as stated by the court in lines 40-42. In what way was the doctrine extended?

☐2 Does the Restatement § 328 D reflect this extension?

☐3 Why was it necessary to extend the doctrine in *Escola*?

☐4 What is the difference between res ipsa loquitur and strict product liability?

Continue reading the case and Justice Traynor's famous concurring opinion:

120 TRAYNOR, JUSTICE.

I concur in the judgment, but I believe the manufacturer's negligence should no longer be singled out as the basis of a plaintiff's right to recover in cases like the present one. In my opinion it should now be recognized that a manufacturer incurs an absolute liability when an article that he has placed on the market, knowing that
125 it is to be used without inspection, proves to have a defect that causes injury to human beings. MacPherson v. Buick Motor Co ... . established the principle, recognized by this court, that irrespective of privity of contract, the manufacturer is responsible for an injury caused by such an article to any person who comes in lawful contact with it ... In these cases the source of the manufacturer's liability was his
130 negligence in the manufacturing process or in the inspection of component parts supplied by others. Even if there is no negligence, however, public policy demands that responsibility be fixed wherever it will most effectively reduce the hazards to life and health inherent in defective products that reach the market. It is evident that the manufacturer can anticipate some hazards and guard against the recurrence of
135 others, as the public cannot. Those who suffer injury from defective products are unprepared to meet its consequences. The cost of an injury and the loss of time or health may be an overwhelming misfortune to the person injured, and a needless one, for the risk of injury can be insured by the manufacturer and distributed among the public as a cost of doing business. It is to the public interest to discourage the
140 marketing of products having defects that are a menace to the public. If such products nevertheless find their way into the market it is to the public interest to place the responsibility for whatever injury they may cause upon the manufacturer, who, even if he is not negligent in the manufacture of the product, is responsible for its reaching the market. However intermittently such injuries may occur and however
145 haphazardly they may strike, the risk of their occurrence is a constant risk and a general one. Against such a risk there should be general and constant protection and the manufacturer is best situated to afford such protection.

The retailer, even though not equipped to test a product, is under an absolute liability to his customer, for the implied warranties of fitness for proposed use and merchant-
150 able quality include a warranty of safety of the product ... This warranty is not necessarily a contractual one ... , for public policy requires that the buyer be insured at the seller's expense against injury ... The courts recognize, however, that the retailer cannot bear the burden of this warranty, and allow him to recoup any losses by means of the warranty of safety attending the wholesaler's or manufacturer's sale
155 to him ... Such a procedure, however, is needlessly circuitous and engenders wasteful litigation. Much would be gained if the injured person could base his action directly on the manufacturer's warranty ...

As handicrafts have been replaced by mass production with its great markets and transportation facilities, the close relationship between the producer and consumer
160 of a product has been altered. Manufacturing processes, frequently valuable secrets, are ordinarily either inaccessible to or beyond the ken of the general public. The consumer no longer has means or skill enough to investigate for himself the sound-

ness of a product, even when it is not contained in a sealed package, and his erstwhile vigilance has been lulled by the steady efforts of manufacturers to build up con-
165   fidence by advertising and marketing devices such as trade-marks ...

The manufacturer's liability should, of course, be defined in terms of the safety of the product in normal and proper use, and should not extend to injuries that cannot be traced to the product as it reached the market.

Questions on the Text

[1]   Give a statement of a) the facts of the case, b) the legal history of the case, c) the issue raised on appeal, and d) the holding.

[2]   Justice Traynor gives a variety of reasons for imposing strict liability on the manufacturer of a defective product. What are they?

[3]   Traynor also bases his arguments on variations of already recognized causes of action for injury caused by defective products. What are they and where can you find them in the text?

[4]   What is the law of products liability in your own country?

B. Design Defects

Greenman v. Yuba Power Products, Inc.
59 Cal.2d 67, 377 P.2d 897 (1963)

TRAYNOR, Justice. Plaintiff brought this action for damages against the retailer
5   and the manufacturer of a Shopsmith, a combination power tool that could be used as a saw, drill, and wood lathe. He saw a Shopsmith demonstrated by the retailer and studied a brochure prepared by the manufacturer. He decided he wanted a Shop-smith for his home workshop, and his wife bought and gave him one for Christmas in 1955. In 1957 he bought the necessary attachments to use the Shopsmith as a lathe
10   for turning a large piece of wood he wished to make into a chalice. After he had worked on the piece of wood several times without difficulty, it suddenly flew out of the machine and struck him on the forehead, inflicting serious injuries. About ten and a half months later, he gave the retailer and the manufacturer written notice of claimed breaches of warranties and filed a complaint against them alleging such
15   breaches and negligence.

After a trial before a jury, the court ruled that there was no evidence that the retailer was negligent or had breached any express warranty and that the manufacturer was not liable for the breach of any implied warranty. Accordingly, it submitted to the

jury only the cause of action alleging breach of implied warranties against the retailer
20 and the causes of action alleging negligence and breach of express warranties against
the manufacturer. The jury returned a verdict for the retailer against plaintiff and for
plaintiff against the manufacturer in the amount of $65,000. The trial court denied
the manufacturer's motion for a new trial and entered judgment on the verdict. The
manufacturer and plaintiff appeal. Plaintiff seeks a reversal of the part of the judg-
25 ment in favor of the retailer, however, only in the event that the part of the judgment
against the manufacturer is reversed.

Analysis

It is somewhat difficult to understand exactly what happened procedurally in
this case. First of all, the plaintiff filed a complaint alleging breach of warranties,
meaning express and implied warranties, and negligence against both the retailer
and the manufacturer of the shopsmith. The trial court judge then submitted the
following causes of action to the jury with the result indicated:

| plaintiff v. retailer | for breach of implied warranties | defendant |
| plaintiff v. manufacturer | for breach of express warranties
for negligence | plaintiff in the amount of
$65,000 |

The judge submits a cause of action to the jury by instructing the jury on the law
with respect to that cause of action and in regard to a particular defendant. It is
therefore left to the judge to determine whether the evidence presented could
support a particular cause of action, which is a legal question. The jury then
deliberates and returns its verdict. In this case the plaintiff lost against the retailer
and won against the manufacturer. The manufacturer then made a **motion for a
new trial**. A motion for a new trial is based on the argument that the trial court
committed **prejudicial error** during the trial. Here, as you will see later in the text,
the manufacturer argued that it was an error for the judge to instruct the jury on
breach of warranties. This type of error is a legal error and can also be the basis
of an appeal. It is **prejudicial** if it could have affected the outcome of the trial.
Otherwise we would say that it is a **harmless error**.

The judge, however, denied the defendant's motion and **entered judgment on the
verdict**, meaning that he officially recorded the jury's verdict thus giving it legal
effect. The manufacturer then appealed the judgment for the plaintiff, and the
plaintiff conditionally appealed the judgment for the retailer. The plaintiff was
interested in appealing this judgment only if the appellate court should reverse
the judgment in his favor against the manufacturer.

Continue reading the case:

Plaintiff introduced substantial evidence that his injuries were caused by defective design and construction of the Shopsmith. His expert witnesses testified that inadequate set screws were used to hold parts of the machine together so that normal
30   vibration caused the tailstock of the lathe to move away from the piece of wood being turned permitting it to fly out of the lathe. They also testified that there were other more positive ways of fastening the parts of the machine together, the use of which would have prevented the accident. The jury could therefore reasonably have concluded that the manufacturer negligently constructed the Shopsmith. The jury
35   could also reasonably have concluded that statements in the manufacturer's brochure were untrue, that they constituted express warranties, and that plaintiff's injuries were caused by their breach.

The manufacturer contends, however, that plaintiff did not give it notice of breach of warranty within a reasonable time and that therefore his cause of action for breach
40   of warranty is barred by section 1769 of the Civil Code. Since it cannot be determined whether the verdict against it was based on the negligence or warranty cause of action or both, the manufacturer concludes that the error in presenting the warranty cause of action to the jury was prejudicial.

Analysis

Again this passage is difficult to understand unless you fully appreciate the nature of a jury trial. In this case the manufacturer argued that the breach of warranty cause of action was barred because the plaintiff had not given timely notice of the breach as required by the **Civil Code**. If we assume for the sake of argument that the manufacturer was right, then we have the following problem. The jury was instructed both on the negligence cause of action and on the breach of express warranties cause of action. After deliberating, the jury returned a **general verdict** in favor of the plaintiff in the amount of $65,000. A **general verdict** does not tell us, however, whether the jury based its verdict on the evidence regarding the breach of express warranties claim or the negligence claim. If the trial court erred as a matter of law by instructing the jury on the breach of express warranties claim and since the verdict might have been based on that claim and not on the negligence claim, then the error could have affected the outcome of the trial. In such case it would be **prejudicial error**, and a new trial would be appropriate.

Continue reading the case:

Section 1769 of the Civil Code provides: "In the absence of express or implied
45   agreement of the parties, acceptance of the goods by the buyer shall not discharge the

seller from liability in damages or other legal remedy for breach of any promise or
warranty in the contract to sell or the sale. But if, after acceptance of the goods, the
buyer fails to give notice to the seller of the breach of any promise or warranty within
a reasonable time after the buyer knows, or ought to know of such breach, the seller
50   shall not be liable therefor."

The notice requirement of section 1769, however, is not an appropriate one for the
court to adopt in actions by injured consumers against manufacturers with whom
they have not dealt ... "As between the immediate parties to the sale [the notice
requirement] is a sound commercial rule, designed to protect the seller against
55   unduly delayed claims for damages. As applied to personal injuries, and notice to a
remote seller, it becomes a booby-trap for the unwary. The injured consumer is
seldom 'steeped in the business practice which justifies the rule,' ... and at least until
he has had legal advice it will not occur to him to give notice to one with whom he
has had no dealings." ... We conclude, therefore, that even if plaintiff did not give
60   timely notice of breach of warranty to the manufacturer, his cause of action based on
the representations contained in the brochure was not barred.

Moreover, to impose strict liability on the manufacturer under the circumstances of
this case, it was not necessary for plaintiff to establish an express warranty as defined
in section 1732 of the Civil Code. A manufacturer is strictly liable in tort when an
65   article he places on the market, knowing that it is to be used without inspection for
defects, proves to have a defect that causes injury to a human being. Recognized first
in the case of unwholesome food products, such liability has now been extended to a
variety of other products that create as great or greater hazards if defective.

Although in these cases strict liability has usually been based on the theory of an
70   express or implied warranty running from the manufacturer to the plaintiff, the
abandonment of the requirement of a contract between them, the recognition that
the liability is not assumed by agreement but imposed by law and the refusal to
permit the manufacturer to define the scope of its own responsibility for defective
products (Henningsen v. Bloomfield Motors, Inc., ...) make clear that the liability is
75   not one governed by the law of contract warranties but by the law of strict liability
in tort. Accordingly, rules defining and governing warranties that were developed to
meet the needs of commercial transactions cannot properly be invoked to govern the
manufacturer's liability to those injured by their defective products unless those rules
also serve the purposes for which such liability is imposed.

Questions on the Text

1. To uphold the verdict in this case, Justice Traynor has taken several courses
    of action. What is the first one? Would it have been sufficient to uphold the
    trial court's judgment in this case?
2. What was Traynor's second course of action? Which of the two holdings do
    you think made this case famous?

[3] Note the ratio decidendi in lines 69-79. Traynor briefly describes case law development in lines 69-76 noting three decisive judicial moves. What were they?

[4] In *Henningsen*, which the court cites, an automobile manufacturer sold its cars with an express **disclaimer** of any warranty other than for replacement of defective parts. Here the court held that the disclaimer was invalid. What do you think might have been the ratio decidendi of *Henningsen*? Perhaps it would help you to know that the form contract used by the manufacturer and dealer was a contract drawn up by an association of automobile manufacturers and that all manufacturers in the U.S. used it.

Continue reading the case:

80 We need not recanvass the reasons for imposing strict liability on the manufacturer. They have been fully articulated in the cases cited above ... The purpose of such liability is to insure that the costs of injuries resulting from defective products are borne by the manufacturers that put such products on the market rather than by the injured persons who are powerless to protect themselves. Sales warranties serve this

85 purpose fitfully at best ... In the present case, for example, plaintiff was able to plead and prove an express warranty only because he read and relied on the representations of the Shopsmith's ruggedness contained in the manufacturer's brochure. Implicit in the machine's presence on the market, however, was a representation that it would safely do the jobs for which it was built. Under these circumstances, it

90 should not be controlling whether plaintiff selected the machine because of the statements in the brochure, or because of the machine's own appearance of excellence that belied the defect lurking beneath the surface, or because he merely assumed that it would safely do the jobs it was built to do. It should not be controlling whether the details of the sales from manufacturer to retailer and from retailer to

95 plaintiff's wife were such that one or more of the implied warranties of the sales act arose (Civ. Code, § 1735). "The remedies of injured consumers ought not to be made to depend upon the intricacies of the law of sales." ... To establish the manufacturer's liability it was sufficient that plaintiff proved that he was injured while using the Shopsmith in a way it was intended to be used as a result of a defect in design and

100 manufacture of which plaintiff was not aware that made the Shopsmith unsafe for its intended use ...

The judgment is affirmed.

Analysis

The last sentence of the opinion is the most important statement of the law in this case and, as it turned out, for many future cases to come. It requires a plaintiff to **plead and prove** 1) injury, 2) product defect that makes the product unsafe for its intended use, and 3) causal relation between the defect and the injury. Saying that the plaintiff must **plead and prove** certain facts is another way of saying that these facts define a cause of action. The plaintiff must **plead** these facts in his complaint and must **prove** them at trial to be successful against the defendant. Another way of referring to what the plaintiff has to plead and prove is to say that a certain set of facts make out the plaintiff's **prima facie case**. Once a plaintiff has offered proof of all of the facts that compose his cause of action, the **burden of proof shifts** to the defendant to disprove them.

The precedents set by this decision and others based on it were included in the *Restatement (Second) Torts*. Traynor obviously intended to establish a precedent for strict products liability in tort. Read the following section of the *Restatement*, and particularly the comments to § 402 A. When is liability really strict and when does it depend on negligence? *Nota bene*: Use of the word **reasonable** is usually an indication that negligence plays some role in the determination of liability.

Restatement (Second) Torts

§ 402 A. Special Liability of Seller of Product for Physical Harm to User or Consumer

(1) One who sells any product in a defective condition unreasonably dangerous to the user or consumer or to his property is subject to liability for physical harm thereby caused to the ultimate user or consumer, or to his property, if

(a) the seller is engaged in the business of selling such a product, and

(b) it is expected to and does reach the user or consumer without substantial change in the condition in which it is sold.

(2) The rule stated in Subsection (1) applies although

(a) the seller has exercised all possible care in the preparation and sale of his product, and

(b) the user or consumer has not bought the product from or entered into any contractual relation with the seller.

Comment:

g. Defective condition. The rule stated in this Section applies only where the product is, at the time it leaves the seller's hands, in a condition not contemplated by the ultimate consumer, which will be unreasonably dangerous to him. The seller is not liable when he delivers the product in a safe condition, and subsequent mishandling or other causes make it harmful by the time it is consumed. The burden of proof that the product was in a defective condition at the time that it left the hands of the particular seller is upon the injured plaintiff; and unless evidence can be produced which will support the conclusion that it was then defective, the burden is not sustained ...

h. A product is not in a defective condition when it is safe for normal handling and consumption. If the injury results from abnormal handling, as where a bottled beverage is knocked against a radiator to remove a cap, or from abnormal preparation for use, as where too much salt is added to food, or from abnormal consumption, as where a child eats too much candy and is made ill, the seller is not liable. Where, however, he has reason to anticipate that danger may result from a particular use, as where a drug is sold which is safe only in limited doses, he may be required to give adequate warning of the danger (see Comment j), and a product sold without such warning is in a defective condition.

The defective condition may arise not only from harmful ingredients, not characteristic of the product itself either as to presence or quantity, but also from foreign objects contained in the product, from decay or deterioration before sale, or from the way in which it is supplied; and the two are purchased by the user or consumer as an integrated whole. Where the container is itself dangerous, the product is sold in a defective condition ...

i. **Unreasonably dangerous.** The rule stated in this Section applies only where the defective condition of the product makes it unreasonably dangerous to the user or consumer. Many products cannot possibly be made entirely safe for all consumption, and any food or drug necessarily involves some risk of harm, if only from overconsumption. Ordinary sugar is a deadly poison to diabetics, and castor oil found use under Mussolini as an instrument of torture. That is not what is meant by "unreasonably dangerous" in this Section. The article sold must be dangerous to an extent beyond that which would be contemplated by the ordinary consumer who purchases it, with the ordinary knowledge common to the community as to its characteristics. Good whiskey is not unreasonably dangerous merely because it will make some people drunk, and is especially dangerous to alcoholics; but bad whiskey, containing a dangerous amount of fusel oil, is unreasonably dangerous ...

j. **Directions or warning.** In order to prevent the product from being unreasonably dangerous, the seller may be required to give directions or warning, on the container, as to its use. The seller may reasonably assume that those with common allergies, as for example to eggs or strawberries, will be aware of them, and he is not required to warn against them. Where, however, the product contains an ingredient to which a substantial number of the population are allergic, and the ingredient is one whose danger is not generally known, or if known is one which the consumer would reasonably not expect to find in the product, the seller is required to give warning against it, if he has knowledge, or by the application of reasonable, developed human skill and foresight should have knowledge, of the presence of the ingredient and the danger. Likewise in the case of poisonous drugs, or those unduly dangerous for other reasons, warning as to use may be required.

But a seller is not required to warn with respect to products, or ingredients in them which are only dangerous, or potentially so, when consumed in excessive quantity, or over a long period of time, when the danger or potentiality of danger, is generally known and recognized. Again the dangers of alcoholic beverages are an example, as are also those of foods containing such substances as saturated fats, which may over a period of time have a deleterious effect upon the human heart.

Where warning is given, the seller may reasonably assume that it will be read and heeded; and a product bearing such a warning, which is safe for use if it is followed, is not in defective condition, nor is it unreasonably dangerous.

k. Unavoidably unsafe products. There are some products which, in the present state of human knowledge, are quite incapable of being made safe for their intended and ordinary use. These are especially common in the field of drugs. An outstanding example is the vaccine for the Pasteur treatment of rabies, which not uncommonly leads to very serious and damaging consequences when it is injected. Since the disease itself invariably leads to a dreadful death, both the marketing and the use of the vaccine are fully justified, notwithstanding the unavoidable high degree of risk which they involve. Such a product, properly prepared, and accompanied by proper directions and warning, is not defective, nor is it *unreasonably* dangerous. The same is true of many other drugs, vaccines, and the like, many of which for this very reason cannot legally be sold except to physicians, or under the prescription of a physician. It is also true in particular of many new or experimental drugs as to which, because of lack of time and opportunity for sufficient medical experience, there can be no assurance of safety, or perhaps even of purity of ingredients, but such experience as there is justifies the marketing and use of the drug notwithstanding a medically recognizable risk. The seller of such products, again with the qualification that they are properly prepared and marketed, and proper warning is given, where the situation calls for it, is not to be held to strict liability for unfortunate consequences attending their use, merely because he has undertaken to supply the public with an apparently useful and desirable product, attended with a known but apparently reasonable risk ...

n. Contributory negligence. Since the liability with which this Section deals is not based upon negligence of the seller, but is strict liability, the rule applied to strict liability cases applies. Contributory negligence of the plaintiff is not a defense when such negligence consists merely in a failure to discover the defect in the product, or to guard against the possibility of its existence. On the other hand the form of contributory negligence which consists in voluntarily and unreasonably proceeding to encounter a known danger, and commonly passes under the name of assumption of risk, is a defense under this Section as in other cases of strict liability. If the user or consumer discovers the defect and is aware of the danger, and nevertheless proceeds unreasonably to make use of the product and is injured by it, he is barred from recovery.

C. Failure to Warn

Failure to warn cases are based on § 402 A as well. As you have just read in Comment h. to § 402 A, a "product sold without [adequate] warning is in a defective condition." Comment k. indicates that unavoidably unsafe products, if accompanied by adequate warnings, are not defective or unreasonably dangerous. Accordingly, a product that cannot be made safe can still be marketed with impunity if it is accompanied by sufficient warning of its inherent dangers. A particular problem is raised when a manufacturer cannot possibly know of the dangers a product poses and thus cannot provide adequate warnings when distributing the product. One type of dangerous activity, the marketing of prescription drugs, has caused the courts considerable problems. If the manufacturer knows of potentially dangerous side-effects, it can provide the appropriate warnings. If it does not, it could simply warn consumers that the drug is experimental, or tell consumers to beware of unknown dangers. The latter warning, however, seems almost empty of effect. The following case has been selected not only for its failure to warn aspect, but also because of the interesting causation issue it raises.

Sindell v. Abbott Laboratories
26 Cal. 3d 588, 607 P.2d 924, 163 Cal. Rptr. 132 (1980)

MOSK, Justice.

5   This case involves a complex problem both timely and significant: may a plaintiff, injured as the result of a drug administered to her mother during pregnancy, who knows the type of drug involved but cannot identify the manufacturer of the precise product, hold liable for her injuries a maker of a drug produced from an identical formula?

10   Plaintiff Judith Sindell brought an action against eleven drug companies and Does 1 through 100, on behalf of herself and other women similarly situated. The complaint alleged as follows:

Between 1941 and 1971, the defendants were engaged in the business of manufacturing, promoting, and marketing diethylstilbesterol (DES), a drug which is a syn-
15   thetic compound of the female hormone estrogen. The drug was administered to the plaintiff's mother and the mothers of the class she represents, for the purpose of preventing miscarriage. In 1947, the Food and Drug Administration authorized the marketing of DES as a miscarriage preventative, but only on an experimental basis, with a requirement that the drug contain a warning label to that effect.

20   DES may cause cancerous vaginal and cervical growths in the daughters exposed to it before birth, because their mothers took the drug during pregnancy … . DES also causes adenosis, precancerous vaginal and cervical growths which may spread to other areas of the body … Women who suffer from this condition must be monitored by biopsy or colposcopic examination twice a year, a painful and expensive proce-
25   dure. Thousands of women whose mothers received DES during pregnancy are unaware of the effects of the drug.

In 1971, the Food and Drug Administration ordered defendants to cease marketing and promoting DES for the purpose of preventing miscarriages, and to warn physicians and the public that the drug should not be used by pregnant women because of
30   the danger to their unborn children.

During the period defendants marketed DES, they knew or should have known that
it was a carcinogenic substance, that there was a grave danger after varying periods
of latency it would cause cancerous and precancerous growths in the daughters of
the mothers who took it, and that it was ineffective to prevent miscarriage. Neverthe-
35   less, the defendants continued to advertise and market the drug as a miscarriage
preventative. They failed to test DES for efficacy and safety; the tests performed by
others, upon which they relied, indicated that it was not safe or effective. In violation
of the authorization of the Food and Drug Administration, the defendants marketed
DES on an unlimited basis rather than as an experimental drug, and they failed to
40   warn of its potential danger.

Because of defendants' advertised assurances that DES was safe and effective to
prevent miscarriage, plaintiff was exposed to the drug prior to her birth ... As a result
of the DES ingested by her mother, the plaintiff developed a malignant bladder tumor
which was removed by surgery. She suffers from adenosis and has constantly to be
45   monitored by biopsy or colposcopy to insure early warning of further malignancy.

The first cause of action alleges that the defendants were jointly and individually
negligent in that they manufactured, marketed and promoted DES as a safe and
efficacious drug to prevent miscarriage, without adequate testing or warning, and
without monitoring or reporting its effects. A separate cause of action alleges that the
50   defendants were jointly liable regardless of which particular brand of DES was
ingested by the plaintiff's mother because the defendants collaborated in marketing,
promoting and testing the drug, relied upon each other's tests, and adhered to an
industry-wide safety standard. DES was produced from a common and mutually
agreed upon formula as a fungible drug interchangeable with other brands of the
55   same product; defendants knew or should have known that it was customary for
doctors to prescribe the drug by its generic rather than its brand name and that
pharmacists filled prescriptions from whatever brand of the drug happened to be in
stock.

Other causes of action are based upon theories of strict liability, violation of express
60   and implied warranties, false and fraudulent representations, misbranding of drugs
in violation of federal law, conspiracy and "lack of consent."

Each cause of action alleges that defendants are jointly liable because they acted in
concert, on the basis of express and implied agreements, and in reliance upon and
ratification and exploitation of each other's testing and marketing methods.

65   Plaintiff seeks compensatory damages of $1 million and punitive damages of $10
million for herself. For the members of her class, she prays for equitable relief in the
form of an order that defendants warn physicians and others of the danger of DES
and the necessity of performing certain tests to determine the presence of disease
caused by the drug, and that they establish free clinics in California to perform such
70   tests.

Defendants demurred to the complaint. While the complaint did not expressly allege
that plaintiff could not identify the manufacturer of the precise drug ingested by her
mother, she stated in her points and authorities in opposition to the demurrers filed
by some of the defendants that she was unable to make the identification, and the

75 trial court sustained the demurrers of these defendants without leave to amend on the ground that plaintiff did not and stated she could not identify which defendant had manufactured the drug responsible for her injuries. Thereupon, the court dismissed the action. This appeal involves only five of ten defendants named in the complaint ...

Questions on the Text

[1] What is the significance of the statement in line 11: "on behalf of herself and other women similarly situated"? You may be confused by the expression "Does 1 through 100." In the United States we often use the fictional names "John Doe" or "Richard Roe" to mean just anyone. "Does 1 through 100" therefore means 100 individuals who remain unnamed, in this case as defendants.

[2] What do the words "knew or should have know" (line 31) refer to in a legal sense?

[3] In line 60 the court indicates that one cause of action was based on "false and fraudulent representations." A **representation** is a statement or claim. What is the difference between a false and a fraudulent representation? Consider the following section of the *Restatement (Second) Torts*:

§. 402 B. Misrepresentation by Seller of Chattels to Consumer

One engaged in the business of selling chattels who, by advertising, labels, or otherwise, makes to the public a misrepresentation of a material fact concerning the character or quality of a chattel sold by him is subject to liability for physical harm to a consumer of the chattel caused by justifiable reliance upon the misrepresentation, even though

(a) it is not made fraudulently or negligently, and

(b) the consumer has not bought the chattel from or entered into any contractual relation with the seller.

Does § 402 B impose strict liability on a manufacturer for misrepresentations? Does every misrepresentation permit a consumer to sue for injury from the product?

[4] The plaintiff here sought **punitive damages**. Punitive damages, as the name indicates, are intended to punish the defendant. They are not accepted in Germany in an action brought by a private party. What arguments can you give in favor of and opposed to private parties being able to sue for punitive damages?

[5] The plaintiff also sought **equitable relief** for the members of her class. Dam-

ages, whether compensatory or punitive, is a common law remedy. Orders issuing from a court commanding individuals to do or not do something are equitable. In Unit I on contracts you have read about some equitable principles. What are they?

6 In line 75 the court states that the "trial court sustained the demurrers of these defendants without leave to amend ... " What do you think was the basis of the demurrers? What do you think "without leave to amend" means?

Continue reading the case:

80   We begin with the proposition that, as a general rule, the imposition of liability depends upon a showing by the plaintiff that his or her injuries were caused by the act of the defendant or by an instrumentality under the defendant's control.

There are, however, exceptions to this rule. Plaintiff's complaint suggests several bases upon which defendants may be held liable for her injuries even though she
85   cannot demonstrate the name of the manufacturer which produced the DES actually taken by her mother. The first of these theories, classically illustrated by *Summers v. Tice* (1948) 33 Cal.2d 80, 199 P.2d 1, places the burden of proof of causation upon tortious defendants in certain circumstances. The second basis of liability emerging from the complaint is that defendants acted in concert to cause injury to plaintiff.
90   There is a third and novel approach to the problem, sometimes called the theory of "enterprise liability," but which we prefer to designate by the more accurate term of "industry-wide" liability, which might obviate the necessity for identifying the manufacturer of the injury-causing drug. We shall conclude that these doctrines, as previously interpreted, may not be applied to hold defendants liable under the
95   allegations of this complaint. However, we shall propose and adopt a fourth basis for permitting the action to be tried, grounded upon an extension of the *Summers* doctrine.

I

100   Plaintiff places primary reliance upon cases which hold that if a party cannot identify which of two or more defendants caused an injury, the burden of proof may shift to the defendants to show that they were not responsible for the harm. This principle is sometimes referred to as the "alternative liability" theory.

The celebrated case of *Summers v. Tice*, ... a unanimous opinion of this court, best
105   exemplifies the rule. In *Summers*, the plaintiff was injured when two hunters negligently shot in his direction. It could not be determined which of them had fired the shot which actually caused the injury to the plaintiff's eye, but both defendants were nevertheless held jointly and severally liable for the whole of the damages. We reasoned that both were wrongdoers, both were negligent toward the plaintiff, and
110   that it would be unfair to require plaintiff to isolate the defendant responsible, because if the one pointed out were to escape liability, the other might also, and the plaintiff-victim would be shorn of any remedy. In these circumstances, we held, the burden of proof shifted to the defendants, "each to absolve himself if he can." ... We

stated that under these or similar circumstances a defendant is ordinarily in a "far
115 better position" to offer evidence to determine whether he or another defendant
caused the injury ... .

Defendants maintain that, while in *Summers* there was a 50 percent chance that one
of the two defendants was responsible for the plaintiff's injuries, here since any one
120 of 200 companies which manufactured DES might have made the product which
harmed plaintiff, there is no rational basis upon which to infer that any defendant in
this action caused plaintiff's injuries, nor even a reasonable possibility that they were
responsible. These arguments are persuasive if we measure the chance that any one
of the defendants supplied the injury-causing drug by the number of possible tortfea-
125 sors. In such a context, the possibility that any of the five defendants supplied the
DES to plaintiff's mother is so remote that it would be unfair to require each defendant to exonerate itself. There may be a substantial likelihood that none of the five
defendants joined in the action made the DES which caused the injury, and that the
offending producer not named would escape liability altogether. While we propose,
130 infra, an adaptation of the rule in *Summers* which will substantially overcome these
difficulties, defendants appear to be correct that the rule, as previously applied,
cannot relieve plaintiff of the burden of proving the identity of the manufacturer
which made the drug causing her injuries ... .

Questions on the Text

[1] What is the real thrust of the defendants' arguments here? Why do they
claim that this case is fundamentally different from *Summers v. Tice*?

[2] Would the defendants in *Summers v. Tice* also be held liable under the law of
your own legal system?

Continue reading the case:

III

135 A third theory upon which plaintiff relies is the concept of industry-wide liability, or
according to the terminology of the parties, "enterprise liability." This theory was
suggested in *Hall v. E. I. Du Pont de Nemours & Co., Inc.* (E.D.N.Y. 1972) 345 F.
Supp. 353. In that case, plaintiffs were 13 children injured by the explosion of
blasting caps in 12 separate incidents which occurred in 10 different states between
140 1955 and 1959. The defendants were six blasting cap manufacturers, comprising
virtually the entire blasting cap industry in the United States, and their trade association ...

The court reasoned as follows: there was evidence that defendants, acting independently, had adhered to an industry-wide standard with regard to the safety
145 features of blasting caps, that they had in effect delegated some functions of safety

investigation and design, such as labelling, to their trade association, and that there
was industry-wide cooperation in the manufacture and design of blasting caps. In
these circumstances, the evidence supported a conclusion that all the defendants
jointly controlled the risk. Thus, if plaintiffs could establish by a preponderance of
150 the evidence that the caps were manufactured by one of the defendants, the burden
of proof as to causation would shift to all the defendants. The court noted that this
theory of liability applied to industries composed of a small number of units, and that
what would be fair and reasonable with regard to an industry of five or ten producers
might be manifestly unreasonable if applied to a decentralized industry composed of
155 countless small producers ...

We decline to apply this theory in the present case. At least 200 manufacturers
produced DES; *Hall*, which involved 6 manufacturers representing the entire blasting cap industry in the United States, cautioned against application of the doctrine
espoused therein to a large number of producers ... Moreover, in *Hall*, the conclu-
160 sion that the defendants jointly controlled the risk was based upon allegations that
they had delegated some functions relating to safety to a trade association. There are
no such allegations here, ...

Equally important, the drug industry is closely regulated by the Food and Drug
Administration, which actively controls the testing and manufacture of drugs and
165 the method by which they are marketed, including the contents of warning labels. To
a considerable degree, therefore, the standards followed by drug manufacturers are
suggested or compelled by the government. Adherence to those standards cannot, of
course, absolve a manufacturer of liability to which it would otherwise be subject ...
But since the government plays such a pervasive role in formulating the criteria for
170 the testing and marketing of drugs, it would be unfair to impose upon a manufacturer liability for injuries resulting from the use of a drug which it did not supply
simply because it followed the standards of the industry.

IV

175 If we were confined to the theories of *Summers* and *Hall*, we would be constrained
to hold that the judgment must be sustained. Should we require that plaintiff identify
the manufacturer which supplied the DES used by her mother or that all DES
manufacturers be joined in the action, she would effectively be precluded from any
recovery. As defendants candidly admit, there is little likelihood that all the manufac-
180 turers who made DES at the time in question are still in business or that they are
subject to the jurisdiction of the California courts. There are, however, forceful
arguments in favor of holding that plaintiff has a cause of action ...

Where, as here, all defendants produced a drug from an identical formula and the
manufacturer of the DES which caused plaintiff's injuries cannot be identified
185 through no fault of plaintiff, a modification of the rule of *Summers* is warranted. As
we have seen, an undiluted *Summers* rationale is inappropriate to shift the burden of
proof of causation to defendants because if we measured the chance that any particular manufacturer supplied the injury-causing product by the number of producers of
DES, there is a possibility that none of the five defendants in this case produced the

190 offending substance and that the responsible manufacturer, not named in the action, will escape liability.

But we approach the issue of causation from a different perspective: we hold it to be reasonable in the present context to measure the likelihood that any of the defendants supplied the product which allegedly injured plaintiff by the percentage which

195 the DES sold by each of them for the purpose of preventing miscarriage bears to the entire production of the drug sold by all for that purpose. Plaintiff asserts in her briefs that Eli Lilly and Company and five or six other companies produced 90 percent of the DES marketed. If at trial this is established to be the fact, then there is a corresponding likelihood that this comparative handful of producers manufac-

200 tured the DES which caused plaintiffs injuries, and only a 10 percent likelihood that the offending producer would escape liability.

If plaintiff joins in the action the manufacturers of a substantial share of the DES which her mother might have taken, the injustice of shifting the burden of proof to defendants to demonstrate that they could not have made the substance which

205 injured plaintiff is significantly diminished. While 75 to 80 percent of the market is suggested as the requirement ... , we hold only that a substantial percentage is required.

The presence in the action of a substantial share of the appropriate market also provides a ready means to apportion damages among the defendants. Each defend-

210 ant will be held liable for the proportion of the judgment represented by its share of that market unless it demonstrates that it could not have made the product which caused plaintiff's injuries. In the present case, as we have seen, one DES manufacturer was dismissed from the action upon filing a declaration that it had not manufactured DES until after plaintiff was born. Once plaintiff has met her burden of joining the

215 required defendants, they in turn may cross-complain against other DES manufacturers, not joined in the action, which they can allege might have supplied the injury-causing product.

Under this approach, each manufacturer's liability would approximate its responsibility for the injuries caused by its own products. Some minor discrepancy in the

220 correlation between market share and liability is inevitable; therefore, a defendant may be held liable for a somewhat different percentage of the damage than its share of the appropriate market would justify. It is probably impossible, with the passage of time, to determine market share with mathematical exactitude. But just as a jury cannot be expected to determine the precise relationship between fault and liability

225 in applying the doctrine of comparative fault ... the difficulty of apportioning damages among the defendant producers in exact relation to their market share does not seriously militate against the rule we adopt. As we said in *Summers* with regard to the liability of independent tortfeasors, where a correct division of liability cannot be made "the trier of fact may make it the best it can." ...

230 We are not unmindful of the practical problems involved in defining the market and determining market share, but these are largely matters of proof which properly cannot be determined at the pleading stage of these proceedings. Defendants urge that it would be both unfair and contrary to public policy to hold them liable for

plaintiffs injuries in the absence of proof that one of them supplied the drug respon-
235 sible for the damage. Most of their arguments, however, are based upon the assumption that one manufacturer would be held responsible for the products of another or
for those of all other manufacturers if plaintiff ultimately prevails. But under the rule
we adopt, each manufacturer's liability for an injury would be approximately equivalent to the damages caused by the DES it manufactured.

240 The judgments are reversed.

BIRD, C. J., and NEWMAN and WHITE, JJ., concur.

RICHARDSON, Justice, dissenting.

Questions on the Text

[1] In lines 180-181, the court refers to the defendants' argument that some of
the DES producers may not be **subject to the jurisdiction** of the California
courts. What does that mean? What difference does that make in this case?

[2] Assuming that the plaintiff manages to join a substantial percentage of the
producers of DES as defendants. What does the court indicate the defendants can do if they are of the opinion that some other manufacturer produced the DES plaintiff's mother took? Will the defendants have some of the
same problems here as the original plaintiff?

[3] *Sindell* is primarily famous for its novel market-share liability holding. The
court, however, notes that there may be a few problems determining exactly
what each defendant's share of the market was at the time the plaintiff's
mother took the drug. The court, however, compares these problems to the
problem of determining **comparative fault** with any degree of exactitude.
Comparative fault refers to the doctrine of **comparative negligence** you have
already read about. What is the important difference between the problems
presented in *Sindell* and the problems presented in determining comparative
fault?

Terminology

manufacturing defect **construction defect**	product defect that affects only a few products of a product line; defect that arises from faulty construction of the particular pro- duct as it moves through the assembly line (**Konstruktionsfehler, der in der Anfertigung eines konkreten Produkts liegt**)
design defect	product defect that affects all products of a product line because

	the product was not conceived in a way that would make it safe to use (**Konstruktionsfehler, der im Design eines Produkts liegt**)
failure to warn	manufacturer's omitting to inform consumers of a danger inherent to a product if it is used incorrectly or because it cannot be made any safer in light of the current state of the art (**Verletzung der Aufklärungspflicht**)
to rest one's case	to close the presentation of one's evidence at trial (**sein Vorbringen vorläufig abschließen**)
express warranty	guarantee that is actually stated; purchaser needs to negotiate with seller to obtain it (**ausdrückliche Zusicherung, ausdrückliche Gewährleistung**)
implied warranty	guarantee that a court will assume exists from the conduct of the party (**konkludente Gewährleistung**); generally courts assume that a product placed on the market is safe for its intended or reasonably foreseeable use (**implied warranty of merchantability**) (**Gewährleistung der handelsüblichen Qualität**); if a seller knew of the particular purpose for which the buyer purchased the product, courts will also assume that the product is safe for this particular use (**implied warranty of fitness for use**) (**Gewährleistung der Eignung für den vertraglichen Zweck**)
privity of contract	legal requirement that one must be a party to a contract in order to be permitted to sue for its breach; doctrine prevented consumers who bought a product from a retailer from suing the manufacturer of the product because the consumer had no contractual relation with the manufacturer (**Stellung als Vertragspartei**)
retailer	merchant who sells to the ultimate consumer (**Einzelhändler**)
wholesaler	middleman in distribution chain, e.g. one who buys from manufacturer and sells to retailer (**Großhändler**)
res ipsa loquitur	the thing speaks for itself; name of doctrine which shifts the burden of proof of the defendant's negligence from the plaintiff to the defendant when the defendant had exclusive control over the thing which caused the plaintiff's injury and the accident would not normally have occurred in the absence of the defendant's negligence
trademark	sign or mark on a product that identifies the manufacturer of the product (**Warenzeichen**)
prejudicial error	an error of law made by the trial court that could have affected the outcome of the case; an error so serious it warrants reversal of the trial court's judgment; also **reversible error** (**Rechtsfehler, der einen Revisionsgrund darstellt**)
harmless error	an error of law that could not have affected the outcome of the trial; an error so insignificant it will not be the basis of reversal on appeal (**unerheblicher Rechtsfehler**)

disclaimer	an express statement that one refuses to include certain types of harm, or that one will pay only for certain types of harm, within the context of a warranty (**Haftungsausschlußklausel**)
sales act	law on the sale of goods (**Kaufrecht**)
assumption of risk	"The doctrine of assumption of risk, also known as volenti non fit injuria, means legally that a plaintiff may not recover for an injury to which he assents, *i.e.*, that a person may not recover for an injury received when he voluntarily exposes himself to a known and appreciated danger. The requirements for the defense of volenti non fit injuria are that: (1) the plaintiff has knowledge of facts constituting a dangerous condition, (2) he knows the condition is dangerous, (3) he appreciates the nature or extent of the danger, and (4) he voluntarily exposes himself to the danger ... " *Black's Law Dictionary* (**volenti non fit injuria**)
misrepresentation	statement or claim that is untrue; any method of expressing s.th. that is not true; also **false representation** (**falsche Angaben, Irrtumserregung, irreführende Angaben**)
alternative liability	responsibility imposed on all potential defendants when one of two or more of them caused plaintiff's injuries and plaintiff cannot prove which one of the defendants actually caused the injury (**Haftung der Beteiligten**); an alternative liability theory shifts the burden of proof on the causation issue to the defendants and if they cannot prove who was not at fault they will be held **jointly and severally liable**
enterprise liability **industry-wide liability**	joint liability of all manufacturers of a defective product when plaintiff cannot prove which one of the defendants actually produced the product that caused plaintiff's injuries; shifts burden of proof to defendants on causation issue; is only applied when all manufacturers adhere to an industry-wide safety standard, all products are generically similar, and plaintiff presents adequate proof that the injury was caused by a product produced by one of the defendants joined in the action
market-share liability	liability of each of a number of defendants all of whom produced a defective product when plaintiff cannot show which defendant actually produced the product that caused plaintiff's injuries; burden of proof on causation issue shifts to the defendants; each defendant held liable for the proportion of the final judgment represented by its share of the market (**Haftung nach dem Marktanteil**)

Terminology Review

to shift the burden of proof (I.I.2)	places burden of proving truth of s.th. on the other party; a shift in the burden of proof occurs when the plaintiff has made a prima facie case, meaning the plaintiff has offered proof of all of the elements of his cause of action; the burden of proof then shifts to the defendant; the burden of proof can also shift when the plaintiff is relieved of proving all of the traditional elements of his cause of action, such as in the res ipsa loquitur cases, where the plaintiff does not have to prove that the defendant was negligent (**Umkehr der Beweislast**)
record (I.I.1)	all of the documents relevant to a law suit assembled by the court (ca. **Gerichtsakten, Protokoll**)
personal jurisdiction (I.II.1)	authority of a court to reach decisions binding on the defendant in the case (**Gerichtshoheit über eine Person**)
cross-complaint (I.III.2)	complaint filed by the defendant to a law suit against any other person who is directly involved in the controversy (**Streitverkündung**)

Vocabulary

to absolve	to excuse, to take away blame from
to adhere to	to stick to, to follow
to belie	to tell lies about s.th.
booby-trap	trap laid to play a trick on s.o.
blasting caps	small closed tubes containing explosives
candid	open and honest, straightforward
chalice	goblet
deleterious	harmful, detrimental
to dispel	to clear away, to get rid of, to drive out
to engender	to bring forth, to create
erstwhile	former, previous
to espouse	to adopt, to accept as one's own
to exonerate	to excuse, to take a burden off of s.th. or s.o.
extraneous	external to s.th., coming from outside

fitfully	irregularly
fungible	interchangeable
haphazard	without plan or pattern, random
to heed	to pay attention to, to follow
infallible	without error or mistake
intermittent	occasional, irregular
intricacy	complexity
ken	range of knowledge or understanding
lathe	machine that turns wood so it can be evenly cut and shaped
to lull	to calm, to quiet
to lurk	to lie hidden waiting to appear or attack
to militate against	to oppose
to preclude	to shut out from the beginning, to prevent
proposition	statement
rabies	fatal disease transmitted through saliva when bitten by a rabid animal
to recoup	to make up for, to get compensation for loss
recurrence	repetition, re-happening
rugged	hardy, heavy-duty
to be shorn	to be shaved, to be cut off from
to steep	to soak in s.th., to saturate with s.th.
tailstock	end of lathe that holds wood and can be swung open and closed
unduly	unreasonably, without good reason
unwary	unaware, not noticing s.th.
workshop	room where one keeps tools and does craftwork

Suggested Reading

Guido Calabresi, *The Costs of Accidents* (1970)

R.H. Coase, "The Problem of Social Cost," *The Journal of Law & Economics*, vol. III, p. 1 (1960)

George P. Fletcher, "Fairness and Utility in Tort Theory," *Harvard Law Review*, vol. 85, p. 537 (1972)

Mark F. Grady, *Cases and Materials on Torts*, West Publishing Co.: St. Paul, Minn. (1994)

Mark F. Grady, "Untaken Precautions," *Journal of Legal Studies*, vol. XVIII, p. 139 (1989)

Mark F. Grady, "Res Ipsa Loquitur and Compliance Error," *University of Pennsylvania Law Review*, vol. 142, p. 887 (1994)

W. Page Keeton, et al. *Prosser and Keeton on The Law of Torts* (5th ed.) West Publishing Co. St. Paul, Minn. (1984)

William Landes & Richard Posner, *The Economic Structure of Tort Law* (1987)

BMW of North America, Inc. v. Gore, U.S. Supreme Court decision, May 20, 1996

Bolton v. Stone, [1951] A.C. 850, 1 All E.R. 1078

Manning v. Grimsley, 643 F.2d 20 (1981)

O'Donnell Transportation Co. v. M. & J. Tracy, Inc. 150 F.2d 735 (1945)

Regina v. Collins [1973] Q.B. 100, [1972] 2 All E.R. 1105

Summers v. Tice, 199 P.2d 1 (1948)

Tarasoff v. Regents of the University of California, 551 P.2d 334 (1976)

Weirum v. RKO General, Inc. 539 P.2d 36 (1975)

Web Sites

http://www.productslaw.com

http://www.law.cornell.edu/topics/torts.html

http://www.findlaw.com/01topics/22tort/index.html

http://lii.zamnet.zm:8000/courts/supreme/tort.htm

Language Exercises
Chapter 3

I. Translate the following terminology into English:

1. verschuldensunabhängige Haftung
2. Fahrlässigkeit
3. Produzentenhaftung
4. Einwilligung
5. Antrag auf Schlüssigkeitsprüfung
6. der vorliegende Fall
7. Sorgfaltspflicht
8. Sorgfaltspflichtverletzung
9. Schaden
10. Schadensersatz
11. Gesamtschuldner
12. Mitverschulden
13. Deliktsrecht
14. Streitverkündung
15. Betrug
16. Fahrnis
17. Einzelhändler
18. Großhändler
19. Warenzeichen
20. conditio sine qua non
21. Körperverletzung
22. Sorgfaltsmaßstab
23. die im Verkehr erforderliche Sorgfalt
24. Beweislast

II. Fill in the blanks:

The trial court **upheld** the defendant's motion =
The trial court _1_ the defendant's motion.

The plaintiff **suffered** physical injuries. =
The plaintiff _2_ physical injuries.

The internal pressure on the bottle was **continued** for one minute. =
The internal pressure was _3_ for one minute.

The appellate court **affirmed** the judgment of the trial court. =
The appellate court _4_ the judgment of the trial court.

The plaintiff **carried** his burden of proof. =
The plaintiff _5_ his burden of proof.

The defendants **openly and honestly** admitted that the evidence was unavailable. =
The defendants _6_ admitted that the evidence was unavailable.
The court cautioned against application of the doctrine **adopted** in *Hall*. =
The court cautioned against application of the doctrine _7_ in *Hall*.

The manufacturers **followed** an industry-wide safety standard. =
The manufacturers _8_ to an industry- wide safety standard.

She brought the action on behalf of herself and others **like her**. =
She brought the action on behalf of herself and others _9_ .

The trial court's error **affected the outcome of the trial**. =
The trial court's error was _10_ .

Such a circuitous procedure **creates** wasteful litigation. =
Such a circuitous procedure _11_ wasteful litigation.

The tests conducted were almost **without error**. =
The tests conducted were almost _12_ .

Answers to Language Exercises

Unit I Chapter 1

I. Terminology and Vocabulary: See pp. 1-21 for use in the original context

Contract Law Terminology

1. offeror
2. offeree
3. accepted
4. closed
5. specialty contracts
6. simple
7. informal
8. consideration
9. deed
10. sealed contract
11. unilateral
12. acceptance
13. consideration
14. bilateral contract
15. breach
16. promisor
17. breaching party
18. promisee
19. non-breaching party
20. liable
21. money damages
22. specific performance
23. revoke
24. retract
25. offer to negotiate
26. offer to receive offers
27. offer to chaffer
28. sufficient
29. inadequate
30. condition precedent
31. condition subsequent

The Legal System

1. plaintiff
2. defendant
3. trial
4. fact
5. law
6. complaint

7. cause of action

8. remedy

9. appeal

10. appellate

11. appellant

12. appellee

General Legal Expression

1. entitled

2. vendor

3. vendee

4. donor

5. donee

6. lessor

7. lessee

8. contend

9. allege

10. maintain

11. agent

12. principal

13. refrain

14. forbear

15. consent

General Vocabulary

1. contracted

2. vague

3. construe

4. subsequently

5. dispense

6. express

7. implied

8. benefit

9. detriment

10. ample

II. Grammar: **See** *Carlill v. Carbolic Smoke Ball Co.*

1. with whom

2. to whom

3. to whom

4. to whom

5. from which

6. on which

7. for which

8. to whose

9. of which

10. to which

III. Definite and Indefinite Articles

1. A

2. the

3. -

4. -

5. the

6. The

7. the	18. the
8. an	19. -
9. the	20. the
10. the	21. a
11. the	22. a
12. the	23. A
13. The	24. the
14. -	25. -
15. the	26. -
16. -	27. the
17. -	28. -

Unit I Chapter 2

I. Grammar

1. a three-year-old child
2. The child is three years old.
3. That is a $5,000 [read: five-thousand-dollar] car.
4. The car costs $5,000 [read: five thousand dollars].
5. He sold the stock for $200 [read: two hundred dollars] per share.
6. This is a thirty-day call option.

Reading and Hyphenation: The following is written as one would read, but not write, the sentence, but includes the appropriate hyphenation.

1. On April fourth nineteen twenty-four there remained unpaid upon the principal the sum of five thousand four hundred fifty dollars.
2. There was a five-thousand-four-hundred-fifty-dollar balance remaining on April fourth nineteen twenty-four.
3. This amount was payable in installments of two hundred fifty dollars on April twenty-fifth nineteen twenty- four, and upon a like monthly date every three months thereafter.
4. Petterson paid two-hundred-fifty-dollar installment payments in a three-month cycle.

5. Thus the bond and mortgage had more than five years to run before the entire sum became due.

6. The bond and mortgage had more than a five-year period to run before maturity.

7. Pattberg wrote that as consideration for Petterson's early payment, Pattberg would allow him seven hundred eighty dollars against the principal due.

8. Pattberg offered Petterson a seven-hundred-eighty-dollar deduction from the principal in exchange for Petterson's early payment.

9. B owes A five thousand dollars payable in installments over a five-year period.

10. A proposes that B discharge the debt by paying four thousand five hundred dollars within one month. B then made a four-thousand-five-hundred-dollar payment.

11. A promises B to sell him a specified chattel for five dollars. A made B a five-dollar offer.

12. B tenders five dollars within a reasonable time. B's five-dollar tender was made promptly.

13. A offers to sell corn to B at five thousand dollars per carload, the current market price.

II. Terminology

1. legal capacity

2. minor

3. option

4. to tender

5. counter-offer

6. immovables

7. real estate

8. realty

9. real property

10. movables

11. chattels

12. personal property

13. personalty

14. mutually bargained-for exchange

15. agent

16. principal

17. irrebuttable presumption

III. Translation

§ 145 [Bindingness of an offer] An offeror is bound to his offer unless he has provided otherwise.

§ 146 [Termination of an offer] An offeree's power of acceptance is terminated by his rejection of the offer.

§ 147 [Time limit on power of acceptance] (2) An offeree's power of acceptance of an offer communicated by a medium and not in the presence of the offeree is terminated at the time at which the offeror could reasonably expect to have received the acceptance.

IV. Prepositions: See the original text on p. 38

1. to	14. into
2. of	15. before
3. in	16. of
4. for	17. in
5. of	18. of
6. by	19. before
7. of	20. upon / for
8. in	21. of
9. of	22. for
10. in	23. at
11. of	24. prior to / before
12. of	25. in
13. prior to / before	

V. Verbs: See pp. 1-41 for use in the original context

1. signed	8. binds
2. sealed	9. to fulfill / to perform
3. delivered	10. breaches
4. supported	11. compensate
5. bargained	12. performing
6. is closed	13. revoke
7. manifest / communicate	14. terminated

15. discharged   18. moved
16. alleged   19. dismissed
17. awarded   20. cited

Unit I Chapter 3

I. Terminology: See pp. 50-66 for use in the original context

1. demurred   23. executed
2. answer   24. constructive
3. admissions   25. symbolic
4. denials   26. repudiated anticipatorily
5. defenses   27. promisor
6. counterclaims   28. promisee
7. exclusive dealing agreement   29. promissory estoppel
8. use best efforts   30. charitable subscriptions
9. promote   31. detriment
10. recitals   32. estate pledge
11. agent   33. endowment
12. principal   34. dies intestate
13. writ of error   35. probate court
14. plaintiff in error   36. administrator
15. defendant in error   37. administratrix
16. writ of certiorari   38. heirs
17. record   39. testator
18. review   40. testatrix
19. supported by consideration   41. executor
20. donative   42. executrix
21. gratuitous   43. executory
22. formalized   44. executed

II. Corrections

1. I do not know *how* to approach the court on this issue. ("the way how" is incorrect)

2. The court based *its* judgment on the *evidence*. (it's = it is; its = possessive of it; "evidence" is never used with the plural "s"; the correct plural is "pieces of evidence")

3. The court *considered whether* the contract was supported by consideration. ("proof" is a noun, "prove" is the verb, but it means "beweisen" and not "prüfen"; "if" is not the correct translation of "ob" in this context)

4. The question *is whether* the contract has already been executed. ("ob" should be translated as "whether" and not "if" in "the question whether," "the issue whether" "it depends on whether"; unlike German, English does not use the comma before the conjunctions "whether," "if," "that," "why," etc.)

5. The plaintiff considered the *information* she had before filing her complaint. (like "evidence," "information" is never used with the plural "s"; the correct plural is "information" or "pieces of information" as in: "She had five pieces of information.")

6. The court *held that* the defendant was liable for breaching the contract. (no comma before "that")

7. The parties *expressly* provided that acceptance was not effective until actually communicated to the promisor. ("expressive" = "ausdrucksvoll"; "expressly" = "ausdrücklich")

Unit I Chapter 4

I. Terminology: See pp. 75-91 for use in the original context

Contract Law Terminology

1. express condition	8. nominal sum
2. implied condition	9. unconscionable
3. vendor	10. voidable
4. vendee	11. avoidance
5. bailor	12. supervening
6. bailee	13. adversely affected
7. bailment	14. negatively affected

15. aggrieved
16. impossibility
17. contract to compose a work

18. mutual
19. common
20. unilateral

General Legal Expressions

21. affidavit
22. counts
23. judgment on the verdict
24. judgment notwithstanding the verdict
25. judgment n.o.v.

26. counsel
27. attorney
28. instant case
29. case at bar

II. Verbs: See pp. 50-91 for use in the original context

1. demurred
2a. sustained
2b. incurred
3. to sustain
4. sustained
5. framed
6a. stipulated
6b. provided
7. was discharged
8. performed
9. allocated
10. extended
11. limited
12. to show
13. directed

14a. denied
14b. counterclaimed
15. tendered
16a. initiated
16b. commenced
16c. filed
17. revested
18. bears
19. had to bear
20. construed
21a. has to meet
21b. to be able to avoid
22. passed
23. rescinded
24. repudiated

Unit I Chapter 5

I. Terminology and Vocabulary: see pp. 100-118 for use in the original context

1. merchant
2. law merchant
3. commercial
4. manifests his assent
5. choice-of-law clause
6. bears
7. forum state
8. conflict of laws

9. parent
10. subsidiaries
11. confirmations
12. battle of the forms
13. open
14. gap fillers
15. in good faith
16. firm offer

II. Translation of terms

1. offeror
2. offeree
3. promisor / debtor
4. promisee / creditor
5. specialty contract
6. donative / gratuitous contract
7. simple contract
8. offer
9. acceptance
10. non-breaching party
11. to revoke an offer
12. condition precedent
13. condition subsequent
14. rebuttable presumption
15. irrebuttable presumption
16. right of avoidance
17. minor
18. counter-offer
19. real property / realty / real estate

20. personal property / personalty / chattels
21. exclusive dealing agreement
22. bailor
23. bailee
24. express condition
25. frustration
26. repudiation
27. mutual mistake
28. unilateral mistake
29. commercial transactions
30. parent
31. subsidiary
32. negotiable instruments
33. letter of credit
34. bill of lading
35. duress
36. merchant
37. securities
38. standard terms

Unit II Chapter 1

I. Prepositions: see pp. 127-134 for the original text

1. on behalf of
2. as
3. of
4. by
5. between
6. to
7. during
8. at
9. as
10. of
11. in
12. between
13. to / by
14. as
15. as
16. until
17. to
18. for
19. for
20. on
21. of
22. for
23. as to
24. whether
25. of
26. to
27. without
28. under
29. for
30. on
31. notwithstanding
32. of
33. of
34. On
35. in

II. Verbs: see pp. 127-138 for use in the original context

1. can be sustained / may be had / lies
2. can be sustained / may be had / lies
3. be sustained / lie
4. constitute
5. filed / brought
6. sought
7a. alleged
7b. committed
8a. moved
8b. to state
9a. denied, held, stated
9b. held
9c. stated
10a. was based / premised / predicated
10b. stand
11. raised

12a. treated
12b. vitiating
13. have revealed
14. is imposed

15. have adopted
16. overruled
17. intended

III. Terminology: see pp. 127-139 for use in the original context

Torts

1. defamation
2. libel
3. slander
4. consent
5. express
6. implied in fact
7. implied in law

8. false imprisonment
9. fault (*not* guilt!)
10. intent
11. tortfeasor
12. recklessness
13. negligence
14. strict

Legal System

1. demurrer
2. motion to dismiss
3. general verdict
4. special verdict
5. instant case

6. case at bar
7. class action
8. federal question jurisdiction
9. judgment on the merits

Unit II Chapter 2

I. Terminology: see pp. 148-177 for use in the original context

1. duty of care
2. breach of duty
3. damage
4. cause in fact
5. proximate cause
6. tortfeasor

7. plaintiff
8. defendant
9. Good Samaritan duty to render aid
10. special relationship
11. gratuitous undertaking
12. occupation of land

13. affirmative act
14. reasonable person standard
15. master-servant
16. respondeat superior
17. vicarious liability
18. joint tortfeasors
19. Joint and several liability
20. primarily liable
21. secondarily liable
22. contributory negligence

23. comparative negligence
24. standard of care
25. cause in fact
26. but-for
27. proximate
28. direct consequence
29. reasonably foreseen
30. transferred intent
31. battery

II. *General Legal Expression:* see pp. 148-171 for use in the original context

1. action
2. plaintiff
3. burden
4. duty
5. defendant
6. standard
7. legal cause
8. suffered
9. damages
10. has reason
11. harm/injury
12. danger
13. duty

14. reasonable/due
15. whether
16. evidence
17. jury
18. rise
19. part
20. conduct
21. case
22. reasonably
23. applicability
24. law
25. cause
26. compensable

Unit II Chapter 3

I. Translation

1. strict liability
2. negligence
3. product(s) liability

4. consent
5. demurrer
6. the instant case / the case at bar

7. duty of care

8. breach of a duty of care

9. damage

10. damages

11. joint tortfeasors

12. contributory negligence

13. torts / tort law

14. cross-complaint

15. fraud

16. chattels

17. retailer

18. wholesaler

19. trademark

20. cause in fact / but-for cause

21. battery

22. standard of care

23. reasonable person standard

24 burden of proof

II. Synonyms

1. sustained

2. sustained

3. sustained

4. sustained

5. sustained

6. candidly

7. espoused

8. adhered

9. similarly situated

10. prejudicial

11. engenders

12. infallible

Answers to Questions on the Text

Unit I Chapter 1

Questions p. 11

1. A statement of facts should be quite short and include only the information one needs for consideration of the legal issue involved. Usually students include too many details, like the names of the parties, the name of the bank (Alliance Bank, Regent Street), the dates (November 20, 1891, to January 17, 1892). A proper statement of facts would be: The defendant published a newspaper advertisement stating that it would pay a reward to anyone who used its product for a specified period of time and still contracted the influenza. Furthermore, the defendant claimed to have deposited money in a bank to show that the advertisement was serious. The plaintiff, in response to this advertisement, bought and used the product for more than two weeks and then contracted the influenza. When the defendant refused to pay her the reward, she brought this action.

2. The trial court held that the plaintiff was entitled to the reward. The defendant appealed.

3. This question is primarily designed to encourage discussion and not to find some "right" answer.

4. The defendant is the offeror and the plaintiff the offeree.

5. It is a simple contract.

6. It is an offer for a unilateral contract. The defendant is not requesting people who read the advertisement to promise to use the medication. Instead the defendant wants people to actually use it.

7. The plaintiff accepted the offer by using the smoke ball.

8. The defendant was bargaining to get people to use its product. The plaintiff was bargaining to receive the reward, assuming she then contracted the influenza.

Questions p. 13

1. The court is discussing the question of whether the defendant actually made an offer to contract. Any question that relates to whether one or the other party will be successful is an issue raised on appeal. If the newspaper advertisement was not an offer to contract, the plaintiff would lose the case. Therefore, this question is one of the issues on appeal.

2. The answer can be found in lines 18-36 of the opinion.

3. This question should encourage class discussion and argumentation, but the court provides the arguments for the plaintiff in lines 37-46.

4. The offer must be made seriously and not as a joke. The offer must be specific, particularly as to whom it is addressed.

Questions pp. 19-20

1. The facts of the case are in lines 7-24. The legal history of the case is in lines 4-6. The point of these questions, however, is to get you to formulate the answers simply in your own words, and not just to read them from the text.

2. Ideally, students should split up into groups and argue this case in class. It is much better for them not to read the rest of the case before doing so.

3. This is a writing exercise and can be checked against the formulation of either the *Carlill* opinion or the actual opinion of the *Lefkowitz* court.

4. The main issue on appeal is whether the newspaper advertisement constituted an offer and whether the plaintiff's conduct constituted an acceptance of that offer. A secondary issue on appeal is whether the defendant can modify his offer by later announcement of his "house rule."

5. The holding of the court is that the advertisement was an offer and the plaintiff's conduct constituted acceptance of that offer. Furthermore, the house rule does not modify the offer.

6. The ratio is contained in lines 39-47 (first issue) and lines 59-61 (secondary issue).

Unit I Chapter 2

Questions p. 34

1. B would not be able to take advantage of A under the common law rules because his acceptance is binding as of the date on which he sent it. He therefore cannot call in an effective rejection after he has posted the acceptance.

2. B has given A nothing in return for A's promise to keep the offer open.

Accordingly if the common law theory of what makes an agreement binding is that it must be supported by consideration, this agreement cannot be binding.

Questions p. 38

1. The facts of the case are stated in lines 5-28. The plaintiff won at the lower court (line 31-32)

2. The trial court apparently thought so. The answer to this question depends on whether Petterson accepted Pattberg's offer and whether the contract is supported by consideration. You will find out what the New York Court of Appeals thought by finishing the case. You, however, should think first about it and try to resolve the issues yourself.

3. The offer is stated in lines 13-16. Whether this offer was accepted is the question open to debate and will be explained in the following pages.

4. Analyze the wording of the offer to help you decide whether it is an offer for a unilateral or a bilateral contract. Does Pattberg request the performance of an act or the making of a return promise? The answer to this question will become apparent on reading the rest of the case.

5. Yes. If the offer was an offer for a bilateral contract, presumably Petterson accepted it at the very latest when he stated "I have come to pay off the mortgage." Before that point in time, Pattberg had not yet revoked his offer. If the offer is an offer for a unilateral contract, the case is more problematic. Petterson had not actually paid off the mortgage, which was the act requested, before Pattberg revoked. He had paid the April 25th payment, but that may not have been enough to close the contract. Please read on to find the answer, but discuss it first in class.

6. If it was an offer for a bilateral contract, Pattberg was bargaining to get Petterson to promise to pay back the mortgage sooner than Petterson was bound to do under the original loan agreement. If it was an offer for a unilateral contract, Pattberg was bargaining to actually receive the money. In either case Petterson was bargaining to get a $780 allowance against the outstanding principal.

7. The answer depends on the relevant legal system. Presumably in Germany Petterson would win the case because Pattberg would be bound to his offer for a reasonable time and Petterson accepted it before the time contemplated in the offer (May 31) had expired.

8. Pattberg was bound to his offer as long as he did not revoke it before it was accepted. He would not be permitted to revoke it if Petterson gave him consideration for keeping it open. Assuming Pattberg could revoke the offer, stating that he had already sold it to a third party would be sufficient as a

revocation. The offeror does not have to use the words "I revoke." It is sufficient if he communicates to the offeree information that indicates his intention to revoke. Selling the mortgage to a third party makes Pattberg's performance impossible and thus clearly indicates that he has no intention to fulfill any potential obligations to Petterson.

Questions pp. 39-43

1. Since "tendering" in this context means actually holding out the money for the other party to take, Petterson did not tender performance. He could not tender performance because Pattberg refused to open the door. Petterson's statement "I have come to pay off the mortgage" is only an indication of his intent to do so.

2. Acceptance of an offer for a unilateral contract does not take effect until the offeree fully performs the act requested by the offeror's promise. In the example of A and D, A is not bound to the offer under the rule announced in *Petterson v. Pattberg*. The result seems unjust, but at least it is logically consistent with common law rules. The real problem seems to lie in the common law rules. The answers to the rest of the questions will become obvious when you continue reading, but first try to come up with your own solution.

3. The answer to this question depends on whether Petterson actually began performing or proffered the beginning of performance before Pattberg revoked his offer. Certainly Petterson's reliance on the promise seems justified under Comment b and Illustration 1, because Pattberg did not reserve the right to revoke his offer. Furthermore, Comment c also seems to pose no problems for Petterson, because Petterson can tender performance without any further cooperation by Pattberg. He just has to hold the money out for Pattberg to take. Pattberg does not actually have to take it. One could take two different approaches to arguing the case for Petterson. One could claim that Petterson began performing when he made the April 25th payment. There is, however, a major problem with this approach that will be obvious when you read the next question and § 73 of the *Restatement*. One could also claim that Petterson began performing when he withdrew the money to make the final payment from his bank account and started walking to Pattberg's house. The problem with that argument is that Pattberg was not bargaining to get Petterson to go to the bank or to walk to his house. Since performance of the act requested in an offer for a unilateral contract is also consideration for the contract, it would be hard to claim that withdrawing the money and walking to the house was the beginning of performance. Note that if A posts a reward for the return of his lost dog, and B finds the dog and is on the way to A's house with it, the analysis would be somewhat different. A here would be bargaining to have someone find the dog and bring it back. Accordingly, under § 45 of the *Restate-*

ment, B would have begun the invited performance. Although § 45 was intended to compensate for the unjust result reached in this case under the common law, it hardly seems to be adequate for this purpose.

4. No.

5. Petterson had a duty under the original loan agreement to make the regular April 25th payment. Consequently, making this payment cannot be consideration for any option contract that would bind Pattberg to his offer. Since the offeree's performance is consideration for a unilateral contract and making this payment cannot be consideration for the contract, making the payment cannot be the beginning of performance.

6a. A has breached the contract. As noted above, A is bargaining to get someone to find his lost property. By finding it, B has begun the invited performance.

6b. A has breached the contract. A is bargaining to get someone to sell magazines, which B has already done by obtaining subscriptions. B's right to the prize depends on a condition precedent, namely whether B sells more subscriptions than anyone else. But A is bound to the promise, and therefore cannot revoke, as soon as anyone sells a subscription in reliance on the prize offer.

6c. A is bound to her promise. B has begun the invited performance by coming to the farm and caring for A. The exception to § 45 stated in Comment b is not applicable, because A did not reserve the right to revoke the offer, but instead gave B the right to terminate the agreement.

6d. A is bound. A made an offer of an option contract to B, which B accepted by hiring experts and paying for their transportation to the land.

7a. false (§ 54, p. 16)

7b. true (§ 23, p. 16)

7c. true (§ 63, p. 31)

7d. false (§ 42, p. 33)

7e. true (binding as of March 5, p. 32)

7f. true (§ 45, Comment b, p. 40)

7g. false (§ 73, p. 41)

7h. false (§ 40, p. 34)

7i. false (A does not have a duty to pay immediately. Therefore agreeing to pay before payment is due is the consideration A gives to B. B does not have any duty to accept less than the full amount. Therefore agreeing to accept $4,000 instead of the $5,000 owed is the consideration B gives to A.)

7j. false (§ 73, p. 41. The amount of the debt here seems to be the "subject of honest dispute" between A and B. Therefore A's promise to pay $500 more than he honestly thinks is due is consideration for B's promise to accept $500 less than B honestly thinks is due)

7k. false (A's offer is for a unilateral contract, which B accepts as soon as he ships the corn. Under *Restatement* § 54, p. 16, B is not required to notify A of his acceptance)

7l. false (A's offer was for the immediate shipment of 1000 bushels; a shipment two weeks later was not the act requested by the offer and thus does not constitute valid acceptance; B's shipment of 500 bushels cannot be seen as the beginning of invited performance and thus enough to create an option contract in his favor, because A is not bargaining to get 1000 bushels of corn, a commodity that can suddenly and dramatically change in price, at some time in the future)

7m. true (A can bargain for a performance rendered after A's own death)

7n. true (§ 73 *Restatement (Second) Contracts*, p. 41)

7o. true (A sacrifices a right A otherwise has, namely the right to bring suit against B for payment of the undisputed debt; B's promise to pay, however, is not consideration for A's promise to forbear and therefore A is not bound (see no. 7n.)

7p. false (§ 73 *Restatement (Second) Contracts*)

7q. true (the primary remedy for breach of contract is money damages and not, as under German law, specific performance; accordingly a contracting party will have to pay for the luxury of not performing, but he will not be forced to perform unless his performance is in some way unique and cannot be measured in money damages)

7r. false (peppercorn doctrine; A is paying for something that is of value to collectors of coins)

Unit I Chapter 3

Questions pp. 51-52

1. The defendant in this case granted the plaintiff the exclusive right to market her fashion designs. The profits from the plaintiff's sales were to be split 50-50 between the plaintiff and the defendant. The plaintiff claimed that the defendant breached the contract by placing her designs on sale without his knowledge and keeping 100% of the profits.

2. The plaintiff brought action against the defendant and the defendant demurred to the complaint. The case is now before the New York Court of Appeals (highest appellate court in the State of New York) on the demurrer issue.

3. The defendant clearly offered to give the plaintiff the exclusive right to sell her fashion designs. What exactly the plaintiff promised to do for the defendant is the main issue of the case and will become clear as you read on. The issue should be discussed now, but answered later.

4. No real question asked here.

Questions p. 53

1. The contract is not an employment contract in the traditional sense. Usually employees are paid for the time they are on the job, but Wood will only receive remuneration if he actually sells Lady Duff-Gordon's fashions.

2. The problem in this case is that Wood does not really promise to do anything. Sometimes students will argue that he promised to give Lady Duff-Gordon half of the profits he received. But any profits attained on the fashions belong to her anyway. Actually she promises to give him half of the profits on any sales he makes (regardless of the wording of the text "[i]n return she was to have one-half of 'all profits and revenues' ... ").
    If Wood does nothing, it would be hard to argue that he had breached any agreement to do something. The agreement seems to be of the form "if I sell any fashions, you will pay me half the profits." The court, as you have read, concludes that Wood intended to make a promise to use best efforts to make sales. That would be consideration for her promise to give him the exclusive sales right.

3. The German equivalent is "der besagte Otis F. Wood."

4. The Appellate Division is the intermediate appellate court, and the court which wrote the decision you have just read is the highest court in the State of New York, the Court of Appeals.

5. The main issue in this case is whether Wood gave Lady Duff-Gordon consideration for her promise to give him an exclusive right to sell her fashions. The holding is that he did and therefore that she was bound by her promise. The ratio is stated in *U.C.C.* § 2-306(2). This principle permits the court to reach the resolution it did in the case.

6. The section contains a rebuttable presumption. You can tell that because the section states "unless otherwise agreed," which means that the presumption can be rebutted by showing a contrary agreement.

Questions p. 55

1. The defendant's demurrer means that the defendant does not believe that the plaintiff's notice of motion is based on a cause of action. The most likely argument to be made in support of the demurrer is that the contract is not

valid because it is not supported by consideration. The defendant will argue that the plaintiff did not give the defendant anything in return for the defendant's promise to give the winner of the drawing an automobile.

2. This question should be discussed in class first before proceeding.

3. Again these questions are intended to stimulate discussion first and will be answered later after you have finished the case.

Questions p. 57

1. It does not seem that the plaintiff here can rely on *Spooner*. If the defendant had intended to transfer the automobile, he could have given the plaintiff the keys to the car and told her where the car was located for her to pick up, or he could have given her a document indicating a transfer of title to the automobile.

2. A gratuitous promise is also binding if already executed, as was the holding in *Spooner*. Under German law, an executed gift is also binding on the donor.

Questions p. 58

1. It was consideration for the defendant's promise because the defendant was interested in attracting a large crowd to his auction.

2. A only benefits from D's abstinence because A is interested in his daughter's welfare. This example points out that the benefit analysis of consideration is not particularly satisfying. It is much better to approach the question from the point of view of what the promisor was bargaining to obtain. A certainly was bargaining to get D to abstain from smoking and drinking, even though the abstinence would have been a greater benefit to D herself than to A.

Questions p. 58

1. The offer is contained in the newspaper advertisement. It is an offer for a unilateral contract. The acceptance is the act of coming to the auction. Since the act requested in an offer for a unilateral contract is simultaneously acceptance and consideration for the agreement, then coming to the auction would also be the consideration the plaintiff gave the defendant. The defendant was bargaining to get people to attend the auction, of course in the hope that they might bid on the residence lots. Still, having a large crowd, even of some non-bidders, at an auction has its advantages.

2. Having your number drawn was a condition precedent to your right to the automobile, and quite similar to contracting the influenza in the *Carlill* case.

3. The answer depends on the legal system. In Germany lotteries are not generally prohibited but are subject to state regulation. Games of chance, like

poker, played within a private group of people, do not give the winner the right to enforce any contractual obligation.

4. The $5 could have been consideration if it had been demanded and paid *before*, rather than after the drawing of the winner. Since it was paid after the winner was drawn, it is **past consideration,** which does not support a contractual obligation. If the $5 were the consideration here, the company would not have been bound until the plaintiff had already paid it to the auctioneer. Under the court's analysis, the contract was binding as soon as the plaintiff appeared at the auction, meaning that at that point in time the defendant was bound to give the plaintiff a slip of paper to deposit in the lottery box.

Questions p. 60

1. Again this should be discussed first and the answers will become clear as you proceed. Try to approach the case in the alternative as if it involved a) an offer for a unilateral contract, or b) an offer for a bilateral contract. If you are working in a classroom setting, have some argue for the college and some for the executors of the plaintiff's estate.

2. If the agreement was binding, the promisor was not free to repudiate, but if it was a gratuitous promise she was.

3. If in accepting the $1000, the college began to perform on a unilateral contract, then the promisor might be bound through the creation of an option contract to the college's benefit. That would be one advantage for the college if the case is analyzed as involving an offer for a unilateral contract. On the other hand, the college might be just as well off with the bilateral contract interpretation. Accepting the $1,000 might be seen as assuming an obligation to establish the scholarship fund. That would make the contract binding at that point in time as well. The court will discuss this issue later in the case.

4. The clause contains a condition precedent. The executors are bound to pay the college the $4,000 only if the money is left over after the other beneficiaries under the will have been satisfied.

5. Since the other beneficiaries under the will had to be paid first and the college had a right only to the remainder, the college would have to wait to bring suit until it was determined whether they had any right at all to the money.

Questions p. 65

1a. lines 97-102; 1b. lines 114-115; 1c. lines 112-117.

2. From the facts as we know them, it does not appear that the college has done anything more than set the money aside for the purpose designated by the plaintiff. Presumably by accepting the $1,000 on account, however, the col-

lege bound itself to establish the scholarship fund in the plaintiff's name on the condition that the rest of the money was paid.

3. If the contract became binding on the defendant as soon as the college accepted the $1,000, then it also became binding on the college at that time. The college would then be in breach of contract.

Questions p. 66

1. If the transaction was a gift, then the college would have been free to do what it wanted with the money. The gift would have been executed as soon as the plaintiff handed the money over to the college. Since the college, however, was bound under the terms of the agreement, the college was not free to do what it wanted with the money. Although this case discusses promissory estoppel, it really involves a binding contract supported by consideration. The plaintiff promised to give the defendant $5,000 and in return the defendant promised to establish the scholarship fund in the plaintiff's name. Neither party was free after the agreement was closed, which was at the latest when the college accepted the $1,000 on account.

2. As you can tell from lines 151-153, the plaintiff lost both at the trial and on the first appeal. The holding is that charitable subscriptions which involve a return promise by the recipient of the donation are supported by consideration and thus binding contracts. You can find dicta in lines 43-82, 97-102, 107-114; 144-150.

3. Mr. French could have argued that Burma Shave made an offer for a unilateral contract. By collecting the 900 empty jars, Mr. French accepted the offer and gave consideration for the company's promise to give him a trip to mars. Burma Shave could have argued that its performance was impossible (we will discuss the defense of impossibility in the next chapter) and that it was thus excused. It could also argue that anyone reading the advertisement would have realized that it was not intended to be an offer because of impossibility of promised performance.

Unit I Chapter 4

Questions p. 75

1. Answer depends on the legal system involved. Under German law, *BGB* § 275(I) would excuse the owner of the music hall from performance and *BGB* § 323 would excuse the plaintiff from paying rent for the use of the music hall. If, as here, the defendant was not at fault for the destruction of the music hall, then he would also be free from paying damages to the plaintiff.

The conditions of the defense are that the contract became 1) impossible to perform, 2) after it was closed 3) through no fault of the promisor.

2. German law distinguishes between performance that was impossible at the time the contract was closed and performance that became impossible after the contract was closed. *BGB § 306* provides that if performance was impossible at the time the contract was closed, the contract is void. In that case the promisor is liable for damages if he knew or should have known that performance was impossible (*BGB § 307*). The damage award is calculated on the basis of the so-called "negative interest," which in our case would have been £58. The negative interest is the amount of money it would take to put the non-breaching party back in the position he was in before the contract was closed and, therefore, does not include lost profits. If performance became impossible after the contract was closed, *BGB § 275* provides that the promisor is excused from performance. *BGB § 280*, for contracts not supported by consideration, and *§ 325*, for contracts supported by consideration, provide that the promisor has to pay damages if he was at fault for the impossibility. Here the damages are calculated on the basis of the so-called "positive interest," which is the amount of money necessary to put the non-breaching party into the position he would have been in had the contract been performed, and, therefore, includes lost profits. German law also distinguishes between objective impossibility, meaning that performance is impossible for all individuals, and subjective impossibility, meaning that performance is only impossible for the promisor himself. If performance is objectively impossible, the rules just stated apply. If performance is subjectively impossible at the time the contract is closed, then the promisor is liable for damages calculated on the basis of the positive interest. If performance becomes subjectively impossible after the contract was closed, the rules stated above apply (*BGB § 275(II)*). This book is not intended to be a course in German law. On the other hand, it is important to be able to formulate the law of your own legal system in the English language.

3. These questions are merely intended to encourage discussion. The German, English and U.S. American legal systems all recognize impossibility of performance as a defense to a breach of contract cause of action.

Questions p. 80

1. If ownership was transferred at the time of the sale, the vendee owned the property. Generally the principle of law is that the owner of property bears the risk of accidental destruction.

2. The bailor owned the horse and the bailee merely had possession of it.

3. The extension of past precedents in *Taylor v. Caldwell* is particularly interest-

ing because in both of the former cases the court discusses of the vendor and vendee, and the bailor and bailee, it is the owner of the property who bears the loss. That conclusion can be reached by applying the principle *casum sentit dominus*, meaning that accidental loss of property falls on the owner of that property. Accordingly, impossibility of performance is not really needed to explain these cases and they do not, at least not completely convincingly, support the holding in *Taylor v. Caldwell*.

4.   In *Taylor v. Caldwell*, the owner bears the loss of his music hall, but does not have to bear the consequences of its loss, because he does not have to compensate for the expenses incurred by the other party in reliance on the contract. Accordingly, the past precedents the court cites do not really support the court's holding in *Taylor v. Caldwell*, because they are different in a legally significant way.

5.   The German law of bailments is contained in *BGB* §§ 688-700. Essentially, the bailor bears the risk of accidental loss of his own property. The bailee is responsible for the loss only if he was at fault.

6.   See answer no. 2 to questions on p. 75.

Questions p. 83

1.   The facts of the case are contained in lines 4-12, 34-45; legal history in lines 4, 8-15; issue raised on appeal in lines 17-20 and modified in lines 21-29; holding in lines 71-80. The issue is not the same in this case as in *Taylor v. Caldwell* because here both parties are capable of performing. The plaintiff can let the defendant use the rooms and the defendant can pay for them under the contract. The problem is that the whole purpose of the contract has been thwarted through the King's illness and the resulting cancellation of the processions.

2.   *Krell v. Henry* extends the precedent in *Taylor v. Caldwell* considerably, because it applies it to a completely different set of facts and really creates a new defense, the defense of frustration.

3.   The German *Civil Code* does not contain any provision on frustration. German courts, however, do recognize the defense and base their decisions on *BGB* § 242 (Treu und Glauben), the "back door" courts can use to avoid unjust results in cases not expressly governed by the code.

Questions p. 85

1.   The facts of the case are stated in lines 11-51; legal history in lines 4-11. The issue on appeal will be stated in the next passage of the case.

2.   In Germany *BGB* §§ 119-124, 142-144 govern the effects of mistakes. If a

seller (or buyer) is mistaken as to the value of what he is selling (or buying), the mistake is irrelevant under German law. If the mistake relates to a characteristic of the object sold that is of central importance to its value, the mistaken party can rescind the contract. If both partes are mistaken, then the case might be dealt with under *BGB* § 242 (Treu und Glauben) as a case of frustration. Since in *Wood v. Boynton*, neither of the parties was mistaken, because they both realized that they did not know what the stone was, German mistake provisions would not permit Wood to rescind the contract. Potentially, Wood could argue that the contract was frustrated, then *BGB* § 242 might apply, and the result is always a bit unpredictable in these cases.

3. Ms. Wood should have said "and I said, ..."

Questions p. 88

1. Mr. Boynton was not fraudulent in his dealings with Ms. Wood and he did not materially misrepresent any facts to her. To be fraudulent, he would have to know or strongly suspect that what he said was untrue and would have to have said it with the intent to get Ms. Wood to agree to sell the stone to him. To materially misrepresent facts he would have to know that his statement was likely to cause Ms. Wood to part with the stone. Here it was Ms. Wood who approached him with the offer to sell, and Mr. Boynton admitted to her that he did not know what type of stone she had.

2. The mistake the court refers to regards the identity of an object sold. If Ms. Wood had two stones, a topaz and a diamond, which looked similar, and she sold the topaz, but accidentally gave Mr. Boynton the diamond, then she would not have passed title to the diamond to Mr. Boynton.

3. In Germany, *BGB* § 119(I) governs mistakes as to the contents of one's declaration of will, e.g. A thinks he is selling residential lot no. 2500, but in fact is selling lot no. 5200. This mistake is similar to the mistake the court in *Wood* considered in lines 57-61. *BGB* § 119(I) also governs a mistake as to whether one is making a declaration of will, e.g. A attends an auction and while it is in progress waves to a friend across the room, not meaning to bid. *BGB* § 119(II) concerns a mistake as to a characteristic that is of central importance regarding a person or a thing, e.g. A thinks he is hiring a trained pharmacist, but the person never studied pharmacy, or A thinks that a stone is a topaz but it really is a diamond. In all of these cases, *BGB* § 142(I) provides that the contract is voidable by the mistaken party. The German system distinguishes between rescission (Anfechtung), which dissolves the contract from the beginning, and money damages.

Questions p. 91

1. The mistake was shared by Wood and Boynton. Section 152 would apply to this case.

2. Section 154(b) allocates the risk to Ms. Wood.

3. In the stock market example, both parties, the buyer and the broker are aware that they do not know what is going to happen to the price of the shares. If *Wood v. Boynton* had been decided in Ms. Wood's favor, that precedent, if applied consistently to the stock market example, would also permit a buyer of stock to declare the contract void whenever the shares fell in price.

4. Under § 154(b) of the *Restatement*, Boynton would also have to bear the risk, assuming that he was aware of the fact that he did not know what the stone really was when he bought it. If the parties both thought they knew that the stone was a diamond, then the contract would be voidable by the disadvantaged party under § 152(1).

Unit I Chapter 5

Questions p. 108

1. The answer to the question depends on Spanish choice-of-law rules. Therefore in order to answer it you would need to know more about Spanish law.

2. The basic difference between § 1-105 and § 2-207 is that the former is meta-level law, meaning it is law about law, namely about what law is to be applied. Section 2-207, on the other hand, is substantive law relating to interpretation of the parties' transaction. Again to answer the question you would need to know more about Spanish law. It is possible that Spanish law requires the judge 1) to apply Spanish choice-of-law rules to determine whether the law of Spain or New York applies, and if the latter then to apply only the substantive law of New York; or 2) to apply Spanish choice-of-law rules to determine whether Spanish or New York law applies, and if the latter then to apply New York choice-of-law rules to determine whether the law of New York or Spain applies. The first alternative raises few problems. But the second alternative can be quite complicated, especially if New York choice-of-law rules point back to Spanish law. If so and "Spanish law" includes Spain's choice-of-law rules, we are back in N.Y., and so on *ad infinitum*. This type of back and forth in choice of law is referred to as *renvoi*.

3. As you know from § 1-105, whether New York law will apply (meaning the U.C.C. and any other applicable New York law on contracts) depends upon whether the transaction bears an "appropriate relation" to the State of New

York. From no. 3 of the Official Comment to § 1-105, you know that this determination is left to the judge's discretion. One indication of an answer to this question is contained in comment no. 2, which mentions the place of contracting and the place of contemplated performance as relevant to the choice of law. Usually the place of contracting is considered to be the seller's location. Similarly, the place of performance, particularly if performance involves merely the shipment of goods, is the seller's location. Accordingly, since the seller here is located in New York, most likely New York law would apply under the choice-of-law rule stated in § 1-105.

4. Under *U.C.C.* § 2-207 the parties have closed a binding contract. XYZ's inclusion of its own choice-of-law clause in contradiction to what ABC specified in its offer does not prevent the formation of a binding contract, since XYZ did not make its acceptance conditional on ABC's agreement to the Spanish choice-of-law clause (§ 2-207(1)).

5. Even scholars disagree on the answer to this question. The answer, however, seems to depend on whether 1) the Spanish choice-of-law clause is a "different" or an "additional" term within the meaning of § 2-207; and 2) if it is a different term, can it still be part of the contract under § 2-207(2). Although § 2-207(2) expressly refers to "additional" and not "different" terms, still Official Comment no. 3 refers to both. Unfortunately there is no easy answer to this question, but it provides an opportunity to debate about the wording of § 2-207 and the Official Comment.

Questions p. 111

1. A and B have closed a binding contract under both the *U.C.C.* and the common law. Under the common law, the purchase order will most likely be interpreted to be an offer for a bilateral contract which B accepted on sending notification to A. If the purchase order had stated "I will pay $10 per bottle for 100 cases of champagne if shipped immediately," it might be interpreted to be an offer for a unilateral contract. If so, B has not accepted by beginning to pick the grapes, because A was bargaining for shipment and not grape picking. Under the *U.C.C.*, B has accepted the offer by sending A notification of acceptance. B has not accepted under § 2-206(1)(b) by beginning to pick the grapes either. If B does not ship the champagne immediately, he is in breach of contract.

2. A and B have not closed a binding contract under either the *U.C.C.* or the common law. Under the common law, the offer would be deemed to be an offer for a bilateral contract requiring promissory acceptance, and not performance of the act of shipping the champagne. Furthermore, B would have had to respond by facsimile or some equally speedy means of communica-

tion, because that was the means A selected. Under *U.C.C.* § 2-206(1)(b) shipment would constitute acceptance, but in the absence of notification within a reasonable period of time, A would not be bound by the contract. No option contract was created by the act of shipping the champagne, because the *U.C.C.* does not so provide and the rule of *Restatement (Second) Contracts* § 45 does not apply to acceptances of offers for bilateral contracts.

3.   A is bound under the common law and under the *U.C.C.* A made an offer for a unilateral contract. Under the common law, B accepted the offer by immediately shipping the champagne. B is not required to notify A of his acceptance, other than through A's receipt of the champagne within the normal time required for trans-Atlantic shipment. Accordingly, B's tardy notification of acceptance is irrelevant. Under the *U.C.C.*, B's notification was not acceptance of A's offer because it was not communicated within a reasonable period of time. B's immediate shipment, in the absence of notification within a reasonable period, is also not sufficient as an acceptance under *U.C.C.* § 2-206(2). Sill, Comment 3 preserves B's rights under *Restatement* § 45. By shipping, B has performed, and thus B has also begun to perform. An option contract has been closed which prevents A from revoking his offer.

4.   A and B have closed a binding contract under the common law. A made an offer for a bilateral contract, which B accepted by sending the telefacsimile. B was permitted to use that mode of communication, because it was the same as that selected by A. Under the mail box rule, the acceptance was valid as soon as it was sent off through the telefax machine, regardless of whether A ever received it. Under the *U.C.C.*, shipment would constitute acceptance. Still § 2-206(2) requires that A actually be notified of B's acceptance, and not that B simply send notification of his acceptance. Since the offer is an offer for a bilateral contract, B would not get the benefit of *Restatement* § 45 either. One could argue that *U.C.C.* § 1-103 preserves the common law and thus the mailbox rule, which could save this contract. This argument could be strengthened by relying on the *U.C.C.*'s general orientation toward upholding a contract even in cases in which it would not be binding under the common law. Therefore, one could argue that it would contradict the general intention of the *U.C.C.* not to uphold a contract in cases in which the common law would.

Questions p. 115

1.   No. A and B are still at the negotiating stage. The facts do not indicate that A and B agreed to contract as required by § 2-204(1) or that they intended to contract as required by § 2-305(1).

2.   Yes. Under § 2-204 B's act of shipping and A's act of paying for the goods indicates agreement. A is therefore bound and cannot reship the goods and

receive a return payment from B. The fact that the price has dropped significantly is a risk A assumed when he accepted B's suggested price by paying for
the goods.

3. No. The parties have entered into an agreement under § 2-204 but have left
    the price to be fixed by the seller, B. Under § 2-305(2), however, B must fix the
    price in good faith. The fact that B has increased her prices by 40%, 75% of
    which exceeds what other suppliers are charging, indicates B's bad faith.
    Under § 2-305(3), B is at fault for the failure, which permits A to cancel the
    contract.

4. No. Under § 2-305(3) A may either treat the contract as canceled or himself
    fix a reasonable price. A reasonable price will not always be the market price
    for the goods, but rather will depend on the general business arrangement
    between A and B. Since B has always charged around 10% less than the top
    ten leading suppliers, the reasonable price should reflect that difference.

Questions p. 118

1. No. A is not a merchant who deals in automobiles and therefore is not subject
    to the rule of § 2-205.

2. No. A's offer was not in writing as required by § 2-205.

3. No. A was only bound for three months under § 2-205, namely until Decem-
    ber 19, 1996. Accordingly, the offer expired and A was free to sell the rug to
    someone else.

Unit II Chapter 1

Questions p. 138

1. see lines 6-25 of the court's opinion

2. No, the action was originally filed in the U.S. District Court. The District
    Court is the trial court in the federal system. The same court will hear the
    trial. The decision you have read is the trial court's decision on a pretrial
    motion to dismiss the complaint. Of course, the defendants, who lost on the
    motion to dismiss, can appeal this decision all the way to the U.S. Supreme
    Court before any trial will be held, but if they do not then the trial will take
    place following this decision. If you are having problems answering these
    questions, refer to *Einführung in die anglo-amerikanische Rechtssprache /
    Introduction to Anglo-American Law & Language*, Unit II and Appendix II,
    and to line 6, lines 33-34 of the court's opinion

3. See lines 37-38 for the main issue of the case (Can this case involve a battery?)

and lines 105-108 for the subordinate issues (Did the defendants act intentionally? Did their acts result in offensive contact with the plaintiffs? Did the plaintiffs consent to the contact?)

4.   The holding is that the facts can support a battery cause of action and that the plaintiffs have to prove that the defendants intentionally acted resulting in offensive contact to which the plaintiffs did not consent.

5.   See lines 45-85 (main issue), 109-112 (intent), lines 113-119 (offensive contact), lines 123-140 (lack of consent).

Questions p. 140

1.   *Mink* provides a good example of a battery that was not an assault. It was not an assault because the plaintiffs were not aware that they were being treated with the experimental drug DES. Therefore they were not put in imminent apprehension of harmful or offensive contact with the drug, as is however required for the tort of assault (*Restatement (Second) Torts* § 21 (1)(b)). The Prosser and Keeton text gives the example of aiming a gun at someone who is unaware of it as not being an assault, of striking a sleeping person as being a battery but not an assault, and of shooting at but missing a person who is aware of being shot at as being an assault and not a battery. If you compare subsections (b) of *Restatement* §§ 13, 18 and 21 you will see that battery requires either a harmful contact or an offensive contact, but assault requires imminent apprehension of contact rather than actual contact. A plaintiff does not have to be aware of the threat of contact to maintain an action for battery. A plaintiff does have to have been aware of the threat of contact to maintain an action for assault.

2a. D is liable neither for a battery nor for an assault. D is not liable for a battery because D did not come into physical contact with P. D is not liable for an assault because P, not thinking that D has her address, cannot reasonably have any imminent apprehension of contact.

2b. D is not liable for a battery because he had no physical contact with P. D is not liable for an assault, because he threatened to hit P only if the policeman were not standing at the corner. Since the policeman is standing at the corner, P knows that D will not hit her.

2c. D is not liable for a battery because he did not come into physical contact with P. D is not liable for an assault, because P knows that D is locked in the jail cell and therefore cannot have any imminent apprehension of contact with D.

Unit II Chapter 2

Questions p. 157

1. Answer depends on the legal system chosen. The answer for the German system is in the text. § 831(1) *BGB* makes liability for the torts of an employee depend upon the employer's fault, whereas § 278 *BGB* does not require the employer to be a fault for contract breaches committed by his employee. The common law has the same rule for contracts and torts, holding the master liable for both the torts and the contract breaches committed by the servant. Accordingly, the common law system does not need a *culpa in contrahendo* theory. A *culpa in contrahendo* theory treats what in the common law would be seen as a tort, as a breach of contract. It does that to get the victim of the tort within the more advantageous rule of § 278, so that the master can be held strictly liable for the servant's torts, which are considered to be breaches of contract under the theory. A classic example of how this theory works is the case of a shopper going into a shop to look around and falling on a banana peel, or soapy water, negligently left on the floor by the cleaning lady. Under a German law tort theory, the shop owner is liable to the customer only if he was himself negligent in monitoring the activities of the cleaning lady. If he was not, the customer can sue the cleaning lady for damages, which, in light of the wages cleaning ladies earn, is not a particularly promising law suit. The theory of *culpa in contrahendo* constructs a pre-contractual relationship out of the shopper's coming into the shop to look around. Once a fictional contractual relationship has been constructed, the shopper can sue the shop keeper independently of the shopkeeper's fault.

2. In Germany, the statute of limitations (**Verjärhungsfrist**) is longer for contract claims than for tort claims, providing another reason why a German lawyer might prefer a contract cause of action to one in tort.

3. You may need to refer to *Einführung in die anglo-amerikanische Rechtssprache / Introduction to Anglo-American Law & Language*, Unit II, to help you answer this question. A trial court, often through a jury, is responsible for determining the facts of a case and for applying the appropriate law to those facts to reach a verdict and judgment. An appellate court is responsible for deciding legal issues, but not factual. Accordingly, Judge Hand as a judge here on the U.S. Court of Appeals, is bound by the determinations of fact reached by the trial court, unless of course he orders a new trial because he finds some legal error that was made during the original trial. Hand is not bound by the trial court's conclusions of law, because it is exactly the law as interpreted by the trial court that Hand is called upon to review as an appellate judge. In line 54, Hand refers to the trial court's finding that the harbormaster was an

employee. That is an issue of fact. In line 55, Hand refers to the trial court's conclusion that the Grace line was responsible for the harbormaster's negligence. Liability for someone else's negligence is a conclusion of law. Hand is not bound by that determination as he is by the factual finding of the trial court. Accordingly, Hand indicates in lines 56-57 that he cannot give the same weight to the conclusion of liability as he would to a finding of fact.

The "tenth finding" in line 68 is a finding of fact. It only determines what happened and not the legal relevance of what happened.

4.   This question is intended to get students to argue by analogy. In *Rice* apparently the tug boat acted under the orders of a harbormaster, whereas in *Carroll Towing*, the harbormaster acted under the orders of the captain of the tug Carroll, albeit without any express instructions. If the tug in *Rice* was held liable, then Hand reasons that clearly the tug Carroll and the Grace Line can be held liable where the situation was reverse and it was the tug boat's captain who was giving the orders to the harbormaster employed by the Grace Line.

Questions p. 164

1.   The plaintiff specifies the breach of duty in her complaint by alleging that the defendant failed to do something he had a duty to do and that this failure resulted in the plaintiff's injury.

2.   The bargee's absence was not the cause in fact of the barge breaking away from the pier, because the harbormaster was in charge of releasing and tying the lines. Even if the bargee had been present, he could not have stopped the harbormaster. The bargee's absence was a cause in fact of the barge's sinking, because if the bargee had been present he could have noticed the leak in the barge and could easily have got help to drain off the water. It obviously would not have been a wise move to specify the bargee's absence as the breach of duty with regard to the collision, since it was not a cause in fact of this collision. Accordingly, the defendant, who is relying on a comparative negligence defense, could not have carried his burden of proof on the causation issue.

3.   Answer depends on the legal system involved. The question is intended to encourage discussion of the relevant legal system in the English language.

4.   The first issue on appeal is stated in lines 51, namely whether the Grace Line is partly liable for the damage to the Anna C. That in turn depends on whether it was vicariously liable for the harbormaster's negligence. The holding on this issue is in lines 80-81. The second holding, namely that Conners is not barred from full recovery for the collision damages, is in lines 90-92; and the third, namely that Conners is 33 1/3% at fault for the sinking damages, is in lines 135-138. Dicta is contained, for example, in lines 122-125. You can easily spot dicta from the court's statements such as "we do not hold," "we

leave that question open," "we need not say." This opinion in general does not contain much dicta, but rather is confined to a statement of the facts (lines 6-44), the legal history of the case (lines 10-17), the issues raised on appeal (lines 45-80), the holdings and the ratio (lines 72-81, 86-90, 110-117).

Questions p. 166

1. Answer depends on the legal system chosen. The question is intended to encourage discussion of one's own legal system in the English language.

2. The defendant operated a railway for the public and thus owed the plaintiff, a passenger, a duty of care through its contractual relation with her. Whether the defendant breached its duty of care depends on whether the defendant failed to take some precaution it had a duty to take to avoid the harm caused the plaintiff. Furthermore, if we follow the Learned Hand formula for the standard of care owed, the breach of the duty would depend on whether this untaken precaution was less costly than the probability that an accident of this type would occur times the gravity of the harm caused. As you have read in the last section, deciding what that untaken precaution was might make a big difference in whether you, as counsel for Ms. Palsgraf, can prove that the untaken precaution was also the cause in fact of your client's injury. One untaken precaution might be keeping railway employees from helping passengers onto moving trains. Another might be prohibiting passengers from taking uninspected packages onto the platform, or bolting heavy scales to platforms, or keeping passengers who are waiting for later trains off platforms. At this stage of the case it is better to think first about these and other alternatives. The answer to this question will be revealed later in the text. The answer to the question of whether the breach was the proximate cause of the injury is the main problem in the case and should first be discussed.

3. The defendant could have forbidden guards from helping passengers onto moving trains or forbidden passengers from carrying explosives onto trains. Either one of these precautions would have avoided the injury to Ms. Palsgraf. The primary risk was the risk of harm to passengers trying to get onto moving trains. The ancillary risk was the risk to bystanders from exploding packages.

Questions p. 167

1. It raises the issue of vicarious liability. The defendant, Long Island R.R., can be held vicariously liable for the torts of its employees.

2. Ms. Palsgraf did not claim that there was any intentional invasion of her bodily security. If she had, she would have based her claim on the tort of

battery. The tort the court refers to in lines 24-26 is negligence. Ms. Palsgraf did base her claim on negligence.

3. The court distinguishes Ms. Palsgraf's claim from the claim of the passenger who was helped onto the train, and presumably anyone else who was standing near to where the package dropped. It seems probable that the Long Island R.R. would be liable to these potential plaintiffs.

4. The primary issue in this case is not whether the defendant owes passengers, and therefore also Ms. Palsgraf, a duty of care. The central issue here is one of proximate cause. In the terms of Clerk & Lindsell, the issue is whether plaintiffs like Ms. Palsgraf should be able to file suit against a railway in this type of case. In the words of Prosser & Keeton, the issue is does the railway's failure to guard against reasonably foreseeable harm to the passenger with the package make it liable for the consequences to Ms. Palsgraf, which it could not possibly have anticipated. In the words of Grady, the issue is whether the railway, which has breached a duty with respect to the passenger with the package, the primary risk, will be held liable to Ms. Palsgraf for harm which arose from an ancillary risk.

Questions p. 171

1. You can find this type of legal reasoning in lines 37-51; 76-80.

2. The doctrine of transferred intent does not apply in this case because the defendant's employees did not intentionally throw down a package of what they thought was explosives. Presumably if they had, the doctrine of transferred intent would have provided a basis of liability toward Ms. Palsgraf. If the guards had intended to throw a package on the ground, not knowing that it contained explosives, it seems doubtful that the doctrine of transferred intent would apply. The court notes in lines 39-41 that a bundle which appeared to be abandoned waste could be kicked with impunity. Presumably the court means intentionally kicked. If there is no reason to think that a bundle contains explosives, then someone kicking it would not intend to cause an explosion. It is this intent that is relevant when determining whether the doctrine of transferred intent applies.

3a. German criminal law theorists differ on the appropriate treatment of these cases. Some, perhaps the majority, say that if A aims and shoots to kill B, but fatally hits C, then A is guilty of the attempted homicide of B and the negligent homicide of C. Some adhere to the transferred intent doctrine as it is followed in the common law.

3b. If A aims and shoots to kill B, but fatally hits C, then A would be liable in tort to C's heirs regardless of whether A hit C intentionally or negligently. Accordingly, German tort law does not distinguish these two cases as far as tort liability is concerned. Under the common law, a plaintiff can sue for **punitive damages** if the tort was committed intentionally, so the doctrine of transferred intent would help a plaintiff in these cases. In Germany, punitive damages are not awarded by courts in torts cases, so again whether A hit C intentionally or negligently is irrelevant.

4. The range of apprehension refers to how remote a risk might be before harm caused when the risk materializes is no longer proximately caused by the defendant's conduct. This question will sometimes be one the court will answer if it finds that the evidence cannot reasonably support a finding of proximate causation (*Restatement* § 328 B(a), (e)), and sometimes the jury will answer it in light of what an individual can reasonably foresee (*Restatement* § 328 C(c)). As you will see from the next excerpt from the opinion, however, Judge Cardozo prefers to treat the issue here as one of whether the defendant owed the plaintiff a duty of care. Framed that way, the question is one for the court alone (*Restatement* § 328 B(b)).

Questions pp. 173-174

1. The Prosser & Keeton text on p. 94, particularly the section of the text dealing with the intentional torts of servants, seems to indicate that the defendant here would be liable for its employees' attempting to help the passenger onto the train because they were acting within the scope of their employment. It seems most probable that the master would be held liable even if it had expressly instructed them not to help passengers onto moving trains, because it would be the master's responsibility to supervise the employees sufficiently to ensure that they are actually following orders. If an employer could simply instruct his employees to exercise caution at all times and thereby escape tort liability, the master-servant relationship would no longer be an effective basis for vicarious liability.

2. Ms. Palsgraf won at trial and on the first appeal, because Cardozo reverses both of these decisions. The case was very close. If you add up all the appellate judges' opinions you have a 6-6 result (Palsgraf: 3 on the first appeal + 3 on the second appeal; Long Island R.R.: 2 on the first appeal + 4 on the second). In addition the trial court judge apparently thought Ms. Palsgraf had a good cause of action in this case. The defendant at least had the opportunity to demur to Ms. Palsgraf's complaint. If it did, the trial court obviously overruled it. If Cardozo had been the trial court judge he would have sustained the demurrer, because he was of the opinion that the railway owed Ms. Palsgraf no duty of care in this case. Accordingly, even assuming that all of the facts Ms. Palsgraf claimed were true, still her complaint would not have stated a cause of action (standard for sustaining the demurrer).

Questions pp. 177-178

1. She might have lost on the breach of duty issue because fixing the scales firmly enough to the platform to avoid them tipping over from this type of explosion might have cost considerably more than the likelihood that they would tip over times the harm they then would cause. The more unlikely it is that the scales would tip, the lower PL will be in comparison to B.

2. Answer depends on the legal system involved. In Germany the issue is discussed as one of the **Adequanztheorie der Kausalität** or the **Theorie der objektiven Zurechnung**. Certainly any theory of proximate causation will at least consider the issue of intervening causes and reasonable foreseeability.

3a. true (see *Restatement (Second) Torts* § 13(a), 18(a) for battery, and § 21(1)(a) for assault)

3b. false (intent to cause offensive contact or imminent apprehension of contact is sufficient, see, *Restatement (Second) Torts* § 21(1)(a))

3c. false (offensive contact is sufficient *Restatement (Second) Torts* § 18)

3d. false (no imminent apprehension of contact)

3e. true (offensive and, depending on George's tolerance for alcohol, perhaps harmful contact has occurred)

3f. false (no imminent apprehension of contact with alcohol)

3g. false (negligence standard depends on reasonable practices in the medical community)

3h. false (tort was not committed within scope of Fred's employment)

Unit II Chapter 3

Questions p. 191

1. As the court stated the doctrine, the defendant must have had exclusive control over the thing that caused the injury for the doctrine to apply. The court extends the doctrine (lines 43-49) to cover cases where the defendant had exclusive control of the thing at the time of the negligent act but not at the time the harm was caused.

2. Restatement § 328D(1)(b) reflects this extension because it does not require the defendant to have exclusive control over the thing but rather that other potentially responsible causes for the harm be excluded by the evidence.

3. It was necessary to extend the doctrine in *Escola* because there was a period of time between when the bottle left the defendant's plant and when the

accident happened, during which the defendant did not have exclusive control over the bottle.

4. Res ipsa loquitur raises a rebuttable presumption that the defendant's negligence caused the accident. Consequently, the defendant can escape liability if he can prove that he was not negligent. Strict product liability does not require the plaintiff to prove that the defendant was negligent. The defendant will therefore be held liable even though he exercised reasonable care in the circumstances. Fault is not an issue in strict liability cases.

Questions p. 193

1. The facts of the case are stated in lines 4-34; the legal history in lines 9 and 35-37; the issue raised on appeal in lines 38-39; the holding in lines 108-110, 118. The legal history is not completely stated. At any rate the plaintiff won at the trial court and the defendant appealed. The court whose opinion you have just read is the supreme court of the State of California, which you can see from the case cite (see *Einführung in die anglo-amerikanische Rechtssprache / Introduction to Anglo-American Law & Language*, Appendix II for a detailed explanation of English and U.S. American case citations).

2. Traynor's reasons include a) that the manufacturer is in a better position than the consumer to avoid product defects (lines 133-135)); b) that the individual cannot bear the financial loss of product defects (lines 135-137); c) that the manufacturer can effectively spread the risk and insure the product (lines 138-139); d) that strict liability has a deterrent effect (lines 139-140).

3. The arguments are based on a tort cause of action for negligence, except that Traynor suggests keeping the tort cause of action but eliminating the requirement of fault (lines 123-133); and on breach of warranties, except that Traynor suggests abolishing the privity requirement and permitting the consumer to directly sue the manufacturer, rather than only the retailer (lines 148-157).

4. In Germany the law was quite similar to that applied in *Escola* before the EC directive on products liability was transposed into German law. The EC directive requires the member states to adopt legislation providing for strict product liability (in Germany, see Produkthaftungsgesetz, 15 December 1989).

Questions p. 196

1. First, he has declared the notice requirement of Civil Cods § 1769 inapplicable as between a buyer and a remote seller, here the manufacturer, with whom the plaintiff had no direct business dealings (lines 51-61). This move would have been sufficient to sustain the decision of the trial court in this

case, because if the jury indeed did base its verdict on the breach of express
warranties cause of action, that cause of action has been declared valid.

2. Traynor goes on to hold that strict liability, the standard for breach of war-
    ranty claims, can be imposed independent of the express warranties that were
    contained in the manufacturer's brochure (lines 62-68). Instead the cause of
    action is one in tort. This holding is what makes the case famous, because it
    is the first head-on precedent for strict product liability.

3. Traynor proceeds from the causes of action for breach of an express or
    implied warranty running from the manufacturer to the plaintiff. He notes
    first that the privity requirement was abolished by referring to "the abandon-
    ment of the requirement of a contract between them" (line 71). He then
    indicates that courts began to recognize that the action was one in tort rather
    than contract by pointing to "the recognition that the liability is not assumed
    by agreement but imposed by law" (line 72). Finally he mentions "the refusal
    to permit the manufacturer to define the scope of its own responsibility for
    defective products" (lines 72-74), citing *Henningsen v. Bloomfield Motors,
    Inc.*

4. The ratio in *Henningsen* revolved primarily around the consumer's inferior
    bargaining position in comparison to the united front presented by the auto-
    mobile industry in America at that time. The consumer either took the con-
    tract as it was drafted, or could not buy an automobile.

Questions pp. 203-204

1. This phrase indicates that the plaintiff has filed a **class action**. Refer back to
    Mink v. University of Chicago for an explanation of the class action if you
    have forgotten the term. You can also tell that this is a class action from line
    16: "the mothers of the class she represents" and from line 66: "For the
    members of her class."

2. They refer to the defendant's potential intent or negligence in marketing DES.
    If strict liability were the standard referred to here, the defendant's fault,
    meaning knowingly or negligently causing injury, would be irrelevant.

3. A false representation, or a **misrepresentation**, is a statement that is not true.
    A fraudulent representation is a statement that is false made by s.o. who
    knows it is false, usually with the intent to gain some sort of advantage by
    making the false claim. Here the advantage would be selling a product that
    the manufacturer knows is defective. You have already read about fraudulent
    misrepresentations in Unit I, Chapter 4 in the contract law context. § 402
    B(a) imposes strict liability. A consumer may sue on the basis of a misrep-
    resentation only if the consumer could have **justifiably relied** on it. Accord-
    ingly, if a reasonable person would have realized that the representation was not

intended to be a statement of fact, but rather only an advertising pitch, or if the plaintiff easily could have realized that the representation was not true and not intended to be a statement of truth, then she could not have justifiably relied on it.

4.   Arguments in favor are a) that the individual will be more likely to file a suit if he can get punitive damages, which relieves the prosecutor of some of her case load while still not failing to punish those who deserve it; b) that the state cannot pursue a policy of protecting industry, because a private party can file the action anyway; c) that the real victim of the tort is the plaintiff and only marginally the community, which requires that the plaintiff receive some satisfaction for the wrong done to him. Arguments opposed are a) that punishment is the sole responsibility of the state because private parties should not be able to seek revenge for wrongs done them; b) that civil wrongs in general should not be punished, but rather only conduct that amounts to a crime; and c) that the prosecutor is more impartial and will be fairer in prosecuting than a victim who stands to gain a large amount of money.

5.   You have read about **specific performance** as a remedy for breach of contract when, for example, the subject matter of the contract is unique (I.1.D). You have also read about **promissory estoppel** as an equitable principle when a party justifiably relies on the promisor's promise to his detriment (I.3.C.). For a full discussion of the development of equity, see *Einführung in die anglo-amerikanische Rechtssprache / Introduction to Anglo-American Law & Language*, Unit I, Chapter 1, 4.

6.   The defendants demurred, meaning they claimed that the plaintiff's complaint failed to state a cause of action. The reason for the demurrer is that the plaintiff could not prove a causal connection between any single manufacturer's defective DES and her injuries. Since the plaintiff bears the burden of pleading and proof on the issue of defect and causation, her complaint would be defective if she cannot plead facts supporting her claim that the defendant caused her injuries. When a trial court sustains a demurrer it usually permits the plaintiff to file a new, or amended complaint which compensates for the deficiency the defendant pointed to in the demurrer. Here since the plaintiff admitted she could not specify which manufacturer produced the drug her mother took, she cannot amend her complaint to make up for its deficiencies.

Questions p. 205

1.   In *Summers v. Tice* there was a 100 percent probability that the plaintiff was injured by one of the two defendants joined in the suit. In *Sindell* there is not that 100 percent probability. Approximately 200 manufacturers produced DES during the time the plaintiff's mother took the medication. The plaintiff

originally joined only eleven drug companies by name and 100 unspecified drug companies. The appeal involves only five of the original defendants. Accordingly ca. 195 other drug companies might have produced the DES that caused plaintiff's injuries. That is the main thrust of the defendants' arguments.

2. Under German law, § 830 I. *BGB*, the *Summers* defendants also would be held liable. The second sentence of § 830 I. essentially contains the holding of *Summers v. Tice*.

Questions p. 208

1. The term **jurisdiction** means the power and authority of a court to hear a case. California courts have **personal jurisdiction**, for example, over residents of California, but not necessarily over the residents of other states. If the California courts do not have jurisdiction over some of the DES producers, then the plaintiff cannot compel these companies to appear in a California court to defend themselves against a law suit. Accordingly, the plaintiff could not join all potential defendants in the law suit. For that reason, *Summers v. Tice* would not apply, unless the court here extends it.

2. The court indicates in line 215 that the defendants may **cross-complain** against any other DES manufacturer. A **cross-complaint** is a complaint filed by a defendant to a law suit against other potential defendants. Of course, if some of the DES manufacturers are not subject to the jurisdiction of the California courts, the defendants will not be able to cross-complain against them anymore than the plaintiff could file a complaint against them in a California court.

3. When a court is apportioning responsibility for harm between the plaintiff, who was harmed, and one defendant, who in part caused the harm, the only error would relate to the exact amount of harm each party had to bear of the total harm they caused together. Accordingly, the defendant might have to pay for 60% of the harm, when he only caused 50% of it. In *Sindell*, apportioning responsibility according to market share could involve two types of error. The court might estimate a defendant's share of the market at 90%, when it was only 80%. The defendant then would have to pay 90% of the damages awarded. The difference between the 90% and the 80% is not much different from the difference between 60% and 50% in the foregoing example. Still, it could be the case in this example that the defendant, although having an 80% market share, did not produce the medication the plaintiff's mother took. It would then be held liable for 80% of harm it did not contribute to causing at all.

Bibliography

(All indicated excerpts are reprinted with permission)

Cases

Allegheny College v. National Chautauqua County Bank, 246 N.Y. 369, 159 N.E. 173
(1927). 59

Butterfield v. Forrester, 103 Eng.Rep. 926 (K.B. 1809) 160

Carlill v. Carbolic Smoke Ball Co., 1 Q.B. 256 [1893]. 10

Cobbs v. Grant, 8 Cal.3d 229, 104 Cal.Reptr. 505, 502 P.2d 1 (1972) 133

Escola v. Coca Cola Bottling Co., 24 Cal. 2d 453, 150 P.2d 436 (1944) 187

Gardner v. Moore's Adm'r, 122 Va. 14, 94 S.E. 162 56

Greenman v. Yuba Power Products, Inc., 59 Cal.2d 67, 377 P.2d 897 (1963) 193

Hall v. E. I. Du Pont de Nemours & Co., Inc., 345 F. Supp. 353 (E.D.N.Y. 1972) 205

Henningsen v. Bloomfield Motors, Inc., 32 N.J. 358, 161 A.2d 69 (1960) 196

Krell v. Henry, 72 L.J.K.B. 794, [1900-03] All E.R.Rep. 20 (1903) 81

Lefkowitz v. Great Minneapolis Surplus Store, 251 Minn. 188, 86 N.W.2d 689 (1957) 19

Maughs v. Porter, 157 Va. 415, 161 S.E. 242 (1931). 54

Mink v. University of Chicago, 460 F. Supp. 713 (N.D. Ill. 1978). 129

Palsgraf v. Long Island Railroad, 248 N.Y. 339, 162 N.E. 99 (1928) 166

Petterson v. Pattberg, 248 N.Y. 86, 161 N.E. 428 (1928) 36

Rice v. The Marion A.C. Meseck, 148 F.2d 522 (2 Cir.) 155

Sindell, v. Abbott Laboratories, 26 Cal. 3d 588, 607 P.2d 924, 163 Cal. Rptr. 132 (1980) . 201

Spooner v. Hilbish, 92 Va. 341, 23 S.E. 751 56

Summers v. Tice 33 Cal.2d 80, 199 P.2d 1 (1948) 204

Taylor and Another v. Caldwell and Another, 32 L.J. Q.B. 164, [1861-73] All E.R.
Rep. 24 (1863). 74

Trogun v. Fruchtman, 58 Wis.2d 569, 207 N.W.2d 311 (1973) 133

United States et al. v. Carroll Towing Co., Inc., et al., 159 F.2d 169 (2d Cir. 1947). . . . 151

Vosburg v. Putney, 80 Wis. 523, 50 N.W. 403 (1891) 135

Vu v. Singer Co., 538 F.Supp. 26 (N.D. Cal. 1981) 149

Wood v. Boynton, 64 Wis. 265, 25 N.W. 42 (1885) 83

Wood v. Lucy, Lady Duff-Gordon, 222 N.Y. 88, 118 N.E. 214 (1917) 50

Legislative Materials

§ 119-124 BGB 243

§ 142-144 BGB 243

§ 145 BGB 35, 48

§ 146 BGB 35, 48

§ 147 BGB 48

§ 242 BGB 243

§ 254 BGB 160

§ 275 BGB 241

§ 278 BGB 157

§ 280 BGB 241

§ 306 BGB 241

§ 307 BGB 241

§ 323 BGB 241

§ 325 BGB 241

§ 688-700 BGB 242

§ 830 BGB 258

§ 831 BGB 157, 249

Law Reform (Contributory Negligence) Act 1945 160

Produkthaftungsgesetz, 15 December 1989 255

Restatement (Second) Contracts § 17. Requirement of a Bargain 5

Restatement (Second) Contracts § 23. Necessity That Manifestations Have Reference to
    Each Other 16

Restatement (Second) Contracts § 25. Option Contracts 35

Restatement (Second) Contracts § 26. Preliminary Negotiations 14

Restatement (Second) Contracts § 29. To Whom an Offer is Addressed 14

Restatement (Second) Contracts § 32. Invitation of Promise or Performance 14

Restatement (Second) Contracts § 35. The Offeree's Power of Acceptance 14

Restatement (Second) Contracts § 36. Methods of Termination of the Power
    of Acceptance 15

Restatement (Second) Contracts § 40. Time When Rejection Terminates the Power of
    Acceptance 34

Restatement (Second) Contracts § 42. Revocation by Communication from Offeror
    Received by Offeree 33

Restatement (Second) Contracts § 45. Option Contract Created by Part Performance or
    Tender 40

Restatement (Second) Contracts § 50. Acceptance of Offer Defined 16

Restatement (Second) Contracts § 52. Who May Accept an Offer 14

Restatement (Second) Contracts § 54. Acceptance by Performance; Necessity of Notification to Offeror 16

Restatement (Second) Contracts § 63. Time When Acceptance Takes Effect 31

Restatement (Second) Contracts § 71. Requirement of Exchange; Types of Exchange . 5

Restatement (Second) Contracts § 73. Performance of Legal Duty 41

Restatement (Second) Contracts § 90. Promise Reasonably Inducing Action or Forbearance 63

Restatement (Second) Contracts § 152. When Mistake of Both Parties Makes a Contract Voidable 89

Restatement (Second) Contracts § 153. When Mistake of One Party Makes a Contract Voidable 90

Restatement (Second) Contracts § 154. When a Party Bears the Risk of a Mistake . . . 90

Restatement (Second) Contracts § 162. When a Misrepresentation Is Fraudulent or Material 87

Restatement (Second) Contracts § 164. When a Misrepresentation Makes a Contract Voidable 87

Restatement (Second) Contracts § 174. When Duress by Physical Compulsion Prevents Formation of a Contract 101

Restatement (Second) Contracts § 175. When Duress by Threat Makes a Contract Voidable 101

Restatement (Second) Contracts § 224. Condition Defined 18

Restatement (Second) Contracts § 230. Event that Terminates a Duty 19

Restatement (Second) Contracts § 265. Discharge by Supervening Frustration 83

Restatement (Second) Contracts § 347. Measure of Damages in General 9

Restatement (Second) Contracts § 357. Availability of Specific Performance 9

Restatement (Second) Contracts § 359. Effect of Adequacy of Damages 9

Restatement (Second) Contracts § 360. Factors Affecting Adequacy of Damages 9

Restatement (Second) Torts § 13. Battery: Harmful Contact 127

Restatement (Second) Torts § 18. Battery: Offensive Contact 128

Restatement (Second) Torts § 21. Assault 139

Restatement (Second) Torts § 314. Duty to Act for Protection of Others 149

Restatement (Second) Torts § 321. Duty to Act When Prior Conduct is Found to be Dangerous 149

Restatement (Second) Torts § 322. Duty to Aid Another Harmed by Actor's Conduct . 150

Restatement (Second) Torts § 328. A. Burden of Proof 148

Restatement (Second) Torts § 328. B. Functions of Court 170

Restatement (Second) Torts § 328. C. Functions of Jury 170

Restatement (Second) Torts § 328. D. Res Ipsa Loquitur.   189

Restatement (Second) Torts § 402. A. Special Liability of Seller of Product for Physical
    Harm to User or Consumer   198

Restatement (Second) Torts § 402. B. Misrepresentation by Seller of Chattels to
    Consumer.   203

Uniform Commercial Code § 1-103. Supplementary General Principles of Law
    Applicable   100

Uniform Commercial Code § 1-105. Territorial Application of the Act; Parties' Power
    to Choose Applicable Law   102

Uniform Commercial Code § 2-104. Definitions: "Merchant"; "Between Merchants".   105

Uniform Commercial Code § 2-204. Formation in General   112

Uniform Commercial Code § 2-205. Firm Offers   116

Uniform Commercial Code § 2-206. Offer and Acceptance in Formation of Contract .   109

Uniform Commercial Code § 2-207. Additional Terms in Acceptance or Confirmation   106

Uniform Commercial Code § 2-209. Modification   116

Uniform Commercial Code § 2-305. Open Price Term   112

Uniform Commercial Code § 2-306. Output, Requirements and Exclusive Dealings . .   54

Uniform Commercial Code § 9-105. Definitions and Index of Definitions   120

Secondary Literature

Clerk & Lindsell, Torts, 16th ed., Sweet & Maxwell: London (1989); Fourth Cumu-
    lative Supplement to the Sixteenth Edition (1994) 149, 150, 165

E. Allan Farnsworth, Contracts, Little Brown & Co.: Boston/Toronto, 1982   18

Charles Fried, Contract as Promise, Harvard University Press: Cambridge, Massa-
    chusetts (1981)   32

Mark F. Grady, Cases and Materials on Torts, American Casebook Series,
    West Publishing Co.: St. Paul, Minnesota (1994) 136, 165

Mark F. Grady, "Untaken Precautions," Journal of Legal Studies, vol. XVIII
    (January 1989) 163, 177

Prosser & Keeton on The Law of Torts, West Publishing Co.:
    St. Paul, Minnesota (1984). 139, 148, 156, 161, 165, 169

J. White and R. Summers, Uniform Commercial Code (4th ed.) West Publishing Co.:
    St. Paul, Minnesota 108, 114, 117

Reinhard Zimmermann, The Law of Obligations. Roman Foundations of the Civilian
    Tradition, Juta & Co. Ltd.: Cape Town, Wetton, Johannesburg (1990).   157

Encyclopedia and Dictionaries

Black's Law Dictionary "anticipatory repudiation" 61

Black's Law Dictionary "assumption of risk" 210

Black's Law Dictionary "bond" 37

Black's Law Dictionary "coercion" 101

Black's Law Dictionary "defamation" 142

Black's Law Dictionary "demurrer" 51

Black's Law Dictionary "duress" 101

Black's Law Dictionary "fraud" 86

Black's Law Dictionary "misrepresentation" 87

Black's Law Dictionary "mortgage" 37

Black's Law Dictionary "negotiable instruments" 119

Black's Law Dictionary "notice of motion" 55

Black's Law Dictionary "principal" 37

Black's Law Dictionary "rescission of contract" 86

Black's Law Dictionary "right of subrogation" 181

Black's Law Dictionary "rule absolute" 79

Black's Law Dictionary "tender" 39

Black's Law Dictionary "writ of error" 56

Newspapers

International Herald Tribune, January 4-5, 1997 66

Terminology

Number after term indicates Unit and Chapter in which term originally appeared and was explained, e.g. (I.1) = Unit I, Chapter 1. The terminology in the Terminology Review sections are *not* contained in this Glossary. They are contained in the Glossary to *Einführung in die anglo-amerikanische Rechtssprache / Introduction to Anglo-American Law & Language*.

The terminology appearing in this book is defined *in the context* in which it appears in the texts. Some terms have more than one usage and the meaning depends on the context. You may therefore not treat this Glossary as an exhaustive dictionary. If you have a German legal term within a text you would like to translate into English, you should first look in a German-English dictionary of legal terms for the possible English equivalents. Once you have the English equivalents, you should check them in an English-English legal dictionary to find out their exact meaning within an Anglo-American legal system. In addition, it is helpful to cross-check the English terms by looking them up in the English-German part of the same legal dictionary you used to find the English equivalents originally. Most likely you will find several German terms indicated for one of the English terms. That should help you understand the possible contexts within which the terms may be used, particularly when translated into another language and another legal system. If you have an English term within a text you would like to translate into German, you probably will not need to do this last cross-check, because you are a native speaker of the German language and have training in German law. You will therefore know which German term to use if you understand the English term sufficiently. Suggestions for German translations of the following terms as they appeared in context are included, if at all feasible. Many terms simply cannot be translated because the two legal systems are different in a fundamental way. Sometimes approximations of terms are indicated with "ca." and sometimes a comparison is suggested or simply an explanation in German given.

acceptance (I.1)	agreement to the terms of an offer; closes the contract (**Annahme**)
actionability (II.2)	the ability to maintain a law suit in the sense that the law supports the particular claim (**Einklagbarkeit**)
action for battery (II.1)	law suit filed against person who committed a battery (**Klage auf Schadensersatz wegen Körperverletzung**)
an action for battery lies (II.1)	indicates that facts support a law suit for a battery; may also be used in the negative: **no action for battery lies** (**eine Klage auf Schadensersatz wegen Körperverletzung ist un/schlüssig**)

an action for battery may be had (II.1)	indicates that facts support a law suit for a battery; may also be used in the negative: **no action for battery may be had** (eine Klage auf Schadensersatz wegen Körperverletzung ist un/schlüssig)
adequate consideration (I.1)	enough to be a fair return for s.th. in the light of general market prices; not a requirement for a contract to be binding, since the parties are free to decide what they want to exchange (**angemessene Gegenleistung**)
administrator (I.2)	male individual appointed by a court to perform the functions of an **executor** in all cases in which an executor has not been named by the decedent (**gerichtlich ernannter Testamentsvollstrecker**)
administratrix (I.2)	female individual appointed by a court to perform the functions of an **executrix** in all cases in which an executrix has not been named by the decedent (**gerichtlich ernannte Testamentsvollstreckerin**)
admissions (I.3)	statements in a defendant's answer that indicate the defendant's agreement with certain facts the plaintiff has claimed in his complaint (**Geständnisse**)
affirmative act (II.2)	basis for the law to impose a duty of care on the actor; used to refer to an act that places s.o. else in danger and thus gives a good reason for requiring the person who committed the act to take measures to protect the potential victim (ca. **Ingerenz**)
agent (I.1)	person who conducts business for another person, who is the principal (**Geschäftsführer, Vertreter**)
age of legal majority (I.2)	age at which the law considers an individual sufficiently mature to enter into legal relations (ca. **Eintritt der Volljährigkeit**)
aggrieved party (I.3)	individual who has been harmed or injured; person who has been negatively affected (**Verletzter, Geschädigter**)
allocation of risk (I.4)	assignment to a certain person or persons of disadvantages that might materialize if some event occurs or facts become known (**Verteilung des Risikos**); also: division and distribution of goods, wealth, entitlements, benefits (**Verteilung von Gütern**)
alternative liability (II.3)	responsibility imposed on all potential defendants when one of two or more of them caused plaintiff's injuries and plaintiff cannot prove which one of the defendants actually caused the injury (**Haftung der Beteiligten**); an alternative liability theory shifts the burden of proof on the causation issue to the defendants and if they cannot prove who was not at fault they will be held **jointly and severally liable**
anticipatory repudiation (I.3)	indication of refusal to perform on a contract before performance is actually due under the contract; repudiation (**Weigerung, den Vertrag zu erfüllen**); anticipatory repudiation (**Weigerung, den Vertrag zu erfüllen, vor Fälligkeit der vereinbarten Leistung**)

argumentation by analogy (I.4)	arguing by comparing a case that has to be decided with other cases that have been decided in the past or to hypothetical cases where the correct solution seems intuitively clear; the purpose of this form of argumentation is convince s.o. of the appropriateness of one's own conclusion regarding the new case, because one claims that it is really no different from these other cases on hypotheticals (**Berufung auf eine Analogie**)
assault (II.1)	tort of intentionally causing the victim to fear that he will be harmfully or offensively touched physically on the instant occasion (**Bedrohung**)
assignments of error (II.2)	list of legal errors appellant claims a lower court, whose judgment the appellant is appealing, made (**Revisionsrüge**)
assumption of risk (II.3)	"The doctrine of assumption of risk, also known as volenti non fit injuria, means legally that a plaintiff may not recover for an injury to which he assents, *i.e.*, that a person may not recover for an injury received when he voluntarily exposes himself to a known and appreciated danger. The requirements for the defense of volenti non fit injuria are that: (1) the plaintiff has knowledge of facts constituting a dangerous condition, (2) he knows the condition is dangerous, (3) he appreciates the nature or extent of the danger, and (4) he voluntarily exposes himself to the danger ..." *Black's Law Dictionary* (**volenti non fit injuria**)
bailee (I.4)	one who holds another's goods in deposit (**Verwahrer**)
bailment (I.4)	deposit of goods with someone for safe keeping or for use for a specified purpose (**Besitzüberlassung an beweglichen Sachen auf Zeit, z.B. Hinterlegung, Verwahrung**)
bailor (I.4)	one who deposits goods with another (**Hinterleger**)
battery (II.1)	tort of intentional harm or offensive contact with the person of another (**Körperverletzung**); cf. **harmful contact battery, offensive contact battery**
battle of the forms (I.5)	conflict between offeror's and offeree's standard terms as incorporated in their order forms or confirmations (**Kollision widersprechender AGB**)
bilateral contract (I.1)	promise in exchange for a promise (ca. **zweiseitig verpflichtender Vertrag**)
bill of lading (I.5)	document of verification of having received goods for shipment, which is issued by the transporter (**Frachtbrief, Seefrachtbrief, Konnossement**)
bond (I.2)	instrument of security for a debt; document indicating existence of a debt and agreement to repay which is secured by a mortgage

	(Schuldschein verbunden mit der Bewirkung einer Sicherheits-leistung)
breach of contract (I.1)	failure to fulfill a contractual obligation when due (**Nichterfül-lung einer vertraglichen Verbindlichkeit zum Fälligkeitszeit-punkt**)
breach of duty (II.2)	failure to meet up to the standard of care imposed by law on a person who has a duty of care to another individual (**Sorgfalts-pflichtverletzung**)
breaching party (I.1)	person who fails to perform on a contract when performance is due (**Schuldner, der seine vertraglichen Pflichten nicht erfüllt**)
non-breaching party (I.1)	person who has either performed or is prepared to perform on a contract that has been breached by the other party to the contract (**vertragstreuer Teil**)
bulk sales (I.5)	sale of more than half of seller's inventory when seller has no intention to continue in the business of selling that type of inven-tory (**Gesamtverkauf**)
burden of proof (II.2)	obligation to provide enough evidence to prove legal claim (**Be-weislast**)
but-for cause (II.2)	test of causation whereby one determines whether A caused B by asking whether if A had not occurred, B would have oc-curred; if not then A was the **cause in fact** or the **but-for cause** of B (**conditio sine qua non; äquivalente Verursachung**)
call option (I.2)	option giving offeree the right to buy s.th. at a set price for a specified period of time (der Ausdruck **call option** wird auch in deutschen Texten benutzt)
cause in fact (II.2)	test of causation whereby one determines whether A caused B by asking whether if A had not occurred, B would have oc-curred; if not then A was the **cause in fact** or the **but-for cause** of B (**conditio sine qua non; äquivalente Verursachung**)
charitable subscription (I.3)	promise to donate money to a charity (**Zusage, eine Spende für eine wohltätige Einrichtung zu geben**)
chattel paper (I.5)	"writing or writings which evidence both a monetary obligation and a security interest in or lease of specific goods" *U.C.C. § 9-105(1)(b)*; when an owner of property leases it to another or sells it on installment payments but retains a security interest in that property, the documents indicating the debt and the security interest are chattel paper (**Papiere, die eine Zahlungsverpflich-tung und zugleich eine Sicherung dafür beurkunden**)
chattels (I.2)	property other than land (**Fahrnis, bewegliche Sachen**)
choice of law (I.5)	determination by the parties to a contract that the law of a

specified nation or state is to apply to their agreement (**Bestimmung des anzuwendenden Rechts**)

civil procedure (I.3)   body of rules governing the manner in which a private law dispute is carried out in the courts (**Zivilprozeßrecht**)

coercion (I.5)   compulsion, force (**Nötigung, Zwang, Gewalt**)

commercial transactions (I.5)   trade, business of buying or selling goods (**Handelsgeschäfte**)

common mistake (I.4)   mistake as to conditions relating to a contract that is shared by both parties; also called **mutual mistake** (**beiderseitiger Irrtum**)

comparative negligence (II.2)   (US) refers to principle of sharing responsibility for harm caused by a tort; damages are apportioned between the plaintiff and the defendant depending on each party's degree of fault (**Mitverschulden**)

modified comparative negligence (II.2)   apportions damages between plaintiff and defendant but imposes a 50% limit on the plaintiff's own fault for the plaintiff to recover any damages (us: **Mitverschulden, das Schadensersatzansprüche proportional mindert und bei einer mehr als 50%igen Selbstverschuldung des Klägers sogar ausschließt**)

pure comparative negligence (II.2)   apportions damages according to each party's fault in causing harm (**Mitverschulden**)

compensatory damages (I.1)   primary common law remedy for breach of contract; puts the non-breaching party in the position he would have been in had the contract been performed (**Schadensersatz wegen Nichterfüllung**)

concurrent efficient cause (II.2)   another term for an intervening cause; one of several but-for causes of plaintiff's harm (ca. **kumulative Kausalität**)

condition (I.4)   assumption, stipulation (**Bedingung**); can be **express** (**ausdrückliche Bedingung**) or **implied** (**Bedingung, die in einem Vertrag konkludent enthalten ist**)

condition precedent (I.1)   some event that must occur before a duty to perform on a contract arises (**aufschiebende Bedingung**)

condition subsequent (I.1)   some event that if it occurs terminates the duty to perform on a contract (**auflösende Bedingung**)

confirmation (I.5)   written statement of terms of an agreement undertaken by the buyer or seller, or both, to verify an oral agreement, or an agreement that has been reached through the exchange of correspondence, also to give the agreement final form; usually contains list of standard terms used by the party writing the confirmation; also: **confirming form** (**Bestätigungsschreiben**)

conflict of laws (I.5)   area of law dealing with decision on which of two or more relevant legal systems to refer to in order to select the law that

	should be applied in a case with relevant connections to one or more states (**Kollisionsrecht, Internationales Privatrecht**)
consent (II.1)	agreement to what would otherwise be a wrongful touching of a person; can justify the commission of a battery (**Einwilligung; Einverständnis**)
consent implied in fact (II.1)	doing or saying s.th. from which a reasonable person would conclude that one is in agreement (**konkludente Einwilligung; stillschweigende Einwilligung**)
consent implied in law (II.1)	circumstances from which one concludes as a matter of law that a person would be in agreement with s.th. (**mutmaßliche Einwilligung**)
consideration (I.1)	mutually bargained-for exchange; requirement for a simple contract to be binding on the parties; whether a contract is supported by consideration is a legal evaluation (**Gegenleistung**)
construction defect (II.3)	product defect that affects only a few products of a product line; defect that arises from faulty construction of the particular product as it moves through the assembly line (**Konstruktionsfehler, der in der Anfertigung eines konkreten Produkts liegt**); also called **manufacturing defect**
constructive delivery (I.3)	not actually transferring an object to another person, but acting in a manner that will be interpreted by a court to be the same as actually transferring or delivering the object (**Übergabesurrogat**)
contract to compose a work (I.4)	agreement requiring one party to make, prepare or create s.th., such as a painting, musical score, book (ca. **Werkvertrag**)
contributory negligence (II.2)	(US) refers to original English doctrine that barred a plaintiff from collecting any damages whatsoever from a defendant if the plaintiff was at all at fault for his own injuries (**Ausschluß des Anspruchs bei Mitverschulden**); (UK) term used today to mean that plaintiff may collect only the amount of damages necessary to compensate for the defendant's share of fault in causing the plaintiff harm (**Mitverschulden**)
counsel (I.4)	lawyer, attorney (**Rechtsanwalt**)
count (I.4)	individual claim against another individual; a **complaint** may include a variety of different claims, each based on a different legal theory and each of which would be one **count** (**Klagepunkt**)
counterclaims (I.3)	allegations of fact in the defendant's answer that would support a legal claim against the plaintiff (**Widerklage**)
counter-offer (I.2)	an offer the offeree makes in response to the offeror's original offer; does not function as an acceptance because the terms of the counter-offer are significantly different from the original offer (**Gegenangebot**)
creditor (I.2)	individual who has loaned money to another (**Gläubiger**), who

is called the **debtor (Schuldner)**; contrast to: **promisor (Schuldner)** and **promisee (Gläubiger)**

damage (II.2)

harm caused the victim of a tort (**Schaden**)

damages (II.2)

remedy in money to compensate for the injury caused a tort victim, as in: **money damages (Schadensersatz)**

deed (I.1)

(UK) formalized contract (**formgerechter Vertrag**); (US) document used to transfer ownership in land

defamation (II.1)

"An intentional false communication, either published or publicly spoken, that injures another's reputation or good name. Holding up of a person to ridicule, scorn or contempt in a respectable and considerable part of the community; may be criminal as well as civil." (*Black's Law Dictionary*),(**üble Nachrede und Verleumdung**); includes both **libel** and **slander**.

default on a mortgage (I.2)

to fail to make timely repayment of a debt that is secured by a mortgage (**Verzug des Schuldners bei einer dinglich gesicherten Forderung**)

defendant in error (I.3)

party against whom a petition for a writ of error has been brought (**Revisionsbeklagter**)

defense to a claim of breach (I.1)

anything a defendant to a law suit for breach of contract can claim on his behalf (**Einwendung gegen eine Klage wegen Nichterfüllung**)

demise (I.4)

transfer of property for life or for a certain number of years

demurrer (I.3)

motion, usually filed by a defendant in response to the plaintiff's complaint, asking the court to dismiss the complaint for legal insufficiency; test for whether the demurrer should be sustained is whether complaint states a cause of action, assuming that all facts plaintiff has claimed are true; raises purely a question of law (**Antrag auf Schlüssigkeitsprüfung**)

denials (I.3)

statements in a defendant's answer that indicate the defendant's disagreement with certain facts the plaintiff has claimed in his complaint (**Bestreiten von Klagebehauptungen**)

design defect (II.3)

product defect that affects all products of a product line because the product was not conceived in a way that would make it safe to use (**Konstruktionsfehler, der im Design eines Produkts liegt**)

detrimental reliance (I.3)

trusting in a promise or statement made by another person under circumstances that would lead reasonable people to trust in that promise or statement and suffering a loss as a result of this trust; as a principle of equity, detrimental reliance will in some cases be a reason for prohibiting the person who made the promise or statement from asserting a right he otherwise would have (**Haftung des Gefälligen für das Nichteinhalten einer Gefälligkeitsabrede**)

to die intestate (I.2) to die without leaving a will or testament (**ohne letztwillige Verfügung sterben**)

direct consequence (II.2) one method of formulating the question of proximate causation; focuses on whether causes other than the defendant's act intervened before the plaintiff was injured (**unmittelbare Folge**)

discharged from performance (I.4) released from the duty to perform according to the terms of a contract (**von einer Leistung befreit worden sein**)

disclaimer (II.3) an express statement that one refuses to include certain types of harm, or that one will pay only for certain types of harm, within the context of a warranty (**Haftungsausschlußklausel**)

to dismiss an appeal (I.4) (UK) to uphold the decision of a lower court in a case against appellate attack by a party dissatisfied with that decision (**die Revision zurückweisen**); opposite of **to allow an appeal** (**der Revision stattgeben**)

donative contract (I.1) contract to make a gift (**Schenkungsvertrag**)

duress (I.5) unlawful use of physical force or threats to cause an individual to act as he otherwise would not act in the absence of the force or threats (**Nötigungsnotstand**)

duty of care (II.2) obligation to take precautions to avoid harming another person (**Sorgfaltspflicht**)

endorsement (I.3) signature of approval or support (**Indossament, Bestätigung, Zustimmung**)

endowment (I.3) an amount of money given for a charitable purpose which is specified at the time of the gift (**Widmung von Stiftungskapital, Stiftung**)

to enter judgment on the verdict (I.4) to officially record, as a judge, the determination made at trial by the factfinder; **entering judgment on the verdict** gives legal effect to the verdict (**ein Urteil im Einklang mit dem Spruch der Geschworenen fällen**); if a jury is used and the judge is of the opinion that no reasonable jury could have reached the verdict the jury did reach, the judge may also **enter judgment notwithstanding the verdict**

to enter judgment notwithstanding the verdict (I.4) to officially record, as a judge, a determination that the jury's verdict cannot be upheld as a matter of law; in order to be able to enter **judgment notwithstanding the verdict**, the judge must view the facts most favorably to the party for whom the verdict was reached and decide on the basis of that view of the facts that still the party should not have been successful in the law suit as a matter of law; either party to the law suit may make a motion at the end of the trial to have the judge **enter a judgment notwithstanding the verdict**; a **judgment notwithstanding the verdict** permits the judge to override the jury's determination and thus ensure that the case is properly resolved; a **judgment notwithstanding the verdict** can*not* be reached if a jury in a criminal case finds the defendant not guilty; also called **judgment n.o.v.**, meaning **judgment** *non obstante veredicto* (**ein Urteil nicht im Einklang mit dem Spruch der Geschworenen fällen**)

to enter a verdict (I.4)   to officially record a decision reached by the **factfinder** (either judge or jury) at trial; more often used in: **to enter judgment on the verdict**

equal fault bar (II.2)   modified comparative negligence rule which bars the plaintiff from recovering any damages from the defendant if the plaintiff's negligence accounts for 50% or more of his own harm; if it is less than 50%, the rule of pure comparative negligence applies (**Mitverschulden, das Schadensersatzansprüche proportional mindert und bei einer mindestens 50%igen Selbstverschuldung des Klägers sogar ausschließt**); cf. **greater fault bar**

equitable remedy (I.1)   remedy, such as specific performance, which was awarded plaintiffs by courts of equity, rather than by courts of law (**Klagebegehren aus Prinzipien von Treu und Glauben, entwickelt für Fälle, die nach reinen Rechtsprinzipien nicht gerecht gelöst werden konnten**)

estate pledge (I.3)   promise to donate money or other assets from property that is left over after one's death (**Erbvertrag**)

exclusive dealing agreement (I.3)   an agreement whereby a seller grants a buyer a right to purchase goods for resale and the seller agrees not to sell the goods to anyone else other than the individual buyer with whom he has closed the agreement (**Alleinbezugsvertrag**)

executed contract (I.3)   a contract that has been fully performed by all of the parties to the contract (**Vertrag, der bereits voll erfüllt worden ist**)

executor (I.2)   male individual designated in a will who is responsible for managing property left after death and eventually distributing it to the deceased's heirs (**Testamentsvollstrecker**)

executory contract (I.3)   a contract that has not yet been fully performed (**Vertrag, der noch nicht ganz erfüllt worden ist**)

executrix (I.2)   female individual designated in a will who is responsible for managing property left after death and eventually distributing it to the deceased's heirs (**Testamentsvollstreckerin**)

express conditions (I.4)   assumptions or stipulations that the parties actually state in their agreement (**ausdrückliche Bedingungen**)

express consent (II.1)   actually saying or writing that one is in agreement with s.th. (**ausdrückliche Einwilligung**)

express warranty (II.2)   guarantee that is actually stated; purchaser needs to negotiate with seller to obtain it (**ausdrückliche Zusicherung, ausdrückliche Gewährleistung**)

to extend a precedent (I.4)   to take an already established precedent and apply it to a new case that is somewhat different in a legally relevant respect to the former case; after the precedent has been extended it applies in more cases than it did before it was extended (**den Anwendungsbereich eines Präzedenzurteils ausdehnen**)

failure to warn (II.3)   manufacturer's omitting to inform consumers of a danger inherent to a product if it is used incorrectly or because it cannot be made any safer in light of the current state of the art (**Verletzung der Aufklärungspflicht**)

false imprisonment (II.1)   tort of unlawful deprivation of the victim's personal liberty through detaining or confining him (**Freiheitsberaubung**)

firm offer (I.5)   an offer to contract that the offeror intends to keep open for a certain period of time (**festes Angebot**)

foreseeability of the risk (II.2)   a method of formulating the question of proximate cause; focuses on whether normal people would have realized ex ante that conduct such as the defendant's would cause a certain kind of harm (**Voraussehbarkeit der Gefahr**)

formalization (I.1)   method of recognition of the binding nature of a contract, usually by a notary who either stamps or seals the contract, often in the presence of witnesses to the contracting parties' signatures (**öffentliche Beglaubigung**)

fraud (I.4)   intentional deceit for the purpose of convincing another person to part with s.th. valuable (**arglistige Täuschung**; strafrechtlich: **Betrug**)

frustration (I.4)   defense to a claim of breach of contract based on a change in circumstances after the contract was closed that make one party's performance worthless to the other party (**Wegfall der Geschäftsgrundlage**)

gap fillers (I.5)   rules on how to determine what the conditions of an agreement are when those conditions have not been specified by the parties (**gesetzliche Auslegungsregeln**)

general verdict (II.1)   conclusion reached by the jury on the final outcome of the case; includes the jury's application of the law, as instructed, to the facts the jury believes true to reach a final determination of the parties' rights (**Endurteil der Geschworenen**)

in good faith (I.5)   honest and without effort to take advantage of another (**nach den Prinzipien von Treu und Glauben, bona fide**)

good Samaritan duty render aid (II.2) — general obligation imposed by law to assist people who are in a dangerous situation in order to to avoid their being harmed (**allgemeine Hilfeleistungspflicht**)

gratuitous contract (I.1) — contract to make a gift (**Schenkungsvertrag**)

gratuitous undertaking (II.2) — basis for the law to impose a duty of care; refers to a situation in which an individual enters into a non-contractual relationship to render services for s.o. else (**Auftragsverhältnis**)

greater fault bar (II.2) — modified comparative negligence rule which bars the plaintiff from recovering any damages from the defendant if the plaintiff's negligence accounts for more than 50% of his own harm; if it is 50% or less, the rule of pure comparative negligence applies (**Mitverschulden, das Schadensersatzansprüche proportional mindert und bei mehr als 50%iger Selbstverschuldung des Klägers sogar ausschließt**); cf. **equal fault bar**

harmful contact battery (II.1) — tort of inflicting physical harm with the intent to do so, or with the intent to offensively come into physical contact with the victim or to make the victim feel threatened with physical harm or offensive contact

harmless error (II.3) — an error of law that could not have affected the outcome of the trial; an error so insignificant it will not be the basis of reversal on appeal (**unerheblicher Rechtsfehler**)

immateriality of breach (I.1) — failure to perform as required by a contract but in a relatively insignificant manner, such as by being in delay for an amount of time that is irrelevant in light of the entire contract; if a breach is **material** it permits the non-breaching party to terminate his own performance and sue the breaching party for damages; if the breach is **immaterial**, the breaching party may insist that the non-breaching party not terminate the contract, or may claim this immateriality in his own defense to an action for breach of contract (**Unerheblichkeit der Nichterfüllung**)

immovables (I.2) — land and everything attached to the land (**Liegenschaften, unbewegliche Sachen**)

implied conditions (I.4) — assumptions or stipulations that are not actually stated but which a court will interpret into a contract based on the parties' behavior and expectations (**Bedingungen, die in einem Vertrag konkludent enthalten sind**)

implied warranty (II.3) — guarantee that a court will assume exists from the conduct of the party (**konkludente Gewährleistung**); generally courts assume that a product placed on the market is safe for its intended or reasonably foreseeable use (**implied warranty of merchantability**) (**Gewährleistung der handelsüblichen Qualität**); if a seller

	knew of the particular purpose for which the buyer purchased the product, courts will also assume that the product is safe for this particular use (**implied warranty of fitness for use**) (**Gewährleistung der Eignung für den vertraglichen Zweck**)
impossibility of performance (I.1)	one defense to a law suit for breach of contract, whereby the defendant claims that through no fault of his own he has become unable to perform his promise (**nicht zu vertretende Unmöglichkeit**)
imputed negligence (II.2)	attributing the negligence of one person to another because of the relationship between the two (**Zurechnung eines Drittverschuldens**)
indorsement (I.3)	signature of approval or support (**Indossament, Bestätigung, Zustimmung**)
industry-wide liability (II.3)	joint liability of all manufacturers of a defective product when plaintiff cannot prove which one of the defendants actually produced the product that caused plaintiff's injuries; shifts burden of proof to defendants on causation issue; is only applied when all manufacturers adhere to an industry-wide safety standard, all products are generically similar, and plaintiff presents adequate proof that the injury was caused by a product produced by one of the defendants joined in the action
informal contract (I.1)	contract that has to be supported by consideration to be binding (**formfreier Vertrag**)
informed consent case (II.1)	tort suit based on the defendant's negligent failure to adequately inform the tort victim of the dangers or risks of undertaking a certain act on the victim to which the victim has consented and as a result of which the victim suffers physical harm (**Klage wegen der Verletzung von Aufklärungspflichten**)
installment (I.2)	regular partial repayment on a debt (**Rate**)
interstate commerce (I.5)	sales of goods across state borders, trade or business conducted across state borders (**grenzüberschreitende Handelsbeziehungen**)
intervening cause (II.2)	a cause in fact of the plaintiff's injury that happened after the defendant's act (**dazwischentretende Ursache**)
to die intestate (I.2)	to die without leaving a will or testament (**ohne letztwillige Verfügung sterben**)
invalidating causes (I.5)	reasons for canceling the legal effect of an otherwise valid contract (**Gesichtspunkte, die die bindende Wirkung eines Vertrages ausschließen**)
irrebuttable presumption (I.2)	legal assumption which is made regardless of what the factual situation might be and which cannot be refuted with any amount of evidence (**unwiderlegliche Vermutung**)

joint and several liability (II.2)	duty each of two **joint tortfeasors (Gesamtschuldner)** has to compensate the victim for the total loss, both individually or together; the victim can execute judgment against either one of the joint tortfeasors for the whole amount of that judgment, or he can execute it against them both (**gesamtschuldnerische Haftung**)
joint tortfeasors (II.2)	two or more persons who act together in committing a tort (**Gesamtschuldner**)
judgment notwithstanding the verdict (I.4)	a judge's official determination that the jury's verdict cannot be upheld as a matter of law; in order to be able to enter **judgment notwithstanding the verdict,** the judge must view the facts most favorably to the party for whom the verdict was reached and decide on the basis of that view of the facts that still the party should not have been successful in the law suit as a matter of law; either party to the law suit may make a motion at the end of the trial to have the judge **enter a judgment notwithstanding the verdict**; a **judgment notwithstanding the verdict** permits the judge to override the jury's determination and thus ensure that the case is properly resolved; a **judgment notwithstanding the verdict** can*not* be reached if a jury in a criminal case finds the defendant not guilty; also called **judgment n.o.v.,** meaning judgment *non obstante veredicto* (**Urteil nicht im Einklang mit dem Spruch der Geschworenen**)
judgment on the verdict (I.4)	judge's official recording of verdict reached by jury (**Urteil im Einklang mit dem Spruch der Geschworenen**); **entering judgment on the verdict** gives legal effect to the verdict; if a jury is used and the judge is of the opinion that no reasonable jury could have reached the verdict the jury did reach, the judge may also **enter judgment notwithstanding the verdict**
justifiable reliance (I.2)	to trust in what another person promises or says under circumstances in which rational people generally would put their trust (**berechtigtes Vertrauen**)
law of delict (II.2)	another term for tort law (**Deliktsrecht**)
law merchant (I.5)	body of law governing commercial transactions (**Handelsrecht**)
Learned Hand formula (II.2)	one way of expressing the standard of care applicable to torts of negligence; determines the defendant's obligation by comparing the burden of his taking a certain precaution against the probability that harm will occur if the precaution is not taken multiplied by the seriousness of that harm if it does occur; if the burden of taking the precaution is less that the probability times the harm, then the defendant has not met the standard of care $(B < PL)$

lease (I.1)   agreement whereby one party, the **lessor**, lets real or personal property to another party, the **lessee**, who pays a certain amount of money to the lessor for the use of that property (**Miete, Pacht, Leasing**)

lessee (I.1)   person to whom property is let for that person's use under the condition that he or she pay a specified amount of money as rent (**Pächter, Mieter, Leasingnehmer**)

lessor (I.1)   person who owns or possesses property and leases it to another, the **lessee** (**Verpächter, Vermieter, Leasinggeber**)

letter of credit (I.5)   promise, usually made by a bank, to pay an amount of money to the person to whom it is issued when that person presents certain documents required in the letter of credit; arrangement undertaken to insure a seller that he will be paid for goods he delivers to a buyer regardless of the buyer's honesty or solvency (**Kreditbrief, Akkreditiv**)

liability based on fault (II.1)   tortfeasor's legal responsibility to compensate for the harm he has caused the plaintiff which depends on whether the tortfeasor acted **intentionally, recklessly,** or **negligently** (**verschuldensabhängige Haftung**)

joint and several liability (II.2)   duty each of two **joint tortfeasors** (**Gesamtschuldner**) has to compensate the victim for the total loss, both individually or together; the victim can execute judgment against either one of the joint tortfeasors for the whole amount of that judgment, or he can execute it against them both (**gesamtschuldnerische Haftung**)

primary liability (II.2)   full responsibility for harm caused through one's tort which is backed up by s.o. else's secondary liability for the damages in case of default by the party primarily liable (**Haftung des Hauptschuldners**)

secondary liability (II.2)   liability to pay the tort damages for s.o. who is primarily liable in case that person defaults and cannot be forced to pay (**Ausfallhaftung**)

libel (II.1)   defamation in printed or written form (**schriftliche oder gedruckte Verleumdung bzw. üble Nachrede**)

to limit a precedent (I.4)   to refuse to apply an already established precedent to a similar but still somewhat different case; after a precedent has been limited it does not apply to as many cases as one might previously have thought or argued (**den Anwendungsbereich eines Präzedenzurteils einschränken**)

mailbox rule (I.2)   principle that makes acceptance effective as soon as it is posted or otherwise sent off to the offeror, assuming that the manner of sending the acceptance was reasonable in light of the offer and the way it was communicated; (UK) **postal rule**

to maintain an action for battery (II.1)	indicate that facts support a law suit for a battery; to allege facts sufficient to support a law suit for the tort of battery; usage, e.g. **an action / no action for battery can be maintained (eine Klage auf Schadensersatz wegen Körperverletzung ist un/schlüssig)**
manifestation of assent (I.1)	communication, express or implied, of agreement (**Erklärung der Zustimmung**)
manifestation of intention (I.1)	communication, explicitly or implicitly, of will (**Willenserklärung**)
manufacturing defect (II.3)	product defect that affects only a few products of a product line; defect that arises from faulty construction of the particular product as it moves through the assembly line (**Konstruktionsfehler, der in der Anfertigung eines konkreten Produkts liegt**); also called **construction defect**
market-share liability (II.3)	liability of each of a number of defendants all of whom produced a defective product when plaintiff cannot show which defendant actually produced the product that caused plaintiff's injuries; burden of proof on causation issue shifts to the defendants; each defendant held liable for the proportion of the final judgment represented by its share of the market (**Haftung nach dem Marktanteil**)
master-servant relation (II.2)	relationship of employer to employee; is a basis for imposing strict tort liability on the employer for the torts of his employee which were committed within the scope of the employment relationship (**Dienstverhältnis, Arbeitsverhältnis**)
meeting of the minds (I.5)	expression used to refer to complete agreement between two parties to a contract (**Einigung**)
merchant (I.5)	person in the business of buying or selling goods (**Kaufmann**)
minor (I.2)	s.o. below the **age of legal majority,** or s.o. who cannot enter into binding legal relations because he or she is not yet old enough to understand the full nature of any obligation assumed (**Minderjährige**)
mirror-image rule (I.5)	common law rule requiring the acceptance of an offer to exactly match the terms of the offer itself (**Regel, die die Entsprechung von Angebot und Annahme fordert**)
misrepresentation (I.4)	intentional false statement (**vorsätzlich falsche Darstellung von Tatsachen**); if used to convince another person to agree to a contract it is a **material misrepresentation** (**rechtlich relevante vorsätzlich falsche Darstellung von Tatsachen**)
misrepresentation (II.3)	statement or claim that is untrue; any method of expressing s.th. that is not true; also **false representation** (**falsche Angaben, Irrtumserregung, irreführende Angaben**)
mistake (I.4)	belief that does not correspond with the truth (**Irrtum**); can be a justification for declaring a contract void; a mistake is **unilateral**

if only one party to a contract has the false belief (**einseitiger Irrtum**), or a mistake can be **mutual** if it is shared by the parties (**beiderseitiger Irrtum**); a **mutual mistake** is also called a **common mistake**

modified comparative negligence (II.2) apportions damages between plaintiff and defendant but imposes a 50% limit on the plaintiff's own fault for the plaintiff to recover any damages (**Mitverschulden, das Schadensersatzansprüche proportional mindert und bei einer mehr als 50%igen Selbstverschuldung des Klägers sogar ausschließt**)

modifying agreement (I.5) an agreement by the parties to a contract to alter in some way the terms of that contract (**vertragsändernde Vereinbarung**)

money damages (I.1) primary common law remedy for breach of contract; puts the non-breaching party in the position he would have been in had the contract been performed (**Schadensersatz wegen Nichterfüllung**)

motion for a directed verdict (I.4) formal request addressed to the court which may be made by either the plaintiff or defendant and which asks the court to determine as a matter of law that the other party cannot win the law suit; if the **verdict is directed**, the jury does not deliberate, but rather the verdict is reached by the judge; the test for whether a party's motion for a directed verdict should be granted is whether a reasonable jury could reach a different result when applying the law correctly even if it viewed the facts in a light most favorable to the non-moving party; thus test is the same as for granting a **motion for a judgment notwithstanding the verdict**, but a **motion for a directed verdict** is made before the case is given to the jury for deliberation, whereas the **motion for a judgment notwithstanding the verdict** is made after the jury has deliberated and reached a verdict of its own (**Antrag auf Erlaß einer bindenden Weisung des Richters an die Geschworenen, ein bestimmtes Urteil zu fällen**)

motion to dismiss (II.1) formal request addressed to the court to declare the plaintiff's complaint deficient for lack of jurisdiction, defective service of process or other procedural flaws (**Rüge der Unzulässigkeit**); used in the federal courts to include also the demurrer, as in **motion to dismiss for failure to state a claim** (**Rüge der Unschlüssigkeit**)

movables (I.2) property other than land (**Fahrnis, bewegliche Sachen**)

mutual mistake (I.4) mistake as to conditions relating to a contract that is shared by both parties; also called **common mistake** (**beiderseitiger Irrtum**)

negligence (II.1) failure to take adequate measures to avoid harming others; failure to act like a reasonable person would to avoid harming others; failure to see a risk of harm that a reasonable person would see (**Fahrlässigkeit**)

negotiable instruments (I.5)	"a written and signed unconditional promise or order to pay a specified sum of money on demand or at a definite time payable to order or bearer" *Black's Law Dictionary*; a check is an example of a negotiable instrument (**begebbare Wertpapiere**)
to negotiate (I.1)	to deal, to discuss in order to reach an agreement or bargain (**verhandeln**)
notice of motion (I.3)	advance formal indication of intent to make a motion to a court for some specific purpose (**Vorankündigung eines Antrags**)
nova causa interveniens (II.2)	(UK) intervening cause
novus actus interveniens (II.2)	(UK) intervening act which was also a but-for cause of the plaintiff's injury
nudum pactum (I.3)	a "naked" agreement; the term is used to signify a contract that is not supported by consideration
occupation of land (II.2)	basis for the law to impose a duty of care; refers to the responsibility the owner or possessor of real property has to keep the property in a condition that others will not injure themselves when they are on the property (**Grundlage einer Verkehrssicherungspflicht**)
offensive contact battery (II.1)	tort of infringing on victim's personal autonomy with the intent to do so, or with the intent to come into harmful contact with the victim or to make him fear either harmful or offensive contact
offer (I.1)	proposal for a specific contract; initiation of the contracting process by the making of a promise which, if accepted and supported by consideration, legally binds the person making it (**Angebot**)
offeree (I.1)	the person to whom an offer to enter into a contract is made (**Angebotsempfänger**)
offeror (I.1)	the person who initiates the contracting process by making an offer (**Antragender**)
offer to chaffer (I.1)	invitation to another person to make an offer (**invitatio ad offerendum**)
offer to negotiate (I.1)	invitation to another person to make an offer (**invitatio ad offerendum**)
offer to receive offers (I.1)	invitation to another person to make an offer (**invitatio ad offerendum**)
onus of proof (II.2)	obligation to provide enough evidence to prove legal claim (**Beweislast**)

open terms (I.5)	conditions of an agreement that are not yet specified (**Vertrags-lücken**)
option contract (I.2)	agreement to keep an offer open for a specified period of time that binds the offeror (**Option**)
parent (I.5)	main company holding a controlling interest in another company (**Muttergesellschaft**), which is referred to as the parent's **subsidiary** (**Tochtergesellschaft**)
party to a contract (I.1)	an individual who has entered into a contractual relationship with one or more persons (**Vertragspartei**)
to pass title (I.4)	to transfer ownership right in property (**Eigentum übertragen**)
past consideration (I.3)	consideration that has been given before any contract was closed; cannot support a contract and make it binding (**Gegenleistung, die schon vor Vertragsabschluß erbracht worden ist**)
peppercorn doctrine (I.1)	principle that even something as valueless as a peppercorn can be sufficient consideration to support a contract if a contracting party actually bargained to get it
personal property (I.2)	property other than land (**Fahrnis, bewegliche Sachen**)
personalty (I.2)	property other than land (**Fahrnis, bewegliche Sachen**)
plaintiff in error (I.3)	party who petitioned for a writ of error (**Revisionskläger**)
prayer for relief (I.3)	formal request that the court grant the plaintiff a specified remedy; part of the complaint in which the plaintiff requests the court to order compensation for the wrong complained of (**Klageantrag**)
pre-existing legal duty (I.2)	a legal obligation one has toward another person which existed before one promises to do the same thing required by that legal obligation; cannot be consideration for a new contract since the person under the obligation no longer can bargain with a promise to fulfill the obligation he already has to fulfill anyway (**(Handlungs- oder Unterlassungs-)Pflicht, die schon vor einem Vertragsabschluß besteht**)
prejudicial error (II.3)	an error of law made by the trial court that could have affected the outcome of the case; an error so serious it warrants reversal of the trial court's judgment; also **reversible error** (**Rechtsfehler, der einen Revisionsgrund darstellt**)
presumption (I.2)	legal assumption which is made regarding the factual situation or the parties' intent; a presumption may be **rebuttable**, meaning a party may offer evidence to disprove it (**widerlegliche Vermutung**); a presumption may be **irrebuttable**, meaning it cannot be refuted by any amount of contrary evidence (**unwiderlegliche Vermutung**)
primary liability (II.2)	full responsibility for harm caused through one's tort which is

backed up by s.o. else's secondary liability for the damages in case of default by the party primarily liable (**Haftung des Hauptschuldners**)

principal (I.1)   person who conducts business through another person, who is the agent (**Geschäftsherr, Prinzipal**)

principal (I.2)   the amount of the original debt excluding interest payments owed under loan agreement; the principal is reduced as repayments on the debt are made (**Kreditsumme**)

privity of contract (II.3)   legal requirement that one must be a party to a contract in order to be permitted to sue for its breach; doctrine prevented consumers who bought a product from a retailer from suing the manufacturer of the product because the consumer had no contractual relation with the manufacturer (**Stellung als Vertragspartei**)

probate court (I.2)   court that deals with inheritance law and family law matters (**Nachlaß- und Familiengericht**)

products liability (II.1)   (UK) **product liability**: strict liability of a producer or seller of a product for any harm caused by that product if the harm resulted from a product defect, from the producer's or seller's failure to warn of potential risks involved in using the product, or from the producer's or seller's misrepresentation of the purpose for which the product can be used (**Produzentenhaftung**)

to proffer performance (I.2)   to actually hand s.th. over for acceptance as opposed to an offer or indication of intent to hand over for acceptance (**die Leistung, wie sie zu bewirken ist, tatsächlich anbieten**)

promisee (I.1)   the person to whom s.th. has been promised, hence either party to a bilateral contract and the person performing the act requested by an offer for a unilateral contract; the term is usually used to designate the plaintiff to a breach of contract suit, because he claims that the defendant has promised something and not performed (**Gläubiger eines Anspruchs aus Vertrag**)

promisor (I.1)   the person who makes a promise, hence either party to a bilateral contract and the offeror for a unilateral contract; the term is usually used for the defendant to a breach of contract suit, because the plaintiff claims that the defendant has promised something and not performed (**Schuldner einer Verbindlichkeit aus Vertrag**)

promissory acceptance (I.2)   to accept an offer by making a return promise (**Annahme des Vertragsangebots**)

promissory estoppel (I.3)   equitable doctrine of contract law which will bar a party from asserting a right he otherwise would have, such as refusing to keep his promise when a contract is not legally enforceable; doctrine applied if when making the promise the promisor knew

	that the promisee would rely on the promise and in fact the promisee did rely on the promise, changed his position, and would suffer a detriment if the promise were not kept (**Verwirkung von Rechten innerhalb einer Vertragsbeziehung**)
proprietor (I.1)	owner (**Eigentümer**)
proximate cause (II.2)	test of causation from the point of view of remoteness of result; for a breach of a duty of care to be actionable, it must have been the proximate cause of the plaintiff's injuries (**Einschränkung der Äquivalenztheorie der Kausalität**; vergleichbar der **Adäquanztheorie der Kausalität** oder der **Theorie der objektiven Zurechnung**)
punitive damages (II.2)	damages awarded to punish tortfeaser (**Zivilstrafe im Gewand von Schadensersatz**)
pure comparative negligence (II.2)	apportions damages according to each party's fault in causing harm (**Mitverschulden**)
put option (I.2)	option giving offeree the right to sell s.th. at a set price for a specified period of time (der Ausdruck **put option** wird auch in deutschen Texten benutzt)
real estate (I.2)	land and everything attached to the land (**Liegenschaften, unbewegliche Sachen**)
real property (I.2)	land and everything attached to the land (**Liegenschaften, unbewegliche Sachen**)
realty (I.2)	land and everything attached to the land (**Liegenschaften, unbewegliche Sachen**)
reasonable foresight doctrine (II.2)	determines the conditions under which tort liability will be imposed on a defendant who could not clearly foresee a secondary risk of his conduct
reasonable person standard (II.2)	one way of expressing the standard of care applicable to torts of negligence; measures defendant against the average person in the community (**die im Verkehr erforderliche Sorgfalt**)
rebuttable presumption (I.2)	legal assumption which is made when facts are insufficient to indicate real state of affairs but which can be refuted by contrary evidence (**widerlegliche Vermutung**)
recitals (I.3)	statements of purpose or reasons given for why the document in which the recitals appear has been adopted by the parties (**einleitende Erklärungen**)
recklessness (II.1)	acting with a total disregard for the consequences of one's action; being aware that one's action creates a risk of harming another person and acting anyway (**bedingter Vorsatz und bewußte Fahrlässigkeit**)
to recover damages (I.1)	to receive a court's award of money damages to be paid by the

defendant to a law suit in order to compensate, e.g. for the defendant's breach of contract

rejection of an offer (I.2)

offeree's communication of refusal to accept offeror's offer; terminates offeree's power ofacceptance (**Ablehnung eines Vertragsangebotes**)

to render performance (I.2)

to actually do what one is required to do under a contract (**den Vertrag erfüllen**)

repudiation of a contract (I.4)

treating a contract as if it were void and demanding to be restored to the position one had before the contract was performed (**Rücktritt vom Vertrag**); compare **anticipatory repudiation** (I.3), which is repudiation before performance under the contract is due

rescission of contract (I.4)

declaration that a contract is void from the beginning; may be made by a party or court (**Rücktritt vom Vertrag, Anfechtung**); if made by a party, that party is called the **rescinding party**

reservation of power (I.2) **to revoke**

offeror's expressly retaining the right to cancel his offer at any time (**Vorbehalt des Widerrufs**)

res ipsa loquitur (II.3)

the thing speaks for itself; name of doctrine which shifts the burden of proof of the defendant's negligence from the plaintiff to the defendant when the defendant had exclusive control over the thing which caused the plaintiff's injury and the accident would not normally have occurred in the absence of the defendant's negligence

respondeat superior (II.2)

another name for the principle of imposing liability vicariously

to rest one's case (II.3)

to close the presentation of one's evidence at trial (**sein Vorbringen vorläufig abschließen**)

retailer (II.3)

merchant who sells to the ultimate consumer (**Einzelhändler**)

to retract an offer (I.1)

to withdraw an offer before it has been accepted (**ein Angebot widerrufen**)

revocation of an offer (I.2)

cancellation of the effect of an offer; extinguishes the offeree's power of acceptance (**Widerruf eines Vertragsangebotes**)

right of avoidance (I.2)

right to have a contract declared void (**Anfechtungsrecht**)

right of subrogation (II.2)

"The substitution of one person in the place of another with reference to a lawful claim, demand or right, so that he who is substituted succeeds to the rights of the other in relation to the debt or claim and its rights, remedies, or securities." *Black's Law Dictionary* (**gesetzlicher Forderungsübergang** bzw. **Anspruch auf Forderungsabtretung**)

rule absolute (I.4)

final rule that is to take immediate effect, often because the person to whom it is directed has failed to **show cause,** or give a good reason, why the rule should not issue (**rechtskräftige richterliche Verfügung**)

sales act (II.3)	law on the sale of goods (**Kaufrecht**)
secondary liability (II.2)	liability to pay the tort damages for s.o. who is primarily liable in case that person defaults and cannot be forced to pay (**Ausfallhaftung**)
secured transactions (I.5)	agreements accompanied by the transfer of an interest in property, usually to a creditor, to ensure that the debtor pays back a loan; a loan accompanied by a mortgage is a secured transaction (**Geschäfte, die mit Sicherungsverträgen verbunden sind**)
securities (I.5)	documents indicating debt issued by an undertaking to an investor; shares of stock in a company are securities (**Wertpapiere, Effekten**)
simple contract (I.1)	contract that has to be supported by consideration to be binding (**formfreier Vertrag**)
slander (II.1)	defamation in spoken form (**mündliche Verleumdung bzw. üble Nachrede**)
slight-gross system (II.2)	bars plaintiff from recovering any damages from defendant if the plaintiff's negligence was not insignificant in comparison to the defendant's negligence; if it was insignificant, the damages are still apportioned according to each party's share of responsibility for the harm
special relationship (II.2)	basis for the law to impose a duty of care; refers to a relationship in which one party has undertaken a responsibility to care for another; exists between a doctor and his patient, a babysitter and the baby (**Schutzverhältnis**)
specialty contract (I.1)	contract that has to be formalized to be binding (**formgebundener Vertrag, formbedürftiger Vertrag**)
special verdict (II.1)	conclusion of the jury on the facts only; list of facts the jury believes true without any application of the law to those facts to reach a final conclusion on the rights of the parties (**Urteil der Geschworenen, durch das der Tatbestand festgestellt wird**)
specific performance (I.1)	equitable remedy for breach of contract which requires the breaching party to actually perform as he promised under the contract (**Anspruch auf Vertragserfüllung**)
standard of care (II.2)	the norm established by law for determining whether an individual has fulfilled a duty of care (**Sorgfaltsmaßstab**)
standard terms (I.5)	the conditions under which an individual generally does business (**allgemeine Geschäftsbedingungen, AGB**)
stipulation (I.4)	provision, agreement or demand regarding a term in a contract, usually on what is to happen in the future or what is taken to be true (**Vertragsbedingung, Vereinbarung, Vertragsbestimmung**)
strict liability (II.1)	principle of responsibility for a tort whereby the tortfeasor's

legal responsibility to compensate for the harm he has caused the plaintiff does not depend on whether the tortfeasor was at fault in causing the harm (**verschuldensunabhängige Haftung, Gefährdungshaftung**)

subsidiary (I.5) — company the controlling interest of which is held by another company (**Tochtergesellschaft**), which is referred to as the subsidiary's **parent** (**Muttergesellschaft**)

sufficient consideration (I.1) — consideration that is viewed by a court to be real in the sense that it was actually bargained for and not just nominal or a sham (**hinreichende Gegenleistung**)

to sustain an action for battery (II.1) — indicate that facts support a law suit for a battery; to allege facts sufficient to support a law suit for the tort of battery; usage, e.g. **an action / no action for battery can be sustained (eine Klage auf Schadensersatz wegen Körperverletzung ist un/schlüssig)**

symbolic delivery (I.3) — not actually transferring an object to another person, but transferring something that is intended to represent the object; for the purpose of a valid gift, symbolic delivery is sufficient (**symbolische Übergabe**)

to tender performance (I.2) — to actually hand s.th. over for acceptance as opposed to an offer or indication of intent to hand to over for acceptance (**die Leistung, wie sie zu bewirken ist, tatsächlich anbieten**)

termination of an offer (I.1) — end to the validity of an offer; once an **offer is terminated**, it can no longer be accepted by the offeree (**Erlöschen eines Angebots**)

testament (I.2) — document containing instructions on how to dispose of a person's property after death; **testament** originally limited to the distribution of personal property and **will** to the distribution of real property, but today terms are synonymous (**Testament**)

testator (I.2) — male person who has left a last will or testament (**Testator**)

testatrix (I.2) — female person who has left a last will or testament (**Testator**)

tortfeasor (II.1) — person who commits a tort (**Täter**)

trademark (II.3) — sign or mark on a product that identifies the manufacturer of the product (**Warenzeichen**)

transferred intent (II.2) — doctrine of English law, applicable today in England and the U.S., which imputes the intent to cause prohibited harm to s.o. who in fact was only negligent with respect to causing that harm, because the actor intentionally attempted to cause a different type of harm, or the same type of harm to a different victim, and as a result negligently caused the harm in question ("**übertragener Vorsatz**" [Annahme, daß der Täter in den Fällen einer aberratio ictus auch mit Bezug auf die eingetretene Verletzung vorsätzlich gehandelt hat])

trespass does not lie (II.2)	expression indicating that the facts do not support a legal claim of trespass (**eine Klage auf Schadensersatz wegen verbotener Eigenmacht ist unschlüssig**)
trespass to chattels (II.2)	tort of unlawful interference with the personal property of another (**verbotene Eigenmacht**)
trespass to land (II.1)	tort of unlawful interference with the real property of another (**verbotene Eigenmacht**)
unconscionable (I.4)	in violation of good moral values, contrary to one's conscience (**gegen die guten Sitten**)
unilateral contract (I.1)	promise in exchange for an act; the act is both acceptance of the offer and consideration for the promise made by the offeror (*nicht:* einseitiges Rechtsgeschäft!; ein Beispiel dieses Vertragstyps ist die Auslobung) (**einseitig verpflichtender Vertrag**)
unilateral mistake (I.4)	mistake as to conditions relating to a contract that only one of the parties makes (**einseitiger Irrtum**)
untaken precaution (II.2)	a measure of care a defendant to a tort claim could have taken but did not take; question for tort liability is whether this untaken precaution was the **cause in fact** and **proximate cause** of the plaintiff's injury; resolving this issue still does not resolve the issue of whether the defendant breached a duty of care to the plaintiff by not taking the precaution, since it may be that the defendant had no duty to take the precaution, e.g. under the Learned Hand formula
validating causes (I.5)	reasons for giving a contract legal effect (**Gesichtspunkte, die die bindende Wirkung eines Vertrages begründen**)
vendee (I.1)	buyer (**Käufer**)
vendor (I.1)	seller (**Verkäufer**)
to vest (I.4)	to become valid and effective, as in: **a right vests, title vests**; if s.th. **revests** it becomes effective or valid again, as in: **title revests** in the seller if the contract is **rescinded**
vicarious liability (II.2)	liability of one person for the torts of another, such as the employer for the torts of the employee (**Haftung für zurechenbares Drittverschulden**)
void (I.4)	empty of legal effect (**nichtig, unwirksam**); contrast to **voidable**
voidable (I.4)	capable of being avoided at the discretion of an adversely affected party to a contract (**anfechtbar**); contrast to **void**, which means empty of effect regardless of the parties' intent or individual discretion

warehouse receipt (I.5)	document of verification of having received goods, which is issued by a person who is in the business of storing goods in exchange for payment (**Lagerschein**)
warranty (I.4)	guarantee, promise that certain facts are true (**Zusicherung, Gewährleistung**); **warranties** can be **express** (**ausdrückliche Zusicherung**), meaning actually stated, or **implied** (**konkludente Gewährleistung**), meaning that one's conduct leads another person to conclude that the **warranty** was intended
wholesaler (II.3)	middleman in distribution chain, e.g. one who buys from manufacturer and sells to retailer (**Großhändler**)
will (I.2)	document containing instructions on how to dispose of a person's property after death; **testament** originally limited to the distribution of personal property and **will** to the distribution of real property, but today terms are synonymous (**Testament**)
writ of error (I.3)	order issued by a court of appellate jurisdiction directed to a lower court to have the lower court send up the record in a case for review because the party petitioning for the writ of error claims that the lower court has made a legal error in dealing with the case; although there are technical differences between an appeal and a hearing on a writ of error, for purposes of understanding the writ of error, one should consider it a form of appeal (**Beschluß, die Revision zuzulassen**)